Legal Issues Across Counselling & Psychotherapy Settings

Legal Resources for Counsellors and Psychotherapists

Legal Resources for Counsellors and Psychotherapists is a series of highly practical books, themed around broad topics, which reflect the most 'frequently asked questions' put to the BACP's professional advice line.

Books in the series:

Therapists in Court: Providing Evidence and Supporting Witnesses
Tim Bond and Amanpreet Sandhu

Confidentiality and Record Keeping in Counselling and Psychotherapy
Tim Bond and Barbara Mitchels

Essential Law for Counsellors and Psychotherapists
Barbara Mitchels and Tim Bond

Legal Issues Across Counselling & Psychotherapy Settings

A Guide for Practice

Barbara Mitchels and Tim Bond

Los Angeles | London | New Delhi
Singapore | Washington DC

British Association for
Counselling & Psychotherapy

First published 2011

SAGE Publications Ltd
1 Oliver's Yard
55 City Road
London EC1Y 1SP

SAGE Publications Inc.
2455 Teller Road
Thousand Oaks, California 91320

SAGE Publications India Pvt Ltd
B 1/I 1 Mohan Cooperative Industrial Area
Mathura Road
New Delhi 110 044

SAGE Publications Asia-Pacific Pte Ltd
33 Pekin Street #02-01
Far East Square
Singapore 048763

Library of Congress Control Number: 2011920329

British Library Cataloguing in Publication data

A catalogue record for this book is available from the British Library

ISBN 978-1-84920-623-5
ISBN 978-1-84920-624-2 (pbk)

Typeset by C&M Digitals (P) Ltd, Chennai, India
Printed by CPI Group (UK) Ltd, Croydon, CR0 4YY
Printed on paper from sustainable resources

Contents

List of checklists, figures and boxes xiii
About the authors xiv
Praise for the book xv
Acknowledgements xvi
Introduction 1

1 Private Practice 3

1.1 Legal features of private practice 3
   1.1.1 Starting up in business 4
   1.1.2 Advertising and the law 5
   1.1.3 Employing others 7
   1.1.4 Equal opportunities, non-discriminatory practice
      and prevention of harassment 9
   1.1.5 Finance and tax 12
   1.1.6 Health and safety 13
   1.1.7 Insurance 14
   1.1.8 Premises 16
   1.1.9 Records, data protection and freedom of information 18
   1.1.10 Out of hours cover 21

1.2 Contractual issues 21
   1.2.1 Contract terms 21
   1.2.2 Therapeutic contracts 21
   1.2.3 Enforceability of contracts 23
   1.2.4 Fees for therapy, and issues of non-payment 23
   1.2.5 Mental capacity 24
   1.2.6 Contracts that must be in writing 25
   1.2.7 Electronic signatures, Internet contracts, etc. 26
   1.2.8 Ethical issues and 'soft law' on contracts 26
   1.2.9 Contracts of employment, contracts for volunteer
      workers and contracts for services 27
   1.2.10 Dealing with legal claims 27

1.3 Practice issues 28
   1.3.1 Currency of information, continuing professional
      development and training 28

1.3.2 Assessment of what to charge for therapy services | 28
1.3.3 Missed appointments | 29
1.3.4 The illness or death of the therapist and 'counselling wills' | 29
1.3.5 Summary checklist: Starting up in business working
from home or in other premises | 30

1.4 Interface and managing movement between
private practice and other contexts | 31
1.4.1 Information sharing and disclosures | 31
1.4.2 Inter-agency working and policy making | 32
1.4.3 Developments in inter-agency collaboration – the
Caldicott Principles | 33
1.4.4 Guidance on information sharing regarding the
welfare of children | 33

2 Commercial and Employee Assistance Programme (EAP) Provision | **35**

2.1 Legal features of commercial and Employee
Assistance Programme (EAP) provision | 35
2.1.1 The emergence of EAPs in response to employers'
legal responsibility to employees | 35
2.1.2 What services might we expect an EAP to provide? | 37
2.1.3 EAP provision and employment issues | 38
2.1.4 Law and guidance on EAP provision | 40

2.2 Contractual issues | 41
2.2.1 Contracts between therapists and EAP providers | 41
2.2.2 Contracts for goods and services relating to
therapy provision | 42
2.2.3 Contracts of employment, contracts for volunteer
workers and contracts for services in EAPs | 43
2.2.4 Therapeutic contracts with EAP clients | 43
2.2.5 Dealing with legal claims | 43

2.3 Practice Issues | 44
2.3.1 Managing confidences | 44
2.3.2 'Whistle-blowing' and reporting bad work practices | 44
2.3.3 Employment tribunal hearings, disciplinary procedures, etc. | 45
2.3.4 Recording and storing client records in an EAP service | 46
2.3.5 Disclosures in the public interest | 46
2.3.6 Contracts forbidding therapists to take a former EAP
client privately | 46
2.3.7 Extra time | 47

2.4 Interface and managing movement between EAP provision
and other contexts | 47

3   Voluntary Work   **48**

3.1 Legal features of the context   49
    3.1.1 What is the legal definition of voluntary work?   49
    3.1.2 Is a volunteer therapist employed, self-employed or
          not employed at all? Does the distinction matter?   49
    3.1.3 What rights does a volunteer have in the workplace?   50
    3.1.4 Relevant law, professional guidance, etc. for volunteers   51

3.2 Contractual issues   52

3.3 Practice issues   53
    3.3.1 Clarity of role   53
    3.3.2 Issues of internal supervision   53
    3.3.3 Should volunteers accept gifts or donations?   54
    3.3.4 Volunteers in training   55

4   Working with Adults in the Context of Social Care Agencies   **56**

4.1 Law and regulation of health and social care   56
    4.1.1 Background legal context of health and social care provision   56
    4.1.2 Summary of the new law regarding standards and
          regulation in health and social care   57

4.2 Mental illness   59

4.3 Clients with special needs, including disability, the elderly
    and vulnerable adults   60

4.4 Contractual issues   64

4.5 Practice issues   64
    4.5.1 Disclosures of abuse   64
    4.5.2 Non-compliance with care plans or contracts for care
          in residential settings – 'whistle-blowing' on bad practice   65

4.6 Interface and managing movement between social care and
    other contexts   66
    4.6.1 Confidentiality   66
    4.6.2 Information about third parties   66
    4.6.3 Referrals   67

5   Education   **68**

5.1 Legal features of education   69
    5.1.1 Legal history of compulsory education   69
    5.1.2 State monitoring and control of education   70
    5.1.3 Teachers' role as being *in loco parentis* to
          children in school   71

5.1.4 Government Inspectorates and audit agencies 73
5.1.5 Statute, subsidiary legislation and guidance relevant to
child welfare in the context of education 74

5.2 Contractual issues 79

5.3 Capacity, consent and confidentiality 79
5.3.1 Definitions of 'child' and 'parent' 79
5.3.2 Parental responsibility 80
5.3.3 Child's capacity to consent to therapy and
request confidentiality 80

5.4 Practice issues 81
5.4.1 Do parents have to give consent for children in
school to have counselling? 81
5.4.2 What if parents or those with parental responsibility
refuse (or cannot agree) to allow their child to have
counselling in school? 81
5.4.3 What if a child needs urgent assessment or treatment but
those with parental responsibility and/or the child refuse? 81
5.4.4 Should parents be given information about their child's
therapy at school? 82
5.4.5 Referrals to other agencies or organisations 82
5.4.6 Child protection situations – what to do 83
5.4.7 CRB checks and the Independent
Safeguarding Agency (ISA) 84
5.4.8 Agreeing length and frequency of sessions in
school counselling 86
5.4.9 Finding designated space for counselling in school 86
5.4.10 Boundary issues and dual roles in schools 86

5.5 The interface and managing movement between
education and other contexts 86
5.5.1 Confidentiality in the school setting 86
5.5.2 Confidentiality in a further education, college or
university setting 87
5.5.3 Keeping records in schools, colleges and universities 88

5.6 Protection of vulnerable adults 89

5.7 Fitness to practise 90

5.8 Tensions between the educational institution and
professional practice guidance 91

6 The National Health Service (NHS) and Private Health Care 92

6.1 Legal features of working in health care settings 94
6.1.1 The Care Quality Commission (CQC) 94

6.1.2 Range of mental health services 97
6.1.3 Law and guidance within health care settings 97

6.2 Contractual and workplace issues 98
6.2.1 I work part time in the local GP surgery. Who do my clients
have a therapeutic contract with – the general practice or me? 99
6.2.2 The doctors in the GP practice want me to keep my notes
at the surgery with their health records. I want to take
them home. Can I insist on this? 99
6.2.3 Can a therapist working part time in a hospital setting
insist on keeping separate records? 100
6.2.4 Where there is a conflict between NHS policy and
procedures and those of a professional organisation,
which takes precedence? In the event of a complaint,
would a practitioner be subject to the hospital disciplinary
procedures, their professional body, or both? 100
6.2.5 If clients tell therapists about bad practice by doctors
or nursing staff, should this be reported? 101
6.2.6 Workplace bullying, harassment and discrimination 103

6.3 Practice issues, the interface and managing information sharing
between the NHS or private health care and other professionals,
agencies and organisations 106
6.3.1 How do agency policies affect therapy clients,
e.g. records, confidentiality and disclosure? 106
6.3.2 Clients' accounts of others' crimes or confessions
of their own criminal acts: Should they be reported? 107
6.3.3 How can I balance my client's well-being against the
safety of others? 109

7 **Counselling in Spiritual or Pastoral Settings** **112**

7.1 Legal and ethical features of the context 113
7.1.1 Confidentiality 113
7.1.2 Counselling in the context of general pastoral care 115
7.1.3 Advice and listening skills used in the context of
pastoral care 116

7.2 Practice issues 116
7.2.1 Keeping appropriate physical, sexual, emotional and
psychological boundaries in pastoral care 116
7.2.2 Meeting the personal needs of clergy and those
involved in ministry 116
7.2.3 Dual roles 117
7.2.4 Appropriate use of power in pastoral relationships 118
7.2.5 Sharing information in shared ministry, or a
pastoral care team 119

7.2.6 Risk of misinterpretations, giving undue weight to
therapeutic interventions, or inadvertent manipulation
in the context of pastoral care   119

7.3 Interface and managing movement between spiritual and
pastoral care and other contexts   121
7.3.1 Child protection   121

8   Working with Children and Young People   123

8.1 Legal features of the context   124
8.1.1 Capacity of children to consent (or refuse) therapy and to
enter into valid and enforceable therapeutic contracts   124
8.1.2 Parental responsibility   126
8.1.3 Consent to therapy and/or sharing information between
professionals working with children and young people   129
8.1.4 Child protection legislation, policies and procedures   131

8.2 Working with children and young people 'in care' or
subject to care proceedings   135
8.2.1 Working in the context of a care order or care proceedings   135
8.2.2 Working in the context of voluntary care   136
8.2.3 Working in the context of residential mental health care   136

8.3 Working with young people in 'secure estate'   137

8.4 Working with young people under a supervision order
or an education supervision order   139

8.5 Working with young people in the context of criminal
proceedings   140

8.6 Working with young people in the context of family proceedings 140

8.7 Working with children and young people in hospital   141
8.7.1 Consent to hospital treatment   141
8.7.2 Record keeping in hospital settings   142

9   Adoption Support Services   143

9.1 Legal context of adoption, adoption agencies
and adoption support services   143

9.2 What are adoption support services?   145

9.3 What is an adoption support agency?   146

9.4 Should therapists in private practice providing adoption
support services register as an adoption support agency?   146
9.4.1 Exceptions to the requirements for registration   147

9.5 Registration process, inspection, enforcement and
  professional standards for adoption support services 148
  9.5.1 Registration 148
  9.5.2 Ofsted inspections 149
  9.5.3 Enforcement 149
  9.5.4 Other professional standards 150
  9.5.5 The Northern Ireland context 150

9.6 Contractual issues 150
  9.6.1 The multi-way contract: agency/local authority/
    parents/child 151

9.7 Practice issues 152
  9.7.1 Assessment of the family situation and needs 152
  9.7.2 Training and information for adoptive families 152
  9.7.3 Understanding and accepting the child's history 152
  9.7.4 Supporting adoptive families 153

9.8 Interface and managing movement between adoption
  support services and other contexts 153
  9.8.1 Liaison with the local authority 153
  9.8.2 Managing differences between attitudes and perceptions 153
  9.8.3 Contact issues and managing contact 154
  9.8.4 Funding 154

10 **Forensic Work** 155

10.1 What is an expert witness? 155

10.2 Why are some therapists treated as experts and others not? 156

10.3 Legal features of forensic work 157
  10.3.1 Experts in Family Proceedings Relating to Children 158
  10.3.2 'McKenzie Friend' 158
  10.3.3 Case law on forensic evidence 159

10.4 Contractual issues in forensic work 161
  10.4.1 Contracting for forensic work/services of expert witnesses 161
  10.4.2 Publicly funded work 161
  10.4.3 General contract issues for experts 161
  10.4.4 Private clients 162
  10.4.5 Unrepresented clients 162
  10.4.6 Court control of evidence 162
  10.4.7 Obtaining clear instructions 162
  10.4.8 What if the solicitors haven't paid me? 163

10.5 Practice issues 163
  10.5.1 Planning and timing evidence in the case 163

10.5.2 Confidentiality and information sharing 164
10.5.3 Evidence on oath or affirmation 164
10.5.4 Authority and reliability of evidence (professional
confidence compared with unprofessional arrogance!) 164
10.5.5 Keep fully informed and be aware of changes 165
10.5.6 Client compliance versus openness in the
therapeutic relationship 165
10.5.7 Risk assessment 166

10.6 Interface and managing movement between forensic
practice and other contexts 167
10.6.1 Managing communication and information
sharing between professionals 167

10.7 Courtroom etiquette 168

11   Counselling in Police and Home Office Settings   171

11.1 Legal features of the context 172
11.1.1 Support for police officers, prison officers and staff 172
11.1.2 Support for adults resident in a custodial setting 173
11.1.3 Support for young people in youth custody 174
11.1.4 Support for asylum seekers, refugees and the staff
caring for them 175

11.2 Practice issues 176
11.2.1 Confidentiality in the context of police and CPS work 176
11.2.2 Confidentiality in the context of work in the prison system 178
11.2.3 Fitness to work: Advice, feedback and management issues 178
11.2.4 Substance misuse in the prison system 179
11.2.5 Violence, harassment and abuse in custodial contexts 180
11.2.6 Equality issues and the balance of power 181

List of Cases, Practice Directions, Government and Professional
Guidance, Statutes, Statutory Instruments and EEC Directives 182
Useful Resources 194
Glossary 199
References and Further Reading 204
Index 210

List of Checklists, Figures and Boxes

Checklists

Starting up in business   4
Employment regulations   9
Health and safety risks   13
Action to minimise health and safety risks   13
Insurance cover   14
Checking an insurance policy   14
Issues to consider when setting up a business   30
Disclosure   31
Issues to be considered in dilemmas over confidentiality   102
Risk assessment for forensic work   166
Practical approaches to OSA issues   177

Figures

Figure 5.1 The Child Assessment Framework   76
Figure 5.2 Flowchart of local authority referral procedures   77
Figure 5.3 Process of a Child Protection Conference   78

Boxes

1.1 Employed/self-employed/or a bit of both?   7
1.2 Legislation against forms of discrimination   10
1.3 Data protection legislation   19
1.4 Examples of brief records of disclosures/referrals   32
2.1 Role of Employee Assistance Programmes   37
2.2 Forms of EAP provision   38
2.3 Statutes and subsidiary legislation relevant to EAP provision   38
7.1 Child protection guidance issued by different faiths   121
8.1 Ability of children under the age of 18 to give legal consent to therapy and/or to make an informed decision to enter into a therapeutic contract   125
8.2 Abbreviations for legislation relating to parental responsibility   127
9.1 Adoption and adoption support services legislation   144
9.2 Documents required for registration as an Adoption Support Agency   148
10.1 Role of a McKenzie Friend   159

About the Authors

Tim Bond BA, CQSW, Cert Ed, PhD, is a Professorial Teaching Fellow at the Graduate School of Education, University of Bristol, who specialises in ethical and legal issues for psychological therapies and other professional roles. He writes widely and runs workshops on these topics.

Barbara Mitchels LLB, UKRCP, Dip Couns, PhD, is a psychotherapist and Director of Watershed Counselling Service in Devon. She is also a solicitor, running Therapylaw, a Web-based legal advice service for therapists. Barbara writes widely and runs workshops on issues relevant to law, therapy, traumatic stress and mediation.

Barbara and Tim are both Fellows of the British Association for Counselling and Psychotherapy.

Praise for the Book

'This text is a "must have" reference source for therapists, supervisors, academics and all agencies employing therapists. Its contents reflect and address many key areas of practice that cause therapists much anxiety! Barbara Mitchels and Tim Bond are to be congratulated again for writing another key text addressing legal issues faced by those in the counselling and psychotherapy profession.'
Dr Colin Lago, independent practitioner, supervisor, trainer and consultant

'*Legal Issues Across Counselling & Psychotherapy Settings: A Guide to Practice* is the fourth book in the series. It is current and relevant in the many different contexts of modern therapeutic practice. It also serves as an excellent reference and is something that I believe will prove to be a valuable resource to practitioners.'
Professor Cary L. Cooper, CBE, Chair of Academy of Social Sciences, Distinguished Professor of Organisational Psychology and Health, Lancaster University Management School

'Many counsellors and psychotherapists feel themselves increasingly oppressed by the litigious nature of our prevailing culture. Anxiety undermines their creativity and fear of complaint or accusation permeates their practice.

This excellent book should do much to offer reassurance and to provide the guidance and information which can bolster therapeutic confidence. Based on the experience of practitioners from a wide variety of settings, it addresses the day-to-day dilemmas of therapists who may be working in difficult legal terrain with clients who are exceptionally vulnerable or confused.

Its scope is impressive and as well as being an invaluable guide to the complexity of the relevant law it is also a mine of useful resources and suggestions for further study. It has the merit, too, of being the work of seasoned writers who know how to capture and retain the reader's attention even when the content may seem to be scarcely the material of high drama.'
Brian Thorne, co-founder, The Norwich Centre, Emeritus Professor of Counselling, University of East Anglia

Acknowledgements

We thank all the counsellors and psychotherapists who provided us with questions and issues for inclusion in this book, and we are greatly indebted to all the professionals who have helped us in many different ways with writing this book.

In particular we are grateful to Ruth Caleb and BACP's AUCC Division, Dominic Davies, John Eatock, Mike Fowler, Lynette Harborne, Chris Jenkins, Mary Lane and Barbara Lawton. We thank Manjula Nayee from the CPS, and Joanne North, Justine Oldfield-Rowell, Andrew Reeves, Alistair Ross and Val Potter, all of whom have given us very valuable feedback and useful ideas for the book.

We also thank Alice Oven and Rachel Burrows from Sage; and copyeditor Elaine Leek, who did a great job.

We want to express our especial thanks and good wishes to Denise Chaytor, whose extensive experience as the former Head of the Information Team, coupled with her consistent patience, optimism and encouragement, made her a great person to work with over the years. We send all good wishes to Kathleen Daymond, Ethics Services Manager, in the Ethics Services Team, her successor and the BACP Information Services Team. We also especially thank Grainne Griffin for all she has done for us and for others. We are very sorry to lose her from BACP, and wish her well for the future. Grateful thanks also to Sarah Millward, John O'Dowd, Jan Watson and all those in BACP who have helped us in many different ways during the production of this book.

Last, but certainly not least, we appreciate the legal expertise of Helen Watts, Advocate, from Edinburgh, who added relevant Scottish law to the text, and Alice Bailie and Mark Thompson from A & L Goodbody in Belfast who together provided a Northern Irish legal perspective for the book.

Introduction

Awareness of context

56. The practitioner is responsible for learning about and taking account of the different protocols, conventions and customs that can pertain to different working contexts and cultures. (BACP 2010b: 9)

Counsellors and psychotherapists work in a wide variety of contexts. Each context has its own specific perspective of therapy practice. Policies, professional practice regulations and guidance all operate in the general framework of local and national law. Civil and criminal law applies to all practitioners and to all aspects of our work.

In order to practise within the law, we need to be aware of what it is and how it works, but don't worry – therapists don't have to become lawyers! It is enough to understand how the law works in the context of therapy practice and to recognise the potential legal pitfalls, enabling therapists to get appropriate professional advice and help when necessary. Each case is different. If a therapist is concerned about their legal position in a particular situation, they are strongly advised to seek professional legal advice on the facts of their specific circumstances. Professional insurers will often provide or fund legal advice, as part of their cover.

The earlier books in the BACP's Legal Resource Series (Bond and Mitchels 2008; Bond and Sandhu 2005; Mitchels and Bond 2010) took a generic approach and addressed the interests of the therapy profession as a whole. This book explores the law in relation to the different contexts in which therapy is practised.

We have listened to the concerns of practitioners working in a wide variety of contexts and, in response, we write about the law in specific areas of work including: private practice, commercial and employee assistance provision, voluntary work, social care, education, National Health Service (NHS) and private health provision, police and home office, youth work, adoption support, forensic work and spiritual and pastoral care.

There are, of course, certain common themes which apply to many different contexts of therapeutic work. These themes are addressed in this book, too, but are explored in greater detail in our earlier books, for example, giving evidence and preparing court reports (Bond and Sandhu 2005), how long to keep records (Bond and Mitchels 2008: 72–8), mental capacity (Bond and Mitchels 2008: 117–25), negligence and professional duty of care (Mitchels and Bond 2010: Chapter 3), criminal activity (Mitchels and Bond 2010: Chapter 5) and professional diligence (Mitchels and Bond

2010: Chapter 11). Where relevant, to avoid repetition, we have briefly mentioned the salient points here and also cross-referenced to these other publications.

We cannot cover everything there is to say in a book of this size, but we have done our best to provide pointers to the relevant law, with an explanation of its impact and to explore the main issues or common dilemmas that might be relevant to each therapeutic context. We are greatly indebted to those practitioners who have shared ideas, concerns and difficulties which they have encountered in their work. Their input has helped us to write this book with the interests and needs of practitioners in mind, and to create what we hope is a direct and practical approach to practice issues and dilemmas.

We have tried to point out the main legal 'elephant-traps' along the paths of therapeutic practice as we explore each different context. Every work situation is different, and each client unique, so there will always be new, unusual or unexpected situations. If dilemmas arise, we hope that this book will provide sufficient information and general principles to create a starting point for consideration and discussion of the issues, with pointers to resources for further specialist help wherever necessary.

Since each therapeutic situation is unique, if a present (or potential) legal dilemma, court case, claim or complaint arises, no book can ever be an adequate substitute for direct legal and professional advice. We recommend that advice is sought from an experienced lawyer or other professional appropriately qualified in the relevant field and that the professional indemnity insurers are notified. Insurers may be able to provide (or fund) legal advice and assistance. At the back of the book we have also included some useful resources and suggestions for further reading.

We refer in the book to *'therapists'* as a generic term which includes counsellors and psychotherapists of all approaches and modalities. 'Therapists' also includes closely related roles such as coaching, mentoring and consultative support or supervision within the specific therapeutic contexts covered here. Where we use 'he' or 'she', we intend these terms to include both genders, and the singular includes the plural, unless we say otherwise.

Note on jurisdiction: This book covers the law in England. The law in Wales, Northern Ireland and Scotland is covered where specifically mentioned.

1 Private Practice

Is therapy a vocation or is it really a business?

Does it matter what time of year I start up in private practice? Is there a best time to do this?

Can I say what I like in an advertisement for my new practice?

He lost his temper and shouted at our receptionist in the office twice last week, in front of all the others, and made her cry – is that harassment?

I work part of the time for myself at home and part of the time in a GP surgery, how can I tell if I am self-employed or employed?

Can I negotiate the terms of my professional indemnity insurance policy or do I have to take what I am offered? What should I be looking for it to cover?

If I work from home, do I have to make disabled access provisions, like a ramp?

Do I have to keep client records?

What can I do if my client does not pay their fees?

Therapy is regarded for tax and other legal purposes as a business enterprise, whether a therapist is a sole practitioner working part-time from home, or part of a large consortium. In private practice, therapists are free to run their business as they wish, provided that they act ethically and comply with local and national law. All the practical aspects of setting up in business – including, for example, advertising, premises, facilities, contracting, finance, employment, tax, data protection, equal opportunities and health and safety legislation – may apply. On top of all this are the guidance and ethics of professional organisations. Practitioners might like to look at *Freelance Counselling and Psychotherapy* (Clark 2002). This book originated from a conference for freelance therapists, at the Univeristy of East Anglia, with contributions from a wide variety of private practitioners exploring some of the advantages and challenges of private work. Useful BACP Information Sheets relevant to private practice are included in 1.1 below.

1.1 Legal features of private practice

Like any business, private therapeutic practice requires attention to setting up, marketing, premises, management and administration, insurance, tax and quality assurance of the service provided. There are many complex specialist areas of law involved, so in this chapter we outline the relevant law, with references to other publications for those who need greater detail or wish to read further, but as all situations are different, if there are important legal issues, we recommend seeking specialist advice. Check with insurers – many of them will provide free legal assistance – after all, it is in their interests to do so!

1.1.1 Starting up in business

'Starting up' has both a colloquial meaning and also, in business terminology it means the official commencement of the business – otherwise referred to as the 'business start date' or the 'starting up date', i.e. the official date on which the business commences, for accounting, tax and other purposes. Accounts are usually produced annually for income and other tax purposes. The business financial year for accounting purposes (also known as the 'fiscal year') may not necessarily be a calendar year. The government fiscal or 'budget' year in the UK runs from 31 March to 1 April in the following year. Some universities have a fiscal year which coincides with the academic year, as they are less busy in the summer months. Many UK businesses, for convenience, choose to adopt the government fiscal year for their own financial accounts.

A careful choice of starting date may be important, especially where there are tax-allowance schemes in operation for new businesses. These schemes are often politically motivated and may vary with the prevailing government plans, so talk with a financial adviser about the choice of starting up date to utilise any possible tax advantage. As an example, a therapist who chooses a start-up date for their business on 1 July 2010 may then choose a business tax year which runs from 1 July 2010 to 30 June 2011, and render their tax accounts accordingly.

Finance is only one aspect of starting up in a therapy business. It all requires some organisation and advance planning, and the checklist below may be helpful.

Checklist: Starting up in business

- Start date
- Set up premises where business operates (and/or services provided)
- Check that premises are covered by appropriate insurance
- Professional indemnity insurance for therapist(s)
- Professional memberships for therapist(s)
- Bank – see advice and special offers for new businesses
- Local authority – training and networking opportunities
- Set up an administrative system for client records, appointments, standard letters, bills and receipts, invoices, etc.
- Staff, reception and administration – will help be needed?
- Computer data held? Data protection notification and registration
- Tax – registration as self-employed (if appropriate)
- VAT – registration (if appropriate)

- Services: business telephone/fax line
- Out-of-hours service arrangements (if appropriate)
- Local professional groups and organisations for marketing and support
- Advertising – local directory, Yellow Pages and websites

For government advice and assistance on business start-up, see www.hmrc.gov. uk/startingup/. Local councils may encourage business groups and offer training or start-up loans, banks often have special offers, including business advice and free banking for the first year.

Useful resources for further discussion of starting up in business are Mitchels and Bond (2010: 102–6) and Gabriel and Casemore (2009a). BACP Information Sheets are free to members, and other helpful titles when starting in private practice include: Anthony (2007); Bond and Jenkins (2009); Bond et al. (2010); Clark (2002); Dale (2009a); Dale (2009b); Jackson and Chaytor (2009); Mearns (2009); Moore (2009).

1.1.2 Advertising and the law

Since therapy is a business, advertising is regulated in the same way as other business enterprises. Therapists must be careful to avoid misleading descriptions of their experience, qualifications or work, and of making promises that they cannot fulfil.

> Providing clients with adequate information
>
> 59. Practitioners are responsible for clarifying the terms on which their services are being offered in advance of the client incurring any financial obligation or other reasonably foreseeable costs or liabilities.
>
> 60. All information about services should be honest, accurate, avoid unjustifiable claims, and be consistent with maintaining the good standing of the profession.
>
> 61. Particular care should be taken over the integrity of presenting qualifications, accreditation and professional standing.
>
> (BACP 2010a: 9)

Under the Trade Descriptions Act 1968 and other regulations, including the Business Protection from Misleading Marketing Regulations 2008 and the Consumer Protection from Unfair Trading Regulations 2008, it is illegal to promote a business with false or misleading information, e.g. if a therapist claims experience or qualifications that they don't have, or makes extravagant claims for their therapy – e.g. promising that they can provide an absolute 'cure' for all their clients. As Cohen (1992) says, '... the wisest of them promise nothing at all!' (Bond 2010: 70).

It is also legally unwise to advertise by making unfavourable comparisons with others; see The Control of Misleading Advertisements (Amendment) Regulations

2000 and 1998. An advertisement is misleading if in any way, including its presentation, it deceives or is likely to deceive the person to whom it is addressed or whom it reaches and if by reason of its deceptive nature, it is likely to affect their economic behaviour, or for those reasons injures or is likely to injure a competitor of the person whose interests the advertisement seeks to promote. An 'advertisement' for the purposes of the regulations means any form of representation (including oral) which is made in connection with a trade, business, craft or profession, in order to promote the supply or transfer of goods or services, immovable property, rights or obligations. For further details, see www.oft.gov.uk.

Applying the advertising regulations to a dispute about dog food advertising, the Court of Appeal held in the case of *Boehringer Ingelheim Ltd and Others v. Vetplus Ltd* [2007] Times Law Reports 27 June, that comparative advertisements must not be misleading, but the judges gave their view that: 'Traders would have nothing to fear if they had sure foundations for claims they made about their products ... Traders who made claims for their products which they could not readily and firmly justify would have to live with the risk that their rivals could honestly and reasonably call those claims into question ...'

One particular case could be applied by analogy to therapy advertising. In 2006, the Office of Fair Trading (OFT) took action against Magna Jewellery Limited. Whilst not admitting that their advertising was misleading, the owners of the business gave certain specific undertakings, i.e.

'Not to give the impression that:

- the therapeutic effect of magnetic products is established or proven by scientific trials. This includes claims like, 'Only Magna Therapy Jewellery is clinically proven to relieve pain,' and that the idea magnetic fields improve circulation, 'has been reinforced by medical research studies'.
- products have a therapeutic effect due to their magnets (or magnetic fields) and/or will in all cases produce a therapeutic effect for those who wear them. This includes claims like, 'The pain relieving properties are derived from tiny but powerful magnets'; and, 'Magnetic pain relief bracelets really work'.

The undertakings also restrict the publication of advertisements using customer testimonials that repeat any of the above claims. Christine Wade, Director of Consumer Regulation Enforcement, said: 'Magna Jewellery Ltd targets its products at consumers who are looking for relief from pain. Where advertisements claim products have therapeutic effects it is important they do not mislead consumers. These undertakings given to the OFT will protect consumers' (OFT 2006).

If the undertakings given to the OFT are breached, a High Court injunction can be sought. Failure to comply with an injunction may result in proceedings for contempt of court. In 2007, the OFT committed to targeting health care as a priority area for the next three years.

BACP's *Ethical Framework* (BACP 2010a) lists practitioners' values as including respect for human rights and dignity, and integrity in practitioner–client relationships. The first ethical principle is:

Being trustworthy: honouring the trust placed in the practitioner (also referred to as fidelity)

Being trustworthy is regarded as fundamental to understanding and resolving ethical issues. Practitioners who adopt this principle: act in accordance with the trust placed in them; strive to ensure that clients' expectations are ones that have reasonable prospects of being met; honour their agreements and promises; regard confidentiality as an obligation arising from the client's trust; restrict any disclosure of confidential information about clients to furthering the purposes for which it was originally disclosed. (BACP 2010a: 3)

Clearly, deliberately misleading advertising would contravene these values and principles.

1.1.3 Employing others

Box 1.1 Employed/self-employed/or a bit of both?

The difference between employment status and 'self-employed' status is a legal minefield. Be careful not to get caught in the trap of taking on someone to help, perhaps for reception duties, or another therapist who describes themselves as 'self-employed' without checking this out carefully. You may find out later that actually, in the eyes of the law, you are employing them – this can be expensive for the employer in terms of possible liability for payment of accumulated tax, national insurance contributions etc., and there may be legal fines.

The distinction is also important for therapists in private practice. Many of us undertake part-time work for GP surgeries, voluntary agencies, and other organisations. We may think that we are self-employed because we work part-time, or work with more than one agency, but we could discover that we are not. For help in making the distinction between self-employment and employment, contact your local branch of HM Revenue and Customs (HMRC) or visit HMRC's website at www.hmrc.gov.uk, which has information about starting up in business, leaflet IR 56, showing how to discover if you should be classified as 'self-employed' for tax purposes. See also the HMRC *Employment Status Indicator (ESI) Tool* at www.hmrc.gov.uk/employment-status/index.htm and the HMRC *Employment Status Manual* at www.hmrc.gov.uk/manuals/esmmanual/index.htm, with links to a helpline for the newly self-employed.

Therapists may be self-employed in their own business, but also need to employ others, for secretarial, administration or reception services, cleaning, etc. See the section on Finance and Tax below for details of PAYE and national insurance contributions. See the section on Equal Opportunities below for the rights of minority groups and those with disability. For an explanation of current employment rights, see the various headings in the government website www.direct.gov.uk, and www.berr.gov.uk or www.lra.org.uk in Northern Ireland from which information can be downloaded. To search for relevant guidance to the Employment Act 2008, go to www.legislation.gov.uk.

Therapists who are employers will have to comply with all the relevant parts of a wide range of employment legislation, including the Employment Acts 2002 and 2008, Employer's Liability (Compulsory Insurance) Act 1969, Equal Pay Act 1970, Redundancy Payments Act 1965, and the Rehabilitation of Offenders Act 1974.

In Northern Ireland, whilst the Employment Acts 2002 and 2008 apply, the remaining Acts do not extend to Northern Ireland. In this jurisdiction the relevant legislation is as follows: Employer's Liability (Defective Equipment and Compulsory Insurance) (Northern Ireland) Order 1972, Equal Pay Act (Northern Ireland) 1970, Contracts of Employment and Redundancy Payments Act (Northern Ireland) 1965 and the Rehabilitation of Offenders (Northern Ireland) Order 1978. Amongst other legislation, the Employment (Northern Ireland) Order 2003 and the Employment Act (Northern Ireland) 2010 also apply.

In particular, note the Safeguarding Vulnerable Groups Act 2006 (the Northern Ireland equivalent being the Safeguarding Vulnerable Groups (Northern Ireland) Order 2007) which regulates employment in work with children or vulnerable adults, barring any person who is on the 'Child First' or 'Adult First' lists. The Act creates requirements when taking on new employees in specified fields of work; failure to comply will be an offence, but its provisions may be changed by new governments. In England, Wales and Northern Ireland, the Vetting and Barring Scheme is implemented by the Independent Safeguarding Authority (ISA) so watch the website www.isa-gov.org.uk for details of the progress of the legislation. Details can also be found with an explanatory note at www.legislation.gov.uk. See also the Safeguarding Vulnerable Groups Act 2006 (Commencement No 1) Order 2007 and the Safeguarding Vulnerable Groups (Northern Ireland) Order 2007, and www.dhsspsni.gov.uk/child_protection guidance. Watch these websites for changes.

In Scotland, a similar Protecting Vulnerable Groups (PVG) Scheme is created by the Protection of Vulnerable Groups (Scotland) Act 2007, with implementation being phased in to minimise the administrative burden on individual organisations. At present, it is anticipated that this scheme will begin to operate from February 2011. For a copy of the Protection of Vulnerable Groups (Scotland) Act 2007 see www.legislation.gov.uk.

In addition, there are a myriad of regulations, which there is insufficient space to explore in detail here, but of which it is helpful to be aware (see Box 1.1).

Checklist: Employment regulations

- Employment Act 2002 (Dispute Resolution) Regulations 2004 (in Northern Ireland, Employment (Northern Ireland) 2003 (Dispute Resolution) Regulations 2004)
- Employment Equality (Age) Regulations 2006 (in Northern Ireland, Employment Equality (Age) Regulations (Northern Ireland) 2006)
- Employment Equality (Religion or Belief) Regulations 2003 (in Northern Ireland, Fair Employment Treatment Order (Amendment) Regulations 2003)
- Employment Equality (Sex Discrimination) Regulations 2005 (SI 2005/2467) (in Northern Ireland, Employment Equality (Sex Discrimination) Regulations (Northern Ireland) 2005)
- Employment Equality (Sexual Orientation) Regulations 2003 (SI 2003/1661) (in Northern Ireland, Employment Equality (Sexual Orientation) Regulations (Northern Ireland) 2003)
- Employment Equality (Sexual Orientation) Regulations 2003 (Amendment) Regulations 2004 (SI 2004/2519)
- Employers Liability (Compulsory Insurance) Regulations 1998 (SI 1998/2573)
- Maternity and Parental Leave, etc, Regulations 1999 (SI 1999/3312) (in Northern Ireland, Maternity and Parental Leave etc. Regulations (Northern Ireland) 1999)
- Part-time Workers (Prevention of Less Favourable Treatment) Regulations 2000 (SI 2000/1551) (in Northern Ireland, Part-time Workers (Prevention of Less Favourable Treatment) Regulations (Northern Ireland) 2000)
- Paternity and Adoption Leave Regulations 2002 (SI 2002/2788) (in Northern Ireland, Paternity and Adoption Leave Regulations (Northern Ireland) 2002)
- Unfair Terms in Consumer Contract Regulations 1999 (SI 1999 No 2083)
- Working Time Regulations 1998 SI 1998 No 1833 and the Working Time (Amendment) Regulations 2001 (*SI 2001 No 325) (in Northern Ireland, Working Time Regulations (Northern Ireland) 1998 and the Working Time (Amendment) Regulations (Northern Ireland) 2002)

For further discussion of these regulations, employment issues generally, PAYE, national insurance etc, see Mitchels and Bond (2010: Chapters 8, 9).

1.1.4 Equal opportunities, non-discriminatory practice and prevention of harassment

The Human Rights Act 1998 establishes general principles of equality and makes certain rights generally enforceable in UK law. This is reinforced by other legislation against specific forms of discrimination, see Box 1.2. Therapists running their own business, even those working alone or working from their own home, must make sure that both employees and clients have equal opportunities and that their practice is non-discriminatory. The *Ethical Framework* (BACP 2010a: 3) requires 'justice: the fair and impartial treatment of all clients and the provision of adequate services'. Therapists are also required to consider conscientiously any legal requirements and obligations and remain alert to potential conflicts between legal and ethical obligations.

Discrimination can take many forms, and Box 1.2 indicates some of the main legislative provisions.

Box 1.2 Legislation against forms of discrimination

- **Discrimination on the grounds of sex, sexual orientation or gender reassignment** (see the Sex Discrimination Act 1975 (in Northern Ireland, the Sex Discrimination (Northern Ireland) Order 1976), the Equal Treatment Directive (76/207/EEC) and The Equal Opportunities Directive 2006/54/EC implementing equal opportunities, e.g. equal pay. See also the provisions relating to sexual orientation and sexual discrimination in the Employment Equality (Sex Discrimination) Regulations 2005, Employment Equality (Sexual Orientation) Regulations 2003 and the Employment Equality (Sexual Orientation) Regulations 2003 (Amendment) Regulations 2004). (The Northern Ireland equivalents of these regulations are provided in section 1.1.3.)
- **Age discrimination** (see the Employment Equality (Age) Regulations 2006, which have been in force since 1 October 2006). (The Northern Ireland equivalents of these regulations are provided in section 1.1.3.)
- **Discrimination on the grounds of religion or belief** (see the Employment Equality (Religion or Belief) Regulations 2003). (The Northern Ireland equivalents of these regulations are provided in section 1.1.3.)
- **Discrimination on the grounds of race** (see the Race Relations Act 1976 or in Northern Ireland, the Race Relations (Northern Ireland) Order 1997).
- **Discrimination on the grounds of disability** (see the Disability Discrimination Acts 1995 and 2005, and website www.direct.gov.uk. Braille, Audio, BSL and Easy read versions are available from The Stationery Office www.tsoshop.co.uk. In the context of employment, see the *Disability Discrimination Act 1995 Code of Practice: Employment and Occupation* (the Code), issued on 1 October 2004, setting out the rights of disabled workers and duties of their employers).

The Code provides that employers should not discriminate against disabled workers, but this is now limited by the House of Lords' decision in *London Borough of Lewisham v Malcolm* [2008] UKHL 43, overruling earlier decisions, which may influence future employment cases. It is now not enough for a disabled person to show that there was some connection between her disability and the reason for the treatment that she challenges. She also needs to show that her disability played some motivating part in the alleged discrimination.

In addition, it is unlawful to discriminate on the grounds of:

- Pregnancy, maternity leave or paternity leave
- Marital or civil partnership status: see the Sex Discrimination Act 1975, Sex Discrimination (Northern Ireland) Order 1976, as amended by the Civil Partnership Act 2004, s. 251(1)–(2).

Part-time workers are protected in relation to pay and other potential detriments by the Part-time Workers (Prevention of Less Favourable Treatment) Regulations 2000 and the Part-Time Workers (Prevention of Less Favourable Treatment) Regulations (Northern Ireland) 2000. The Equal Pay Act 1970 and its Northern Ireland counterpart, as amended by subsequent legislation, expects that women employed in an establishment in Great Britain (whether they are British or not) should receive 'equal pay for equal work' in comparison with men, see s. 1(13) and the *Code of Practice on Equal Pay* issued by the Equal Opportunities Commission in 2003.

The Protection from Harassment Act 1997 and Protection from Harassment (Northern Ireland) Order 1997 were designed to protect victims of harassment, whatever form the harassment takes, wherever it occurs, and whatever its motivation. In the workplace, harassment may involve the violation of self-respect, dignity, or a hostile working environment. Harassment (defined in s. 1 of the Act as pursuing a course of conduct which amounts to harassment of another and which the alleged offender knows or ought to know amounts to harassment of the other) is unlawful and may generate civil liability and/or constitute a criminal offence where the victim is caused 'alarm' or 'distress' (s. 7.2). A 'course of conduct' implies an action on at least two occasions, s. 7(2),(3) and 'conduct' includes speech, s. 7(1),(2). Establishing a 'course of conduct' is more difficult when the actions are separated in time than when actions are close together, e.g. within three months of each other, see *Pratt v DPP* [2001] EWHC 483.

In the case of *Kelly v DPP* [2002] EWHC Admin 1428 166 JP 621, three threatening or abusive phone calls were held to constitute harassment. It is our view that threatening email and Internet communications may also be harassment if they cause alarm and distress to the recipient, see *S v DPP* [2008] EWHC (Admin) 438.

It is possible that a therapist or staff member working in private practice, e.g. as part of a consortium, may experience workplace harassment. Such behaviour is contrary to the *Ethical Framework* (BACP 2010a) and potentially grounds for complaint against a therapist colleague. A therapist employing a member of staff who harasses others may be vicariously liable for the actions of their employee. In *Majrowski v Guy's and St Thomas's NHS Trust* [2006] UKHL 34, a clinical auditor hospital employee was subjected to criticism and bullying by his departmental manager, who was rude, abusive and critical to him in front of other staff, imposing unrealistic targets and threatening disciplinary action if these were not met. In this case, the court supported the concept of the 'vicarious liability' of employers for acts of their employees in the course of their employment, and reiterated that imposing this strict liability on employers encourages them to maintain standards of good practice by their employees. For those reasons, where one employee harasses another, the employer may be held liable. Employers can cover their potential liability with appropriate insurance. For a detailed discussion of the relevant law, see the judgment in the *Majrowski* case and Slade (2008: Chapter 12). Their Lordships' opinions in this leading case about employer's liability for the actions of employees are also reported online at www.publications.parliament.uk.

Careful consideration should be given to providing accessibility and resources in therapy premises for those with disability. See the section on premises below.

In Northern Ireland, additional legislation exists in relation to religious belief and/or political opinion (Fair Employment and Treatment (Northern Ireland) Order 1998).

1.1.5 Finance and tax

Many counsellors are employed part-time and also run their own private self-employed business for another part of the working week. The therapist would be taxed under the PAYE system in respect of their employment and also have to register for self-employed taxation for the business. For employment/self-employment distinctions, see above at 1.1.3.

Business expenditure can be set against profits for tax purposes. Keep receipts for all equipment and bills used for the business. Sometimes only a proportion of the cost of equipment or expenditure can be allowed against income for taxation purposes (e.g. if a therapist uses the car for business, a proportion of the whole car insurance, repair and petrol cost may be allowable; or a proportion of the telephone or heating costs if a therapist works from home).

All self-employed therapists must declare their income (business profits) for tax purposes. HMRC may require to see business records of income and expenditure, created from and supported by all the relevant business documents, including invoices, cheque books, bank statements, paying-in books, and income and expenditure receipts. These records do not necessarily have to be written or audited by an accountant or a book-keeper, but the help of an accountant or book-keeper may be well worth the cost. See www.hmrc.gov.uk/startingup/ for links to sources of advice and help. Data and supporting documents should be kept for seven years. Advice on business record keeping and resources can be found at website: www.hmrc.gov.uk/startingup/keeprecs.htm.

The government website www.hmrc.gov.uk/startingup/taxgate.htm has a good deal of useful information about how National Insurance and taxation might affect the business. VAT limits and the levels of VAT taxation may vary from year to year. Details of the impact of VAT registration, how and where to register, and accounting schemes to simplify VAT accounting are all to be found at the government website www.hmrc.gov.uk/vat/start/register/index.htm.

1.1.6 Health and safety

Under the Health Act 1999 and the Health and Safety at Work Act 1974 (in Northern Ireland the Health and Safety at Work (Northern Ireland) Order 1978), Occupiers' Liability Acts 1957 and 1984, Occupiers' Liability (Northern Ireland) Act 1957, Occupiers' Liability (Northern Ireland) Order 1987 and various asbestos and fire safety regulations, there is a responsibility for employers and those who are in control of work premises to provide a safe environment for workers, clients and visitors. This also applies to therapists who work from home, who should consider safety issues, and therapists who are self-employed must take similar care of themselves and clients under the legislation. Detailed information can be found in the legislation and in resource books such as *The Health and Safety at Work Handbook* (Bamber et al. 2008). Most local authorities have a Health and Safety Officer who may be willing to advise.

Checklist: Health and safety risks

- fire
- asbestos and other dangerous substances in the building
- access to premises
- equipment
- activities
- accidents and emergencies

Checklist: Action to minimise health and safety risks

- assessment of client (customer) needs and abilities
- maintenance of safe access
- fire prevention and control
- first aid facilities and training
- information, training and instruction
- supervision and control
- monitoring
- emergency arrangements

Therapists working from home may use a room in their house for therapy and also for other purposes. If they do not have a part of the house designated solely for their work and they have no employees, they may not be required to comply with the Health and Safety at Work legislation, but they should be aware of (and insure against) possible risks to clients and themselves. They should also bear in mind the general duty of care to clients (and visitors) and take reasonable safety measures, e.g. adequate household fire safety precautions, removal of dangerous substances and keeping a first aid kit available. There is always a possibility in any of our lives that family, clients or visitors may need first aid, and basic first aid training is always useful! Insurance for public and professional liability is considered in the next section.

1.1.7 Insurance

There are considerable numbers of complaints about therapists to their professional bodies each year, and responding to complaints may require legal assistance and prove expensive. Government regulation of the profession is probably imminent and will almost certainly require compulsory insurance cover. Professional bodies (e.g. BACP, UKCP and BPC) recommend insurance in their practice guidance and some, including BACP, require cover as a precondition of accreditation. Insurance is a means of providing a level of protection for the profession, clients and the public interest, and it is our firm view that adequate professional insurance cover is essential for all those in therapeutic practice.

Insurers may be able to provide advice and help on the appropriate levels of cover in relation to workload, place of work and identified risks. Insurance proves its worth when you need it to pay out. Inexpensive insurers may offer cheap deals, but provide only minimum cover.

Checklist: Insurance cover

- ensure premises are covered for repairs etc.
- obtain cover for occupier's liability
- if working from home, ensure this does not invalidate your usual home insurance cover
- obtain cover for life, health, income
- obtain cover for professional indemnity and public liability

Checklist: Checking an insurance policy

Ask whether insurers provide:

- advice and assistance in dealing with professional complaints
- legal assistance in responding to complaints and legal claims
- a telephone helpline for advice and assistance or access to other help and resources

Do the insurers provide cover for:

- claims for negligence
- dealing with allegations of professional misconduct
- claims for libel and slander
- claims for breach of the therapeutic contract
- public liability
- legal fees in dealing with complaints and claims

Additional cover may include:

- directors' and officers' liability
- public relations assistance to mitigate damage to reputation
- assistance with criminal defence

Watch out for limits on indemnity cover and exclusion clauses in the insurance policy. Most insurance companies set a *limit of indemnity,* i.e. a limit on the total amount of money they would pay out on each policy. This will usually be expressed as indemnity 'for any one claim' or indemnity 'in the aggregate' or similar words to this effect. There is a vast difference. Response to even one claim may take a good deal of money, for example, cover of £1 million might soon be used up. Cover for 'any one claim' is best, in that the stated limit applies to each separate claim on the policy in one insurance year. Cover 'in the aggregate' means that the limit applies to all claims in that year, taken together, so if more than one claim arose in a year, there is a risk that the total of all the claims might exceed the limit.

Some insurers impose an 'excess' and usually, the higher the excess, the lower the insurance premium. In other words, the insurer will only pay out on claims that exceed a certain level, the insured having to foot the bill for the 'excess' amount. An excess of £500 would mean that the insurer pays out on claims that exceed this amount, with the insured therapist paying the first £500 themselves.

Ask for a copy of the terms and conditions of the policy before taking it on, and read all the exclusion clauses, particularly those that appear in 'small print' and in less obvious parts of the policy documents. Make sure that the exclusions set out do not compromise the cover that you want to achieve.

When changing insurers, watch out for the exclusion of claims arising from past events that happened when you were covered by another insurer. Look for retro-active cover, under a 'claims made' policy, or, sometimes, as an extension to an occurrence-based policy.

Therapists who are employers must comply with the Employers' Liability (Compulsory Insurance) Act 1969, s. 1(1) or its Northern Ireland equivalent, and arrange cover 'for bodily injury or disease sustained by his employees, and arising out of or in the course of that employment'. The minimum cover required is £5m for any one or more of the employees arising out of any one occurrence, under regulation 3(1) of the Employers' Liability (Compulsory Insurance) Regulations 1998. A certificate of insurance must be displayed in the workplace (or can now be made electronically). Failure to do so is a criminal offence, with a £1,000 fine. Under the Employers' Liability (Compulsory Insurance) Act 1969, s. 2(2)(a) or Employers' Liability (Defective Equipment and Compulsory Insurance) (Northern Ireland) Order 1972, art. 6(a), certain employees are exempt, including family members: spouse, father, mother, son daughter or other close relatives. An exemption now also applies for Limited Liability Companies that have only one employee where that employee is the owner of the business.

The most important thing when arranging insurance cover is to be completely open and honest with the insurance company. Under contract law and the policy terms of most insurers, a policy may be invalidated if it is found that information has been deliberately withheld or is incorrect, e.g. failing to declare a previous conviction, or a professional complaint.

1.1.8 Premises

This is a complex area of law, and we cannot go into great detail here, but we can give some pointers to more detailed sources of information. We also focus on some of the main issues raised by therapists in workshops.

Issues to consider:

- The contract of lease or sale of premises needs to be in writing, signed by both parties and witnessed. It should set out clearly the terms of the sale or lease.
- When buying or leasing premises, it is advisable to take legal advice because there are many issues that might otherwise catch you out. These include title (e.g. you cannot sell or lease land that you do not own), restrictive covenants (e.g. not to carry on a business from that address), rights of way (e.g. the right of a neighbour to use a stairway, or to go through a passageway to get to their dustbin or a shared back gate), planning consents (e.g. an extension built without any necessary planning consent could be subject to an order for demolition), and the respective responsibilities and liabilities of the landlord/tenant; lessor/lessee (e.g. maintenance, decoration, management fees etc.).
- Premises must comply with disability legislation. See the glossary for definition of disability; see also the Disability Discrimination Act 1995 (DDA) and the Disability Discrimination Act 2005 (DDA).
- Health and safety issues must be addressed. Employers and/or those who are in total or partial control of work premises must provide a safe environment for employees, staff and volunteers, clients, customers and those who use the facilities, visitors, neighbours, the public, and even (in some cases) trespassers. The local authority has a Health and Safety Officer who may be willing to advise.
- Therapists working from home, who use a room in their house from time to time for therapy (and therefore do not have a part of the house designated solely for their work) and who have no employees, although perhaps not required to comply with the Health and Safety at Work Act or Health and Safety at Work (Northern Ireland) Order 1978, should be aware of (and insure against) the possible risks to clients and themselves, and bear in mind the general duty of care to clients (and visitors) and take reasonable safety measures, e.g. adequate household fire safety precautions, removal of dangerous substances and keeping a first aid kit available. See the Health and Safety at Work Act 1974 (or, if relevant, the Northern Ireland equivalent), the Regulatory Reform (Fire Safety) Order 2005, Occupiers' Liability Acts 1957 and 1984 and Occupiers' Liability (Northern Ireland Order 1987) and the Control of Asbestos Regulations 2006 (or the Control of Asbestos Regulations (Northern Ireland) 2007).
- Public liability and professional indemnity insurance is essential.
- Accidents or unforeseen events can happen, e.g. an attack by a client on another person, or a client falling over a carpet or stairs. Public liability insurance cover is necessary to protect therapists, clients and the public in the event of an accident in which a member of the public suffers personal injury. Also consider the matter of insurance cover for buildings and contents , so check the terms of the building and contents

insurance policy, and arrange insurance that covers all the necessary aspects of the therapy business at home. Ensure that present policies are not adversely affected by working from home.

- Therapists who own or are in control of premises for work purposes must comply with the Occupiers' Liability Acts 1957 and 1984, the Occupiers' Liability (Northern Ireland) Act 1957, and the Occupiers' Liability (Scotland) Act 1960, which create liability for safety and security of premises, see (Mitchels and Bond 2010: Chapter 7).

Therapists, whether providing paid or free-of-charge therapy, are providing services in the context of a 'profession or trade'. Part III of the DDA 1995 makes it unlawful to discriminate against a disabled person by unjustifiably providing less favourable treatment (s. 20) or failing to take reasonable steps to provide access or facilities (s. 21). The Equality and Human Rights Commission runs a dedicated disability helpline (see Useful Resources at the end of this book), and the Acts and guidance are available on their website www.direct.gov.uk. There is also a useful booklet *Making Access to Goods and Services Easier for the Disabled: a Practical Guide for Small Business and Service Providers* by the Disability Rights Commission, available from the Equality and Human Rights Commission or at www.direct.gov.uk. Braille, Audio, BSL and Easy read versions are available from The Stationery Office, at www.tsoshop.co.uk. An audit of business premises and the feasibility of making disability provisions can be obtained from the *Centre for Accessible Environment* (www.cae.org.uk) or the *National Register of Access Consultants* (www. nrac.org.uk).

Ensure that working from home or other premises does not put you in breach of a mortgage agreement, or planning regulations. A useful resource is the Planning Portal, a UK government online planning and building regulations resource, available at www.planningportal.gov.uk. It was designed to help enquirers to find out whether their proposed action requires planning consent, the relevant building regulations that apply, and to make any necessary application.

Restrictions may be placed on the use of buildings and land for the benefit of neighbours and the community, and they are set out in title deeds and leases. In titles that are registered with the Land Registry, restrictive covenants are entered on the register along with the title to the land, and a copy can be obtained for the payment of a fee from the local Land Registry. For example, many dwelling houses and flats have restrictive covenants forbidding certain uses of the premises (a covenant against business use may prohibit 'any business', or prohibit specific sorts of business, e.g. use of the building as a shop or garage etc.). A covenant against business use may mean that neighbours could object if the therapist begins to work from home, and action could be taken in the local county court to enforce the restrictive covenant. If there are restrictive covenants, seek advice from a conveyancing lawyer. In Scotland, premises may be subject to a 'burden' in the title deeds which restricts their use. The Registers of Scotland will provide details of the burdens pertaining to a particular property in exchange for the payment of a small fee. Further information is available at www.ros.gov.uk.

Working from home can be very convenient, but it has its potential problems, e.g. the use of the premises may be shared with family, pets and general bric-a-brac, any of which may provide unexpected difficulties for clients who may object to being licked enthusiastically by an excited dog as they come through the gate, meeting granny or children in the hall, or simply being faced with family pictures, religious objects, or other things that may constitute unwelcome self-disclosure. The insurance companies report complaints and claims based on issues such as these.

1.1.9 Records, data protection and freedom of information

The *Ethical Framework* (BACP 2010a: 3) refers to trustworthiness, expecting therapists to 'regard confidentiality as an obligation arising from the client's trust; restrict any disclosure of confidential information about clients to furthering the purposes for which it was originally disclosed'.

Therapists are not legally obliged to keep notes, but are increasingly expected by the courts and others to keep appropriate and accurate notes as a routine part of professional practice. Government services and those regulated by the Health Professions Council are expected to keep notes. There are some situations where notes are required, e.g. the Crown Prosecution Service (England and Wales) requires that, when providing therapy for a witness, 'Records of therapy (which includes videos and tapes as well as notes) and other contacts with the witness must be maintained so that they can be produced if required by the court' (CPS, 2005b: s. 11.4) and there are comparable provisions for therapists working with child witnesses (CPS, 2005a: ss. 3.7–3.14). This CPS guidance is currently being revised and updated, so watch out for new versions. The Scottish Government has also issued guidance for therapists in Scotland: *Interviewing Child Witnesses in Scotland* and *Code of Practice to Facilitate the Provision of Therapeutic Support to Child Witnesses in Court Proceedings*. Both of these publications are available on the Scottish Government's website at www.scotland.gov.uk.

The Northern Ireland office has issued guidance in *Achieving Best Evidence in Criminal Proceeding (Northern Ireland): Guidance for Vulnerable Witnesses, including Children*. This is available on the Northern Ireland office website at www. nio.gov.uk.

The *Ethical Framework* (BACP 2010a: 5) states:

Practitioners are advised to keep appropriate records of their work with clients unless there are good and sufficient reasons for not keeping any records. All records should be accurate, respectful of clients and colleagues and protected from unauthorised disclosure. Any records should be kept securely and adequately protected from unauthorised intrusion or disclosure. Practitioners should take into account their responsibilities and their clients' rights under data protection legislation and any other legal requirements.

A therapist who is either under a legal obligation to keep records or is ethically committed to doing so may decline to work with a client who refuses to permit the keeping of records.

Some therapists may wish to see clients without keeping any records. The ethical reasons that they may have for doing so might include the deterrent effect of record keeping on some potential clients, for example young people or others who live at the margins of society and mistrust the authorities. In some circumstances, the therapist may have no secure way of protecting records from unauthorised access. In some cases, this may be an exceptional arrangement for a particular client who will accept therapy only on the basis that records are not kept. These may amount to 'good and sufficient reasons not to keep records' within the context of the *Ethical Framework*.

Box 1.3 Data protection legislation

- Data Protection Act 1998
- Freedom of Information Act 2000
- The Data Protection Act 1998 (Commencement) Order 2000
- The Data Protection Act 1998 (Commencement No. 2) Order 2008
- The Data Protection Act 1998 (Commencement No. 3) Order 2011
- The Data Protection (Monetary Penalties) Order 2010
- The Data Protection (Monetary Penalties) (Maximum Penalty and Notices) Regulations 2010
- Data Protection (Processing of Sensitive Personal Data) Order 2000
- The Data Protection (Processing of Sensitive Personal Data) Order 2006
- The Data Protection (Processing of Sensitive Personal Data) Order 2009
- The Data Protection (Processing of Sensitive Personal Data) (Elected Representatives) (Amendment) Order 2010
- The Data Protection (Notification and Notification Fees) (Amendment) Regulations 2009
- Data Protection (Subjects Access Modification) (Health) Order 2000
- Data Protection (Subjects Access Modification) (Education) Order 2000
- Data Protection (Subjects Access Modification) (Social Work) Order 2000
- The Protection of Vulnerable Groups (Scotland) Act 2007 (Prescribed Manner and Place for the Taking of Fingerprints and Prescribed Personal Data Holders) Regulations 2010

The Data Protection Act 1998 and Freedom of Information Act 2000 govern a client's access to personal records. Under these statutes, all personal data held by public bodies, whether held electronically or handwritten, can be accessed by the client (the data subject), with certain statutory safeguards. These include health, education and social services records, irrespective of when or how they were made and stored.

Client records held by therapists working privately are not subject to the Freedom of Information Act 2000, but if the records are stored electronically (i.e. if notes are held on a compter, video or tape recordings, etc), then therapists must register under the Data Protection Act.

There is often some confusion about two separate concepts:

- **Registration** under the Data Protection Act is compulsory for all electronically held personal records.
- Irrespective of registration, the Data Protection Act provisions still apply not only to all records held electronically (i.e. those which have been registered) and under the Freedom of Information Act to all government departments, but they also apply to **all manual records** held in a 'relevant system'.

The term 'relevant system' means handwritten records kept in a way that would enable a temporary assistant to find a file or a piece of information easily. This means that if therapists in any kind of private practice have neat, tidy records in a 'relevant system', although that therapist might not have to register under the Data Protection Act, the Data Protection Act provisions would still apply to those records.

So the advice we give to therapists is simple: If you keep records on computer or electronically in recordings, etc., register under the Data Protection Act with the Information Commissioner's Office. If your records are handwritten, then keep neat, tidy records, and comply with the Data Protection Act provisions anyway (storage, client right of access etc.). That way, you cannot go wrong!

Clients will have the right to see their notes if the Data Protection Act applies, or if this is agreed in their therapeutic contract.

For further details of how the data protection legislation works, see Bond and Mitchels (2008, Chapter 6), Bond et al. (2010) and Bond and Jenkins (2009), and the website of the Information Commissioner, www.ico.gov.uk. It is always wise to check with the Information Commissioner's office if in any doubt about whether to register. Registration involves completion of a fairly straightforward form, and there is an annual fee to pay.

For discussion and some examples of records of information sharing see 1.4 below.

Record storage

One of the issues for therapists, especially those working from home is the storage of client records and notes. For a full discussion of this see *Confidentiality and*

Record Keeping for Counsellors and Psychotherapists (Bond and Mitchels 2008). We recommend keeping records safely and securely in a locked cabinet or other secure locked filing system (note that some insurers and organisations now require therapists to use metal cabinets for record storage), and ensuring adequate security of any papers, electronic data storage and the premises as a whole, with appropriate insurance cover both for the premises and for professional liability.

1.1.10 Out of hours cover

Therapists are strongly advised to make provision for cover by a trusted colleague or supervisor in the event of death, illness, disability or any other inability of the therapist to work, plus 'out-of-hours' arrangements. Ensure that clients are aware of the therapist's boundaries and arrangements around out-of-hours contact, and negotiate these issues as part of the therapeutic contract where necessary. Protect the duty of confidentiality to clients by ensuring that if there is a telephone line or Internet connection at home, business messages and emails remain confidential. If there is an answer-phone, ensure that clients' messages are confidential, and checked regularly.

1.2 Contractual issues

1.2.1 Contract terms

Therapists in private practice may enter into many different types of contracts in the course of their working life, for example buying, leasing or renting premises from which to work, contracts for insurance, loans and mortgages, telephone, Internet or fuel supply, and perhaps for services, e.g. secretarial help or cleaning. Many of these contracts will apply also to therapists working from their own home. There are also therapeutic contracts with clients. In Scotland, the courts recognise a further requirement for the formation of a binding contract: *consensus in idem*. This requires that parties have reached a mutual understanding and agreement about the terms of the contract. In England and Wales, this concept also underpins contract law, and emphasises the need for mutual clarity and understanding of expectations and promises when making any kind of contract.

For fairness of terms in contracts, see the Misrepresentation Act 1967 (in Northern Ireland, the Misrepresentation Act (Northern Ireland) 1967) and the Unfair Contract Terms Act 1977. Goods purchased must be fit for the purpose for which they were intended, see the Sale of Goods Act 1979, which provides a legal remedy over and above commercial guarantees and manufacturers' warranties.

1.2.2 Therapeutic contracts

In counselling, expectations may not be clearly expressed or understood by both parties. Clients arriving for the first time do not always have a clear idea of what they expect or want from therapy, they may be anxious and forget to ask about the rates charged or whether they have to pay for missed sessions, how long therapy may take, or what to do if they are dissatisfied with their therapy. The therapist may not have a clear policy about missed sessions or late payments. Client and therapist may have different expectations about confidentiality. Contractual terms can be clarified by discussion with new clients at their intake assessment or first session, or by the provision of a leaflet setting out the basic terms of the therapy offered. Verbal contracts made at the first therapeutic session may not be remembered clearly, so it is better, wherever possible, to have a written therapeutic contract for clarity and as an aide-mémoire. See the guidance in Mitchels and Bond (2010: Chapter 4) and BACP Information Sheet P.11: *Making the Contract for Counselling and Psychotherapy* (Dale 2009c).

Discussion of the terms on which therapy is offered does not have to be protracted, difficult or legalistic. Sometimes negotiation of the therapeutic contract can be a helpful part of the therapeutic process, providing an opportunity to build trust, explore relevant issues, create mutual understanding and develop a therapeutic alliance. If a client is anxious or their mental state is not conducive to concentration on details or remembering terms, the contract can always be revisited as therapy progresses.

It is helpful to provide advance information about therapy, and the terms on which it is offered. This can be in various forms, for example leaflets, posters, entries in directories or web pages, and advertisements. Advance information may shorten and facilitate the initial discussion about the terms of the therapeutic contract. If that discussion is then supported by a written or other record of the agreement (e.g. a tape recording or Braille note for clients with visual impairment), clients are helped to assimilate information and to refer to and recall what was agreed. If clients are also made aware that they (or the therapist) can raise issues about their contract again during the course of therapy if they wish to do so, then client autonomy is respected and the contract may be renegotiated at a later date.

Should therapeutic contracts be in writing?

There is no requirement in law that a therapeutic contract should be written down, and in some circumstances verbal therapeutic contracts might not present difficulties. However, a written record is helpful as an aide-mémoire for therapist and client, and without a contract in writing, the absence of any evidence of what was actually agreed might become problematic if a client considers that they have been misled or harmed in any way. In the event of a dispute it would be difficult to establish satisfactorily what had been agreed, as it would be just one person's word against another.

Implied terms in therapeutic contracts

If a legal dispute arose over confidentiality, case law operates in ways that will generally favour a client claiming a right to confidentiality (see Bond and Mitchels 2008: 127–31). The legal presumption in favour of regarding therapy as a confidential activity is so strong that in the absence of any evidence to the contrary, a court may imply a term of confidentiality and then hold a therapist liable for a breach of the terms implied by the court. Similarly, any claims for breach of confidence in common law and under data protection law will start with an assumption of a commitment to confidentiality unless the therapist can establish a legal exception based on the client's consent, a statutory duty or the balance of public interest. This means that clients should be informed of (and agree to) any exceptions to confidentiality, in advance of therapy commencing. For implied terms regarding fees, see 1.2.4 below.

1.2.3 Enforceability of contracts

Legally enforceable contracts embody a number of essential ingredients that may be explicit or implied:

- a promise (for example to do or supply something)
- an agreement, and
- an exchange (for example money given in return for goods or services, in law referred to as the 'consideration').

Consideration is 'the price of a promise' per Lord Dunedin in *Dunlop v Selfridge* [1915] AC 847 at 855. In therapy, consideration is the money paid by the client for their sessions. The therapist in return promises to provide therapy in accordance with their modality, training and experience. The ingredients of contracts are regulated by statute, subordinate legislation and by case law. Some promises are made with no consideration expected in return, for example voluntary gifts of money or land, and wills. These are not contracts (although they may be legally enforceable) and may be recorded in legal deeds, signed and witnessed.

There are time limits for suing for breach of contract, usually six years for commercial contracts (five years in Scotland); see Limitation Act 1980, Limitation (Northern Ireland) Order 1989, Prescription and Limitation (Scotland) Act 1973 and Mitchels and Bond (2008: 72–8).

1.2.4 Fees for therapy, and issues of non-payment

If the fees are not agreed before therapy starts, the parties may have no clear legally enforceable contract. There are also potential ethical issues here, for example failure to support client autonomy and possibly a lack of self-respect for the therapist (BACP 2010a). If the client then receives therapy but refuses to pay any fee, the therapist may have difficulty in enforcing payment. If this should happen, once a therapist realises their mistake and wishes to continue working with that client, they should discuss and negotiate the terms of the therapy as soon as possible for an effective contract to be established, at least for their future work.

There is an old-established rule that if A does work for B, at B's request, in circumstances where *both* parties would reasonably expect A to be paid for it, and

B promises to pay a particular sum for that work, then B's promise would be enforceable; see *Lampleigh v Braithwait* [1615] Hob 105. In Scotland a similar rule, *quantum meruit* (Latin: meaning 'for what it is worth') applies. These rules might rescue the situation if the client is willing to pay a reasonable fee, but prevention is far better than cure. Most therapists would not want to have to take a client to court to obtain payment for past sessions.

Interest for late payment of debts: How to encourage prompt payment!

Some client agencies and commercial organisations (including solicitors!) who commission therapy, will eventually pay up, but seem to keep you waiting for ever. In private practice, working often on a tight budget, this is at the least, frustrating. Constant reminders to pay up are tiring to produce and do not enhance business relationships. Recognising this, parliament passed the Late Payment of Commercial Debts (Interest) Act 1998, which, as amended by subsequent legislation, allows interest to be charged for the late payment of contracts for goods or services where both parties are acting in the course of a business. Interest (currently set by the rules at the generous rate of 8% over the base rate) is payable from either an agreed date in the contract or within 30 days after delivery or invoice, whichever is the later. In Scotland interest at the judicial rate of 8% is usually payable only from the date when court proceedings are served on the Defender, although interest may be payable from an earlier date if it is provided for in the contract between the parties.

Therapists (and other professionals) have told us that they have successfully avoided problems of late payment by simply adding at the end of each invoice a sentence reminding clients of this law, e.g. *'Payment for this invoice should be remitted within 30 working days, after which interest will be charged in accordance with the Late Payment of Commercial Debts (Interest) Act 1998.'*

1.2.5 Mental capacity

A client's ability to give legally valid consent to any medical, psychiatric or therapeutic assessment or treatment, or to enter into either a valid therapeutic contract or a legally binding contract for services, will depend upon their mental capacity to make an informed decision.

Mental capacity is a legal concept, according to which a person's ability to make rational, informed decisions is assessed, and for adults, this is now governed by the Mental Capacity Act 2005, the Mental Health Act 2007 and the Mental Capacity Act 2005 (Appropriate Body) (England) Regulations 2006. Relevant publications and websites are listed at the end of this book. For the relevant provisions in Scotland, see the Adults with Incapacity (Scotland) Act 2000 and the Mental Health (Care and Treatment) (Scotland) Act 2003.

Northern Ireland does not have mental capacity legislation although a Mental Capacity Bill has been proposed, which will be ready for introduction to the Assembly in 2011. Mental capacity issues are dealt with under common law. Please see the Northern Ireland Executive website (www.northernireland.gov.uk) for further details.

There is no single test for mental capacity to consent. Assessment of mental capacity is not on a theoretical ability to make decisions generally, but is situation-specific and depends upon the ability of the person to:

- take in and understand information, including the risks and benefits of the decision to be made, and
- retain the information long enough to weigh up the factors, make the decision and
- communicate their wishes.

Part 1 of the Mental Capacity Act 2005 (MCA) defines 'persons who lack capacity' and sets out relevant principles to be applied, including a checklist to be used to ascertain their best interests. In particular, it requires that a person is not to be treated as lacking capacity simply because they may be making an unwise decision.

Note that a person may be mentally incapacitated on a temporary basis (i.e. following an accident or illness), or on a longer-term or permanent basis (i.e. those who suffer from severe long-term mental illness or other impairment of mental functioning) and in their case capacity to make medical decisions is likely to be assessed by a medical doctor or psychiatrist. The assessment of a person's mental capacity for other tasks may be made by others. For example, the decision on a client's mental capacity to make a will may be made by their lawyer. The decision whether they are able to engage in therapy may be made by their therapist. If there is any doubt, advice from an appropriate registered medical practitioner, psychiatrist or psychologist should be sought. If there is a dispute about a person's mental capacity to make an important medical decision, the matter should be referred to the High Court or Court of Session, which will then assist and, if necessary, make a ruling. A person's capacity is relevant in therapy when considering whether someone can give a valid consent to receive therapy or agree to the contractual terms on which therapy is being provided.

In relation to entering into contracts, for minors, the relevant law is s. 1 of the Family Law Reform Act 1969 and s. 1 of the Age of Majority Act (Northern Ireland) 1969, which lowered the age of majority from 21 to 18, the Minors' Contracts Act 1987, and Minors' Contracts (Northern Ireland) Order 1988, which allows minors (children and young people under the age of 18) to go back on contracts, with some exceptions. In Scotland, young people under the age of 16 cannot usually enter into contracts. From 16–18 years, contracts may be challenged in the Sheriff's court if they are 'prejudicial' to the young person. For further discussion of mental capacity and the ability of minors and vulnerable adults to enter into contracts, see Mitchels and Bond 2010: 63–8.

1.2.6 Contracts that must be in writing

Some contracts, for example for the sale or lease of land, must be 'evidenced in writing' to be legally enforceable (Law of Property Act 1925, s. 52 or, in Northern

Ireland, Statute of Frauds (Ireland) Act 1695, s. 2). It is therefore advisable to ensure that all agreements for a lease or tenancy of premises and sales of land are in writing. It is advisable to obtain legal advice for sales of land and purchasing leases and tenancies, because there are often complex legal and financial issues involved and pitfalls to be avoided, particularly in this current climate of rapid changes in property values.

There are some specific statutory requirements for certain types of contract to be written or evidenced in writing, including insurance (Mitchels and Bond 2010: 87–93), guarantees, hire, consumer credit, and for the sale of certain specified goods and services. Terms of employment, if not provided at the outset, should be confirmed in writing after one month of starting in a statement giving certain specified details, even though other terms of the employment may be verbal. Employment is deduced from the contract and the surrounding circumstances. For discussion of this, and an explanation of the distinction between a 'contract of service' (i.e. employment) and 'a contract for services' or 'contract for the provision of services' (i.e. self-employment) see Mitchels and Bond 2010: 107–11.

In Scotland the statutory provisions relating to which type of contracts require to be evidenced by writing differ from the provisions in England and Northern Ireland. Section 1 of the Requirements of Writing (Scotland) Act 1995 lists some of the situations in which writing is required to make a contract legally enforceable. Examples of such situations include contracts which vary rights in land. There is no requirement for a contract for the provision of therapy to be written down. However, as with the position in England and Northern Ireland, therapists should always ensure that there is adequate written evidence of any contract they enter into, in order to protect themselves in the event of a future dispute.

1.2.7 Electronic signatures, Internet contracts, etc.

In modern times, the use of the Internet for commerce is developing. Electronic communication via emails and documents sent as attachments, and digital signatures have resulted in specific legislation (in the UK, see the Electronic Communications Act 2000, Electronic Commerce (EC Directive) Regulations 2002 and Electronic Signatures Regulations 2002). The general rule is that computer-generated communications, which provide a visible representation or record (which could if necessary be printed out as hard copies), are generally deemed to be 'in writing' as defined in the Interpretation Act 1978. If stored on the computer, documents must be retrievable in visible form. There is an unresolved issue about text and pager messages, which could be seen, but not printed out as hard copies.

1.2.8 Ethical issues and 'soft law' on contracts

Therapists need to consider ethical and professional issues, legal requirements, and any relevant agency policies and procedures. For helpful information from the BACP website, see Information Sheets P.11: *Making the Contract for Counselling and Psychotherapy* (Dale 2009c); P.2: *Charging for Therapy in Private Practice: Pitfalls and Ethical Issues* (Dale 2009a); and the *Ethical Framework* (BACP 2010a). We explore some of these issues in Bond and Mitchels 2008: Chapter 12, using examples of existing contracts in use by colleagues. However, we would encourage therapists to keep an eye on developments in law and practice, and to create their own contracts, compliant with current law and the public interest, and meeting the needs of the therapist, agency and client.

1.2.9 Contracts of employment, contracts for volunteer workers and contracts for services

We have discussed the situation of the therapist as a self-employed business person. Therapists who are self-employed may also be commissioned to undertake pieces of work for businesses, agencies and organisations in a 'contract for services' or 'contract to provide services'.

Therapists may be the employees of a business or organisation. Volunteer therapists are also potentially subject to binding contracts with the agency for which they work, and have many of the legal rights of employees, e.g. health and safety, equality of opportunities, etc. Volunteers will not, of course, have a right to employment pension, maternity/paternity pay or other financial remuneration, as they are unpaid. A contract of service (employment contract) should set out the terms and conditions upon which the worker is employed. Volunteers should also have a clear contract with their terms of work. These terms are legally binding on both parties unless varied by mutual agreement. Contracts of employment ideally should be written, or at least the main terms of employment should be evidenced in a written statement, so that the terms are readily available for reference if a dispute arises (Mitchels and Bond 2010: 107–8).

Therapists may also themselves be employers, e.g. of reception or cleaning staff, or may have other therapists working for them.

1.2.10 Dealing with legal claims

Wherever there is a contracted service, there may be a potential legal claim. There is excellent guidance about making legal claims, and dealing with claims made against therapists on the government website, www.hmcourts-service.gov.uk. For claims in Northern Ireland, see www.courtni.gov.uk, and for claims in Scotland, see www.scotcourts.gov.uk, but if the amount concerned is significant to the therapist, then it is advisable to seek legal advice before taking action. The Citizens Advice Bureau locally usually has free legal advice sessions, and professional insurance may cover free legal advice provided or paid for by the insurer. See also Mitchels and Bond 2010: 120–32.

For advice about claiming payment of unpaid fees, and how to go some way towards avoiding problems with unpaid invoices, see 1.2.4 above.

1.3 Practice issues

1.3.1. Currency of information, continuing professional development and training

One of the main challenges in private practice is the work involved in keeping up to date with ethics, current law, government policy and continuing education in topics relevant to therapeutic practice. It is here that the role of professional organisations, such as BACP, are important in gathering and disseminating information for practitioners. Even though the information is provided, some busy practitioners find it difficult to make the time for catching up by reading journals and newsletters. The *Ethical Framework* (BACP 2010a: 6, paras 7–10) requires therapists to maintain competent practice by regular supervision and consultative support, monitoring and reviewing practice, keeping up to date with knowledge with continuing professional development and educational activities and being aware of and understanding any legal requirements concerning their work.

1.3.2 Assessment of what to charge for therapy services

In private practice a common theme seems to be fees. How much to charge clients and arrangement of fees raises emotional and practical issues. The amount of any fees payable, and terms (e.g. whether payment is required for missed sessions etc.) should be made clear to a client before starting therapy, and form part of the therapeutic contract. In financial arrangements, practitioners are required to be honest, straightforward and accountable in all financial matters concerning their clients and other professional relationships (BACP 2010a: 10, para. 62). If finances are clear, there is less likelihood of this being a cause of difficulty between therapist and client, although it may still trigger issues in the therapy about valuing self and others, reflect aspects of financial struggles, etc. which can be worked through. Fees are difficult to negotiate for some practitioners. In our workshops, therapists sometimes say that, particularly when they started work after training, it was difficult to assess an appropriate fee for their work and also to know how and when to apply a variable fee structure. Equally, practitioners may feel resentful that clients who have asked for reduced fees subsequently talk in therapy about spending money on luxury items that the therapist could not afford. We have to be careful of making assumptions: a client who has therapy for a low £5 weekly fee and then comes in to say joyfully that they have spent £50 on an expensive hairdo may do this for many reasons – varying from the cold-blooded exploitation of a kind-hearted therapist to a real sign of recovery from depression – and so finances can raise important therapeutic issues with which supervision and mentoring by experienced practitioners could help! It is best to be open about finances in therapy and deal with any emotional or process issues that may surround it, and avoid the necessity of having to issue fee reminders or even to take legal proceedings against clients for unpaid fees. For contracting for fees and legal enforcement of non-payment of fees see 1.2.4 above.

1.3.3 Missed appointments

Many therapists seem to struggle with finding the right approach to missed appointments. Some of that struggle may be about self-respect and valuing ourselves and our time. A hard and fast rule is simple to operate, but may cause feelings of resentment or unfairness where the client was unavoidably detained, e.g. through serious illness. For many therapists, therefore, a hard and fast rule does not seem the best approach, preferring to have some flexibility in situations where the client is unavoidably prevented from coming to therapy. Where there is flexibility, a problem may occur in defining what constitutes a 'reasonable excuse' for not coming and to justify waiver of the counselling fee. This in itself may become a matter of friction between therapist and client. How can one decide? What principles might apply? For example, would you consider any of the following client's reasons for non-attendance (all real examples from practice) to constitute sufficient justification for non-attendance and therefore justify a waiver of the counselling fee?

- Sorry, I forgot
- The dog ate the letter with the appointment in it
- I had a cold
- I was ill with the 'flu
- I was in hospital
- My mum/dad/grannie/auntie was in hospital
- I was going to come, but then did not feel like it today
- I decided I was not coming any more but did not know how to tell you
- The voices said I should stay in today
- My boiler broke this morning
- My cat was ill
- My partner did not want me to come
- It was such a lovely day, I went for a picnic instead

The list is endless, but from these examples one can see that, rather than making definite 'rules', it might be easier to have certain principles on which a decision of 'reasonableness' is made. Some therapists might involve the client in the decision making process, e.g. asking them whether they think that their decision not to come was reasonable, or whether they feel that they should pay for the missed session. That kind of involvement would need a good established relationship of trust with the client. Issues such as the strength and quality of the client/therapist relationship, patterns of behaviour, frequency of missed sessions, and the general attitude of the client towards commitment to the process are all relevant.

1.3.4 The illness or death of the therapist and 'counselling wills'

Therapists have a duty of care to clients and this includes making a contingency plan for times when the therapist is unexpectedly ill or dies. Clients' needs must be taken into account in dealing with cancellation of appointments and/or informing clients of the situation and dealing with the impact for the clients of the illness/death of the therapist. This news may be traumatic for clients and would need to be imparted carefully, and the therapist's supervisor or an appointed colleague might be asked to take care of clients' needs in this situation. Supervisors are well placed to undertake this role since they are likely to know the clients' cases through their supervision work with the therapist, even though the clients may not be specifically identified in supervision. The role would require trust, tact and confidentiality and should be carried out by an experienced practitioner.

Counsellors are well advised to consider the possibility of their own illness/unavailability/death and to make what is colloquially referred to as a 'counselling will' i.e. provision for their own illness or death. They might also perhaps take into account the possibility of arranging suitable payment (from their estate or from funds set aside for the purpose) for the person taking on that role. Before making the arrangements, therapists should always ask the person whether they are willing to accept this role, as it may be burdensome in time and energy. Supervisors with many supervisees might also need to consider whether they can handle the additional potential workload, before accepting the role.

1.3.5 Summary checklist: Starting up in business working from home or in other premises

We have discussed each of these topics individually earlier in this chapter, but this checklist may prove useful as a reminder.

Checklist: Issues to consider when setting up a business

- Business start-up advice
- Start date (take financial advice on best date to choose)
- Loans, mortgages and capital (check special offers for new businesses)
- Accounting, book keeping and tax liability
- New bank accounts for the business
- Record keeping and storage, data protection legislation compliance where relevant
- Suitability of the premises/facilities/environment for therapeutic work
- Do I need to make adaptations/changes? If so, do I need planning consent for any change of use, conversions or extensions?
- Admin and services, e.g. telephone line, Internet access, reception, correspondence, out of hours arrangements, etc.
- If renting or leasing, do I need the landlord's consent?
- Are there any restrictive covenants against running a business from home?
- Insurance (professional and public liability, the premises and contents)
- Health and safety
- Disability legislation compliance

- Ethical and, in particular, boundary issues, e.g. confidentiality for the client on arrival and leaving or waiting, use of therapy room, storage of client records, facilities, inadvertent self-disclosure by the therapist through their possessions in the home, etc.
- Marketing: business cards, advertising, e.g. Yellow pages, local papers and shops, websites, etc.
- Check Internet and local resources for support and help, e.g. www.businesslink. gov.uk, a very useful website

1.4 Interface and managing movement between private practice and other contexts

1.4.1 Information sharing and disclosures

Sharing information between professionals is often fraught with difficulties, often because there may be different expectations and obligations in branches of the professions, e.g. health professionals may be used to routine information sharing within a team, and private therapists may be used to keeping one to one confidentiality for their clients.

If in any doubt, first clarify why the information is required, and the basis on which you are being asked to disclose something. Consider whether this is compatible with your professional ethics, the law and the context of your practice. We have developed a checklist of issues for consideration which may help therapists in the decision making process about sharing information: see below and also Bond and Mitchels 2008: Chapter 9.

Checklist: Disclosure

- Is this information regulated by the Data Protection Act 1998; for example, do the records comprise client-identifiable sensitive personal data held on computer or in a relevant filing system?
- Is this information regulated by the Freedom of Information Act 2000; for example, were the notes made by a professional working for a public body in health, education or social care?
- What are the relevant rights of the person concerned under the Human Rights Act 1998?
- If working in the health community, is disclosure compliant with the Caldicott Principles and guidance (see 1.4.3 below)?
- Is there a legitimate requirement to share this information; for example, a statutory duty or a court order?
- What is the purpose of sharing the information?
- If the information concerns a child, young person, or a vulnerable adult, is it in their best interests to share the information?
- Is the information confidential? If so, do you have consent to share it?
- If consent is refused, or there are good reasons not to seek consent, does the public interest necessitate or justify sharing the information?
- Is the decision and rationale for sharing the information recorded?
- What is the most appropriate way to share this information?

Recording any breaches of confidentiality

Recording any breaches of confidentiality is a requirement in some agencies and a wise precaution when working in private practice or as a volunteer. Such a record should include:

- Whether or not the client has consented to disclosure
- Evidence of the client's consent
- What information has been disclosed, to whom, and when
- The justification for the disclosure if it has not been authorised by the client (i.e. in the public interest, required by law, etc.)

Box 1.4 Examples of brief records of disclosures/referrals

1 Re Client [name]. Letter sent (attached) dated 18 May 2010 to Dr X, at client's request and with client's written consent (attached). Client reports severe depressive feelings and would like to explore the possibility of medication.

2 Re Client [name]. Tel. call made at 2.15pm on 18 May 2010 to Ms X at Lyndale Hospital, Social Care Department. Information given: Mrs Z, now aged 89, has been recently feeling very anxious and fearful at home, and she has become afraid that she cannot cope at home alone. She was admitted to hospital today suffering from bruising and scalds resulting from a fall when cooking. Disclosure made without client consent, as client too unwell today to speak. Please explore possibility of appropriate support or residential care for client on discharge from hospital.

1.4.2 Inter-agency working and policy making

In Bond and Mitchels 2008: Chapter 10, we considered the development of agency policies that address the interface between therapy practice and other contexts, for example inter-agency cooperation in child protection, mental health care, crime prevention, care of vulnerable adults, etc. Policies should address any requirements of the courts and comply with the law – for example the Data Protection Act 1988 and Freedom of Information Act 2000.

The issues in the disclosure checklist also apply in this situation, but here we have the added complexity of inter-agency working. Each professional in the team will have their respective professional rules and guidance which may be different from (or even conflict with) those of others in the team. In addition, some professionals may only come together as a team for specific purposes, and individuals may have separate work roles outside the team.

Personal considerations include:

- Is the team fully aware of and operating within the requirements of the law?
- What is required by the applicable professional disciplinary organisations?
- If there are more than one professional disciplinary organisation involved, how compatible are their requirements?

- Does my role in the team conflict at any point with my other roles outside the team?
- Does the team have a clear policy and procedures, e.g. for making and keeping records, protection of client confidentiality, and referrals?
- Can I work comfortably within the team policy and procedures?
- Are the clients of the team fully aware of and in agreement with the team policies and procedures?
- If difficulties arise and my perception of the best interests of a client conflicts with team policy/procedures, how can we address and resolve this potential conflict?
- What professional guidance is relevant to me and helpful to the team as a whole?

1.4.3 Developments in inter-agency collaboration – the Caldicott Principles

Increasing attention has been given to standards for confidentiality and protection of information, resulting in a plethora of guidance, departmental circulars, codes of practice, charters, and recommendations in departmental and inter-departmental reports. In 1997, the Caldicott Committee delivered the Report on the Review of Patient-Identifiable Information (available from the Department of Health website www.dh.gov.uk). That report included recommendations on information sharing within the NHS and between the NHS and non-NHS organisations, embodied in six principles (the 'Caldicott Principles'):

Principle 1 – Justify the purpose(s) for using confidential information
Principle 2 – Only use it when absolutely necessary
Principle 3 – Use the minimum that is required
Principle 4 – Access should be on a strict need-to-know basis
Principle 5 – Everyone must understand his or her responsibilities
Principle 6 – Understand and comply with the law

The Department of Health has produced *The Caldicott Guardian Manual* (DH 2010b) for the guidance of 'Caldicott Guardians', who are people appointed to protect patient information in health and social care. They are usually existing members of the management board or senior management team, senior professionals, or hold responsibility for promoting clinical governance or equivalent functions within organisations providing health or social care. This manual can be obtained by post or at the websites listed at the end of this book. Following the Caldicott Report, the Department of Health made a commitment to develop protocols for information sharing between agencies and organisations, for example in investigations into abuse, professional misconduct, etc.

1.4.4 Guidance on information sharing regarding the welfare of children

The Department for Education website (www.education.gov.uk) provides detailed online child protection guidance documents, some of which are listed in the 'Government Guidance' section at the end of this book, including when and how information should be shared legally and professionally. See *Working Together to Safeguard Children: A Guide to Inter-Agency Working to Safeguard and Promote the Welfare of Children* (DCSF 2010) and its supporting materials. Other useful resources are *Information Sharing: Guidance for Practitioners and Managers* (DCSF 2008a) and *What to Do If You're Worried a Child Is Being Abused* (DfES 2006). Also see *Confidentiality: NHS Code of Practice* (DH 2003 and the supplementary guidance, DH 2010a). The DfE website site informs visitors that as a new UK government took office on 11 May 2010, the content on this website may not reflect current government policy, but all statutory guidance and legislation published continues to reflect the current legal position unless indicated otherwise.

In England, the guidance in Part 1 of *Working Together to Safeguard Children* (DCSF 2010) carries the force of statute under s. 7 of the Local Authorities Social Services Act 1970. It sets out the standards and procedures with which local authorities are to comply. The Children Act 1989 (CA 1989) places a statutory duty on health, education and other services to help the local authority in carrying out its functions under the CA 1989 (similar provisions exist in the Children (Scotland) Act 1995 and *Protecting Children – A Shared Responsibility: Guidance on Inter-Agency Co-operation* (The Scottish Office, 1998: www.scotland.gov.uk). See this website for other useful information). There is a statutory duty to work together, including information sharing, in conducting initial investigations of children who may be in need or subject to abuse and in the more detailed core assessments carried out under s. 47 of the CA 1989. For details of the assessment process see also the Department of Health publication *Framework for Assessment of Children in Need and their Families* (2000b). Adults and children over 16 or children under 16 but 'Gillick competent' may refuse to cooperate with assessments. In these cases, practitioners concerned for the welfare of the child should refer the matter to the family court under the relevant provisions of the CA 1989. The legal department of the local authority may be approached for advice and assistance. See the glossary for an explanation of 'Gillick competence' and also Bond and Mitchels 2008: Chapter 11 for a detailed discussion of capacity and consent.

2 Commercial and Employee Assistance Programme (EAP) Provision

What services might we expect an Employee Assistance Programme (EAP) to provide?

If I work for an EAP, will I be employed or self-employed? Can I elect to be self-employed? How can I know which employment status is correct?

What might happen if either I or my EAP provider gets my employment status wrong?

I work for an Employee Assistance Programme provider which is commissioned by a large UK organisation. What are my duties to the organisation and to the EAP provider?

How should I respond to a request from the manager of an organisation using EAP services for information about my client?

2.1 Legal features of commercial and Employee Assistance Programme (EAP) provision

2.1.1 The emergence of EAPs in response to employers' legal responsibility to employees

The role of counselling and psychotherapy in the context of employee assistance provision has developed gradually over time in response to better perception and understanding of workplace pressures and employee mental health needs, coupled with demands for increased efficiency in the workplace. Employers have come to realise that a reasonably contented workforce may be more productive than a body of dissatisfied and unfulfilled employees. Legislation has had a part to play in bringing about this change.

In *Hatton v Sutherland; Barber v Somerset County Council; Jones v Sandwell Metropolitan Council; Bishop v Baker Refractories Ltd.* [12 February 2002] CA, Times Law Reports, the Court of Appeal (CA) heard a number of appeals from employers against liability for an employee's psychiatric illness alleged to be caused by stress at work.

From the discussion on the law, the following propositions emerged:

1   There were no special control mechanisms applying to claims for psychiatric or physical, illness or injury arising from the stress of doing work the employee was required to do. The ordinary principle of employer's liability applied.

2   The threshold question was whether such harm to that particular employee was reasonably foreseeable. That had two components: (a) an injury to health, as distinct from emotional stress, which was (b) attributable to stress at work, as distinct from other factors.

3   Foreseeability depended upon what the employer knew, or ought reasonably to have known, about the individual employee. Because of the nature of mental disorder, it was accepted that this is harder to foresee than physical injury, but might be easier to foresee in a known individual than in the population at large. The report also indicates that an employer was usually entitled to assume that the employee could withstand the normal pressures of the job unless the employer actually knew of some particular problem or vulnerability of the employee.

4   The test was the same whatever the employment: there were no occupations that should be regarded as intrinsically dangerous to mental health.

5   Factors likely to be relevant in answering the threshold question included:
    a   The nature and extent of the work done by the employee.
    b   Signs from the employee of impending harm to health.

6   The employer was generally entitled to take what he was told by his employee at face value, unless he had good reason to think to the contrary.

7   To trigger a duty to take steps, the indications of impending harm to health arising from stress at work had to be plain enough for any reasonable employer to realise that he should do something about it.

8   The employer was in breach of duty only if he failed to take reasonable steps, bearing in mind the magnitude of the risk, the gravity of any harm, the costs and practicability of preventing it and justifications for running the risk.

9   The size and scope of the employer's operation were relevant, including, for example, re-distribution of duties to other employees and the need to treat them fairly.

10   An employer could reasonably be expected only to take steps that were likely to do some good.

11   An employer who offered a confidential counselling or treatment service was unlikely to be in breach of duty.

12   If the only reasonable step would be to demote or dismiss the employee, the employer would not be in breach in allowing a willing employee to continue working.

13   It was therefore necessary to identify the steps the employer should have taken before finding him in breach.

14   The claimant had to show breach of duty had caused the harm. Occupational stress was not enough.

15   Where the harm had more than one cause, the employer was liable for only his contribution.

16   The assessment of damages would take account of any pre-existing disorder or vulnerability.

It is clear from this case that the employees' burden of proving harm was not easy. Before the employer has a duty to take steps, the indications of impending harm to an employee arising from stress at work would have to be sufficiently obvious to indicate that something should be done. Prevention of workplace stress therefore seems to be regarded, in law, as less significant than watching out for indications of impending actual harm. *Hatton v Sutherland* is an English decision, but is likely to be highly persuasive in Scotland. We do not yet know the impact of this case for personnel in risky and highly stressful occupations, e.g. active service in the armed services, etc.

Nevertheless, from the legal point of view, EAP provision is not only supportive of an employer's general duty of care, but it provides a means of watching out for indications of existing or potential psychological harm to employees and provides an opportunity to take appropriate action in time before any potential liability arises.

2.1.2 What services might we expect an EAP to provide?

We appreciate that there may be many definitions of the functions of an Employee Assistance Programme (EAP). We liked the comprehensive model of the Employee Assistance Professionals Association (EAPA UK, www.eapa.org.uk/) and, with their permission, we have adapted it to create our working definition of the role of EAPs, set out in Box 2.1. The list is not intended to be exhaustive, and readers may wish to add further EAP functions.

Box 2.1 Role of Employee Assistance Programmes

EAPs help to make the workplace more efficient and improve the work experience for both the workforce and management by assisting individuals and organisations to do any or all of the following:

- Cope with work-related and personal problems and challenges that have an impact on performance at work
- Improve productivity and workplace efficiency
- Reduce absenteeism and staff turnover
- Manage or reduce workplace stress
- Promote workplace cooperation
- Reduce conflict in the workplace
- Reduce grievances
- Improve staff morale and motivation
- Assist line managers in identifying and resolving staff problems
- Decrease work-related accidents
- Manage or reduce the risk of unexpected events
- Manage or reduce the impact of traumatic events that impact on the workplace or the workforce
- Encourage organisations to be caring employers and to demonstrate a caring attitude to their employees
- Recruit and retain staff
- Assist in addiction problems
- Provide a management tool for performance analysis and improvement

---

The EAPA UK lists a number of EAP providers at its website and suggests that 'EAPs represent a proven, cost-effective solution to many of the people problems employers face today. The UK EAPA therefore would recommend all organisations to consider seriously how a relevant form of EAP can be introduced into their organisation.' Different forms of EPA are detailed in Box 2.2.

Box 2.2 Forms of EAP provision

EAP provision may take various forms including:

- telephone, email, internet or face to face counselling and psychotherapy
- therapy with individuals, couples or groups
- team building and other activities
- defusing and debriefing activities for individuals and groups
- mediations
- training in relevant topics e.g. self-awareness, communication skills, assertiveness, time management, stress reduction
- providing access to legal, financial and consumer advice
- providing management information
- distributing information and resource materials

2.1.3 EAP provision and employment issues

As discussed earlier, there is no formal general statutory requirement for EAP provision in the workplace. However, once EAP provision is set up, a variety of statutes may apply to the EAP service, in various ways.

EAP providers as employees of an organisation

Box 2.3 Statutes and subsidiary legislation relevant to EAP provision

- Disability Discrimination Act 2005
- Employment Act 2008
- Employment Act (Northern Ireland) 2010
- Employment Act 2002
- Employment (Northern Ireland) Order 2003
- Employment Relations Act 1999
- The Employment Relations (Northern Ireland) Order 1989
- Employment Tribunals Act 1996
- Industrial Tribunals (Northern Ireland) Order 1996
- Employment Rights (Northern Ireland) Order 1996
- Employer's Liability (Compulsory Insurance) Act 1969 (and, where relevant, its Northern Ireland equivalent)
- Equal Pay Act 1970 (and, where relevant, its Northern Ireland equivalent), Unfair Contract Terms Act 1977
- Health and Safety at Work Act 1974 (and, where relevant, its Northern Ireland equivalent)

Therapists providing an EAP may be employees of the organisation using that service, for example, a large factory or insurance company might have its own in-house EAP service. It may contract with each therapist directly as an employee. They would then be subject to all the rights and duties that flow from a contract of employment, including provision for health and safety at work, equal opportunities, holiday entitlement, sick leave, maternity and paternity leave, redundancy provision, pension provision, etc. Many statutes may then apply – see Box 2.3.

For further discussion of contracts, employment, tax, equal opportunities, disability discrimination, pensions and health and safety, see the relevant chapters in Mitchels and Bond (2010).

Where the EAP provider is an employee, they will have a binding contractual relationship with their employer organisation. Their clients will also be employees. This situation needs to be discussed and clarified with the employer and the EAP providers at the outset, to avoid any conflicts of interest, for example between an employer requiring information about a client who is requesting confidentiality, or where lines of management converge in a situation involving both client and therapist. Therapists in this situation need to have clarity in their own minds about policies and procedures with which they have to comply within the organisation. They will need to be clear with clients about any relevant requirements made by their employer (for example reporting to management, health or human resources any risk of harm to the client or others, other issues that may affect the employee's work, or the client's take-up of therapy) and the responsibilities owed to their clients (for example a duty of confidentiality).

EAP provider businesses as employers of therapists

An EAP provider may be commissioned by a business or an organisation to provide a service, but it may have an employer/employee relationship with its therapists. In this case any or all of the statutes listed in Box 2.3 may apply, and see Chapter 9 in Mitchels and Bond (2010) for the rights of employees, e.g. pay, annual leave, maternity and paternity leave and allowances, taxation and redundancy.

Therapists working as independent external consultants with EAP provider businesses

On the other hand, therapists working for an EAP provider may be regarded as independent external consultants, each providing services on a franchised, client-by-client, and/or an hourly basis. In this situation therapists will have a professional duty of care to their clients and also to the commissioning organisation. The therapist's services may be commissioned through an EAP provider organisation, or commissioned directly by the employer. In either case the therapist, if self-employed, will be held responsible for payment of their own income tax and national insurance contributions, and they will also usually be expected to provide and pay for their own professional indemnity insurance.

How can I tell whether I am employed or self-employed?

A clear understanding as to whether a therapist is employed or self-employed is vitally important for tax and other purposes. For discussion and ways of differentiating between the two, see Mitchels and Bond (2010: 107–9). Her Majesty's Revenue and Customs (HMRC) provides a chart for guidance on determination of status, see www.hmrc.gov.uk/paye/employees/start-leave/status.htm and also the Employment Status Indicator at www.hmrc.gov.uk/calcs/esi.htm.

Since employers can get into legal difficulties if they do not set up 'Pay As You Earn' (PAYE) tax and National Insurance deductions for their employees, some EAPs provide detailed questionnaires for therapists wanting to work with them to complete, to resolve the employed/self-employed issue before engaging their services.

What might happen if either I or my EAP provider gets my employment status wrong?

A person who behaves as though they are self-employed but who should be treated as employed will have been doing their own tax returns, etc. In theory, they should not be treated punitively by HMRC provided that they acted in good faith and they have correctly accounted for their income and paid the correct tax on it. However, if they have not paid their correct National Insurance contributions, and other deductions, they may find their national pension entitlement reduced and any tax owed to HMRC treated as a debt.

An employer who makes a mistake by allowing a person to act as self-employed when they should be an employee, may find themselves subject to inspection and punitive measures by the HMRC, with a potential liability to pay to HMRC the income tax and any other money that they should have deducted from the therapist's wages under PAYE.

2.1.4 Law and guidance on EAP provision

We have already mentioned that employers have a general duty of care to their employees, but this does not quite extend to the elimination of employees' workplace stress. However, if circumstances arise in which an employer should reasonably be aware of impending harm to an employee, they should take steps to deal with it; see the *Hatton v Sutherland etc.* case, mentioned above.

EAP provision is subject to government guidance, some of which may be enforceable by the courts by statutory regulation, e.g. for therapists working with children and families, *Working Together to Safeguard Children* (DCSF 2010) is relevant. Part 1 of this guidance carries the force of statute.

Therapists should also be aware of the accepted general standards of practice in the therapy profession, for which the best evidence is the guidance of professional associations, e.g. the *Ethical Framework* (BACP 2010a), the *UKCP Ethical Principles and Code of Professional Conduct* (UKCP 2009), and where applicable, the GMC guidance (GMC 2004, 2006). In cases of alleged breach of duty of care or negligence, accepted professional standards may be taken into account by the courts as a measure of competence. Please also refer to any other professional codes of conduct relevant to your practice.

In relation to EAP provision, there is the professional guidance of specialist organisations for EAP providers, for example, the *Code of Ethics of the Employee Assistance Professional Association* (2002) available at www.eapa.org.uk

2.2 Contractual issues

In private practice, therapists might enter into a wide variety of contracts. Contract law is complex, so we cannot venture into detail here, but we will address the questions that we are asked most often by therapists working with EAPs and summarise some of the main points. Further details about contractual issues in private practice are included in Chapter 1 at 1.2, and see also Mitchels and Bond 2010.

2.2.1 Contracts between therapists and EAP providers

Whether working as an employee or self-employed, with EAPs, therapists working with clients whose employment involves sensitive areas of information, e.g. government, armed forces, police and Home Office staff, may have constraints relating to their use of client material disclosed in therapy. This may leave little room for therapists to negotiate the terms of their contracts of service with EAP providers, and so therapists working for EAPs may have to choose simply whether (or not) to accept the terms of the EAP contract proposed.

Having said in the previous paragraph that there is little room for negotiation, we do advise that some contracts might be properly challenged and re-negotiated. We have seen poorly drafted contracts offered to therapists, which contain unfair contract terms and have clauses that are unclear. Some of these poorly drafted contracts may be unenforceable or unworkable. If the contract offered to you by an EAP seems unclear, muddled, unfair, or difficult to comply with, we suggest that you take legal advice, before committing to the contract.

We suggest that therapists look carefully at the definitions of the terms in their contract, and clarify with the EAP exactly what is meant by them, where necessary. Examples might be: 'confidential material', 'ownership of client notes', 'ownership of all content of client notes' etc. Client notes can physically be owned, but the content of sessions, i.e. the client's recorded material and the therapist's recorded responses, must be dealt with in accordance with the therapist's duty of care and the therapeutic contract. This means that the therapist should be clear about (and agree with) the policies of the EAP about issues such as confidentiality, and the client should be informed of these terms, and agree to them, before therapy starts. Usually the EAP will have written policies to which the client is asked to agree, before referral is made to an individual therapist. The terms of the client's therapeutic contract with the therapist should therefore sit comfortably with the therapist's own professional contract with the EAP.

Examples of unfair terms in some circumstances might be:

- to claim ownership (by the EAP) of all records and at the same time to make the therapist alone liable for any damage resulting from storage or otherwise dealing with those records;
- attempts to limit the EAP's liability to pay compensation to a therapist in certain circumstances;
- requirements for the therapist to comply with EAP systems for online filing and storage of client notes, whilst at the same time making the therapist liable for what happens to those notes (therapists' professional insurers may not be willing to cover a loss incurred in these circumstances);
- requirements for therapists to agree not to upload viruses onto an EAP's website and imposing liability on the therapist for any damage if this occurs (we can only agree to not to so do deliberately, and otherwise to take reasonable precautions by having anti-virus software, but all of these software programs are fallible, and we can never know with certainty that we are not sending viruses with our emails etc.). Therapists' professional insurers may not be willing to cover a loss incurred in these circumstances.

Record systems may be created and stored electronically (e.g. on the database of the therapist or EAP, or in 'cloud storage'), with records sent to the EAP online. We would expect these online systems to lie within the definitions for registration set out in the Data Protection Act, and therapists using them should therefore check whether they are liable to register with the Information Commissioner's Office. Guidance as to the scope of the data protection legislation is available on the Internet at www.dataprotection.gov.uk, and see also Bond and Mitchels 2008: 58–66.

2.2.2 Contracts for goods and services relating to therapy provision

Therapists providing EAP services may work from home or from premises in which they may incur office expenses, i.e. photocopier rental, purchase of office goods and computer equipment, cleaning services, telephone and Internet access, etc. They may also need to commission services, e.g. of an accountant or a lawyer, cleaner or receptionist. Such contracts are enforceable in the courts if necessary, provided that they fulfil the necessary criteria (Mitchels and Bond 2010: 129–31). Enforcement is usually by way of either an order to fulfil the terms of the contract (e.g. to pay the money owed, if therapy has been provided) or monetary compensation for breach (e.g. where an office computer breaks down, if it is still in warranty, the supplier might offer a repair or a replacement, or the money to replace it).

2.2.3 Contracts of employment, contracts for volunteer workers and contracts for services in EAPs

In Chapter 1 we have discussed the situation of the therapist as a possible employer or employee in a business or organisation, including those providing EAP services, see 1.2.9. Volunteer therapists, like employees, are also subject to binding contracts with the agency for which they work. A contract of service (employment contract) should set out the terms and conditions upon which the worker is employed, and ideally should be written, or at least the main terms of employment should be evidenced in a written statement, so that the terms are readily available for reference if a dispute arises (Mitchels and Bond 2010: 107–8).

Therapists who are self-employed may also be commissioned to undertake pieces of work for businesses, agencies and organisations in a 'contract for services' or 'contract to provide services'.

2.2.4 Therapeutic contracts with EAP clients

Therapists make contracts with their clients, which clarify mutual expectations and impose a legal duty on both parties. Therapeutic contracts may include a wide range of terms, e.g. fees, frequency of appointments, charges for non-attendance, holidays, records and confidentiality, referral policies, etc. It is vital to ensure that the therapist's own ethical and professional standards are compatible with those of the EAP for which they work. Most clients of an EAP have agreed in advance to comply with the EAP's policies and procedures. The client's employer will have usually provided standard information and obtained an agreement from employees in advance of use of the EAP service. In the same way, therapists working for an EAP will have been asked to agree to those same standard policies and procedures. Therapists must then be careful to ensure that whatever terms are agreed directly with the client are compliant with the policies and procedures of the EAP for which the therapist works.

The issues concerning contracts are similar throughout all aspects of therapy, and are explored in Chapter 1 at 1.2.2 to 1.2.10, where there are references for further reading.

2.2.5 Dealing with legal claims

Wherever there is a contracted service, there may be a potential legal claim. There is excellent guidance about making legal claims, and dealing with claims made against us on the government website, www.hmcourts-service.gov.uk. For claims in Northern Ireland, see www.courtni.gov.uk , and for claims in Scotland, see www.scotcourts.gov.uk. If the amount concerned is significant to the therapist, then it is advisable to seek legal advice before taking action. The Citizens Advice Bureau locally usually has free legal advice sessions, and professional insurance may cover free legal advice provided or paid for by the insurer. See also Mitchels and Bond 2010: 120–32.

For advice about claiming payment of unpaid fees, and how to go some way towards avoiding problems with unpaid invoices, see Chapter 1 at 1.2.4.

2.3 Practice issues

2.3.1 Managing confidences

EAP provision raises many issues for both the employer commissioning the service, the providers of the programmes, therapists and their clients. Perhaps one of the most complex issues, and certainly one that arises frequently in workshops, is managing confidences. Employers may be most concerned about safety in the workplace and need to maintain efficiency and productivity levels, which may be in conflict with the perceived needs of the workforce. An employer's expectation from EAP provision might be that it will reduce employee absence, but in fact therapy is likely to encourage workers to monitor their stress levels and to take time out before they become too stressed to continue efficient work. Employers may also be motivated to provide EAPs in order to be (and be seen as) caring and considerate, and perhaps to improve working conditions to avoid claims being made against them.

Therapists may hear client material about difficulties in conditions of work and workplace relations, and sometimes they may long to feed back information to the employer to try to stop bad practice or make improvements. One way forward here is to empower clients to make their own representations to the employer wherever they can. Clients may request therapists to raise matters with the employer on their behalf, but this should only be done at the request of the client and with their knowledge and consent. It is fraught with risks, since the timing and method of sharing information can influence the way in which it is received and implemented. If an employer is likely to act punitively if an employee complains about conditions, it may be best for information to come from a neutral source.

2.3.2 'Whistle-blowing' and reporting bad work practices

'Whistle-blowing' (reporting colleagues' bad professional practice) may be an issue for therapists or clients who may struggle to know when it is professionally necessary and appropriate to report colleagues, and to whom a report should be made. This is an issue that can be explored in supervision, and also with the therapist's professional association, which will usually provide help and guidance. In some situations 'whistle-blowing' may be necessary to maintain good professional practice, and it may be permitted or even required within agency policy (contractually agreed by all the agency's employees) or required by law (e.g. reporting terrorist activities under the Terrorism Act 2000 or by an order of a court).

There are other situations where the law leaves whistle-blowing to the therapist's discretion, for example where the therapist becomes aware of criminal acts (for example, a therapist sexually assaulting clients, or mistreating vulnerable adults), or bad practice leading to the risk of potential harm to a child or vulnerable adult, where whistle-blowing may be morally justified. The issue then for the therapist is whether whistle-blowing is *legally* defensible, for example, in the public interest (i.e. that the protection of the general public may justifiably outweigh personal or private rights, such as confidentiality).

In the case of EAP provision, whistle-blowing is much more complex an issue when the therapist becomes aware during therapy of the bad practice of their client's colleagues through something that their clients tells them in a session. Remember that this information is second-hand, and it is the client's reported perception and interpretation of events. The therapist has a discretion about the detail and extent of the notes they may make, but session notes should always be accurate and 'fit for purpose' therapeutically. Any important factual details such as names, dates etc. (for example the name of a person who has attacked the client, and the place and date of the attack) if they are recorded, should be checked with the client to ensure that the client record is correct. In this way, the client is aware that the therapist has a record of what was said, and is reassured that the record reflects accurately their account of events. Client records are confidential, but they may be requested in evidence for disciplinary, legal or other purposes later. If a court orders disclosure, the therapist must comply or be in contempt of court. The limits of confidentiality are discussed in detail in Bond and Mitchels 2008.

A preferable course is for the therapist to empower the client to take the appropriate action, and to help them to do so by providing therapeutic support and referral to other resources where appropriate, for example, a client who is being bullied at work, or suffering from sexual harassment or racial discrimination may want to bring a complaint or legal action, and they may benefit by therapeutic support and a referral to their Trade Union or other resources for confidential legal advice.

If the issue is one where the law requires disclosure (e.g. acts of terrorism), the matter is clear. Where there is discretion, the consideration which applies is whether disclosure is *legally* defensible in the public interest, as described in the preceding paragraph.

2.3.3 Employment tribunal hearings, disciplinary procedures, etc.

In the course of employment, disciplinary hearings may arise in which an EAP client is the subject of a complaint, or the client may be the complainant. In either case, the clients' records may only be disclosed with the consent of the client. Tribunals do not have the power to order disclosure of records in the same way that a UK court may do.

Be aware that employer/employee contracts and agency policies may sometimes conflict with the general law (for example where these contracts require you to do something that the law forbids, or forbid you to disclose information when the law may require it), or they may conflict with what you see as your moral duty. A contract to do something illegal is, by its very nature, legally unenforceable in the courts. A contract with which you morally disagree may nevertheless still be legal and enforceable. If a stark choice arises between compliance with a policy with which you disagree and dismissal, get legal advice and check first whether the policy is legally correct. If it is questionable, then you must consider what is legally right and professionally and ethically correct. The courts would be very likely to support you if the agency then sought to dismiss you for breach of the terms of your contract, since certain unfair contract terms are unlawful (see Mitchels and Bond 2010: Chapter 4).

2.3.4 Recording and storing client records in an EAP service

The therapist has a duty of care to their clients to maintain their notes and records in a confidential manner. The organisation that has commissioned the EAP service has no right to see the client records or seek information from them, unless the client has given consent for this, or where there is a court order.

2.3.5 Disclosures in the public interest

In work contexts where the public or colleagues should be protected, sometimes, there is a three-way contract in which the employer agrees with the client and the therapist that disclosure about the client's physical or mental health may be made, in the public interest, in specific situations, e.g. where the client may cause a serious risk to safety in the workplace. In the absence of such a contract, the therapist may have to make decisions about what the public interest requires, and whether this justifies overriding the contractual rights of the client. Supervision and/or legal advice may be helpful in these situations.

2.3.6 Contracts forbidding therapists to take a former EAP client privately

EAPs usually provide a limited number of client sessions. Part of the therapist's role is to assess the client and to immediately refer on any who are more suitable for long-term work. It is not usually considered good practice in an EAP to see a client for a limited number of sessions and then to send them on to another therapist afterwards with whom they have to make a fresh relationship, unless referral at that stage is justifiable, for example, when the client requires an additional specialist service.

EAPs are not usually willing to allow therapists to continue working with clients privately after they have had their limited number of sessions from the EAP service. They may have several reasons for this, some in their interests and some in the interests of the client. It is therefore common for EAPs to require their therapists to refrain from subsequently taking on in a private capacity clients they have seen in the context of the EAP service.

2.3.7 Extra time

Therapists working with EAPs have to function in a very boundaried setting, with restrictions that may be imposed by financial considerations, e.g. a general limit on the number of sessions provided may be imposed for clients in response to the commissioning organisation's financial needs. Therapists (particularly those who have experienced open-ended work in the context of private practice where they made their own decisions and clients had the ability to work slowly towards an ending) may sometimes have difficulty in completing a piece of work with a client in the limited number of sessions that they are allowed by the EAP provider. Sometimes extra sessions are permitted after negotiation with the EAP clinical advisor, who may, of course, also refuse extra time. Some therapists have expressed to us their dissatisfaction with this process, which prevents them from making their own decision in the best interests of the client. However, therapists are contractually bound to accept the boundaries of their work as it is set out in their contract with the EAP provider. They are providing brief therapy appropriate to the context of their contract for EAP provision. In this context, the initial assessment is vitally important, as it can identify those clients who need longer-term work, or for whom the brief therapy is not useful.

2.4 Interface and managing movement between EAP provision and other contexts

Information may be requested by courts, tribunals or others concerning EAP client records. Usually EAP providers control records and wish to control responses to any requests for disclosures. The general rule is that the therapist should have regard to their duty of care to the client and their professional ethics, and that legally they should comply with the agency policy and the therapeutic contract (which should, hopefully, be compatible).

The therapist is entitled to refuse disclosure unless the client consents or the law requires it, e.g. statutory disclosure or they are ordered by the court to provide information. For general discussion of information-sharing between professionals, see Bond and Mitchels (2008).

3 Voluntary Work

What do we mean by voluntary work?

Do volunteer counsellors need a contract with their organisation?

In legal terms, is a volunteer counsellor employed, self-employed, or not employed at all? Does this matter?

What rights does a volunteer counsellor have in the workplace?

Should a volunteer counsellor accept or refuse gifts or donations?

Should a volunteer counsellor accept compulsory supervision with a person who has line management over them in their organisation?

We are grateful for some thoughts from Val Potter, Chair of BACP's Third Sector Expert Reference Group, the members of which all have some involvement in working with voluntary counsellors. She clarifies a common confusion, pointing out that people often assume that everyone working in the Voluntary Sector is doing so voluntarily. In fact, counselling in the 'Third Sector' (sometimes called the Voluntary Sector) may be provided by counsellors working voluntarily, paid counsellors, or a mix of the two.

Also it is important to note that therapists working voluntarily are subject to the same requirements regarding training, ethics and insurance, etc. as paid counsellors.

Organisations in the voluntary sector are frequently committed to making counselling available to people who would not otherwise have access to it, often for reasons of finance. It follows that therapists in the sector are often working with clients who are very vulnerable and may have a mix of psychological and social problems to contend with. The voluntary sector may work with drink- or drug-related problems, all forms of abuse, immigrants and refugees, family problems and mental health issues. This may mean that there is an increased likelihood of therapists and clients being involved in legal processes.

Particular issues arise in small communities where therapists in the voluntary sector and clients are bound to have interlocking social networks, for example those working in a village or in a defined group in the community, e.g. counselling deaf people who may all have attended one of very few boarding schools in the area. Thought should be given to how both will react when they may encounter each other socially, and how therapists will check for and deal with potential conflicts of interest between clients who may know each other.

Therapists working with people who share the same health problem in organisations set up to cater for their needs may encounter legal disputes between people who think that every penny should go to research into a cure and others who want funds to be invested in therapy for the people with that health problem.

Labelling and self-description is important. Inadvertent mis-descriptions by therapists may lead to legal problems. It is important, for example, that the term 'counsellor' is not used for volunteers who use counselling skills. Some people describe this as 'embedded counselling' but this may be, at best, confusing. The only way that therapists' titles will be clarified may be through eventual statutory or other forms of regulation.

3.1 Legal features of the context

3.1.1 What is the legal definition of voluntary work?

The definition of 'voluntary work' is work for which no payment is made. Payment for reasonable expenses and subsistence solely related to the voluntary work done does not count in this definition. Reasonable expenses might include food, drink, travel and necessary accommodation whilst working away from home.

Training might be provided for volunteers and this, too, unless disproportionate to the work done, is unlikely to be considered as 'remuneration' for employment (see 3.1.2).

3.1.2 Is a volunteer therapist employed, self-employed or not employed at all? Does the distinction matter?

Volunteers have been held not to be employees because they receive no payment for their work, see *Melhuish v Redbridge Citizens Advice Bureau* [2005] IRLR 419, EAT. However, it is possible (although perhaps rare) that a volunteer therapist might be given substantial gifts in return for their work, e.g. expensive holidays, household goods or services by way of exchange for their work, or a debt owed by the therapist to the agency is 'written off' (in legal terms, 'forgiven') in exchange for work.

These gifts might be construed by Her Majesty's Revenue and Customs (HMRC) as not receiving money directly, but receiving 'remuneration' or 'money's worth' in goods/services, and therefore it may be counted as income for tax purposes, incurring an income tax liability. Not only that, but working and being paid in kind or services could also potentially be construed as employment, and a contract of employment implied (Mitchels and Bond 2010: Chapters 8, 9). If in any doubt about whether you are receiving income or not, consult HMRC; their contact details are in the Useful Resources section at the end of the book. If unsure whether you are self-employed or not, a useful website is www.hmrc.gov.uk/paye/employees/start-leave/status.htm.

It is possible to have several roles and so a mixture of employment statuses. A therapist might, for example, work for one day each week day as an unpaid volunteer for a charitable counselling organisation (not 'employed' at all); work three days for a salary on a contract of employment for another organisation (an employee); and also work from home as a self-employed therapist (self-employed).

The distinction between being employed (or self-employed) or not matters, because, as seen in the preceding paragraphs, income tax may be payable on gifts as remuneration (and tax could be demanded for past years – see Mitchels and Bond 2010: 102–4). The contractual and workplace rights of volunteer therapists may also be different from those who are employees.

Beware of the term 'worker' on its own. A 'voluntary worker' might be construed as a volunteer, but the term 'worker' is used in legislation generally to infer working under a contract of employment, e.g. the Interpretation section 2(a) of the Working Time Regulations 1998, defines a worker to include 'an individual who has entered into or works under a contract of employment.' Interestingly though, 2(b) includes 'an individual who undertakes to do or perform personally any work or services for another party to the contract' but then excludes work carried out 'for a client or a customer of any profession or business carried on by the individual'. In other words, an employed therapist can also see clients in their own time as a self-employed person. (See Mitchels and Bond 2010: Chapters 8, 9 for discussion of some of the legal implications of these separate roles.)

3.1.3 What rights does a volunteer have in the workplace?

Volunteers do not receive some of the statutory rights that are linked in with employment, for example, protection from unfair dismissal, redundancy payments, leave entitlements, pension rights, etc.

Volunteers are, however, entitled to other workplace rights that apply to all staff in a workplace, e.g. the benefit of health and safety regulations, public liability insurance, protection from harassment, disability discrimination, etc.

A volunteer may feel the need for a certain degree of protection of their right to work, since voluntary placements are often vitally important to trainee therapists to acquire the hours of work experience necessary for completion of their training, and/or professional accreditation. Usually such protection is afforded by their workplace disciplinary and complaints procedures, and is contractual, but not necessarily part of a contract of employment. For discussion of the rights of employees, see Mitchels and Bond (2010: 107–18). Information can also be obtained from the Advisory, Conciliation and Arbitration Service (ACAS), www.acas.org.uk/, or the local Citizens Advice Bureau (CAB), www.citizensadvice.org.uk.

The government website www.directgov.co.uk provides general information and opportunities for volunteers, which may also be of interest to therapists. Given the decision in the *Melhuish* case (see 3.1.4 below), the site rather confusingly refers to 'your employment rights as a volunteer' but goes on to explain that:

> Most volunteers don't have a contract of employment and so don't have the rights of an ordinary employee or worker. These include the right to a minimum wage, holiday and sick pay, and other statutory rights.

But it then adds that volunteers should have a 'volunteer agreement' explaining their rights, i.e.

- what supervision and support you will get
- insurance cover
- equal opportunities
- how disagreements will be resolved (see www.direct.gov.uk).

Sample volunteering agreements are available at www.volunteering.org.uk.

Note that these examples are not specific to therapists, so a therapist volunteer should have specific additional clauses in their volunteer agreement dealing with therapy-related matters including their agency's policies, their professional responsibilities and duties, client rights and complaints procedures, etc.

3.1.4 Relevant law, professional guidance, etc. for volunteers

Some statutes apply to everyone in the workplace. Others apply to voluntary workers only if they are deemed 'employed'. In summary, the law on data protection, disability and discrimination, freedom of information, health and safety and safeguarding vulnerable groups all apply to everyone, whether employed or volunteers.

Other law specific to employment includes legislation on equal pay, employment rights and responsibilities, equality of treatment, hours of work, and equal opportunities.

In the leading case of *Melhuish v Redbridge Citizens Advice Bureau* [2005] IRLR 419, EAT, the court held that volunteers are not employees if they are unpaid, so they will not be entitled to statutory employee rights, e.g. maternity or paternity leave, etc. However, many statutory protections, for example non-discriminatory work practice, health and safety provisions and protection from harassment in the workplace, will in practice apply equally to employees and to volunteer workers.

In agencies and organisations providing therapeutic services, volunteer therapists would be expected to comply with the government and agency policies and practices, and to be subject to the same disciplinary proceedings as employed therapists. Where the agency provides professional or any other insurance cover for its workers, check with the agency or insurer whether volunteers working at the agency are covered by the policy.

Most professional guidance is specific to professions and professional organisations. Volunteer therapists should therefore look to their professional organisations for policies and accepted standards of practice in the therapy profession, e.g. the *Ethical Framework* (BACP 2010a), *UKCP Code of Professional Conduct* (UKCP 2009), etc. and where applicable, the relevant GMC guidance (GMC 2004, 2006). In cases of alleged breach of duty of care or negligence, accepted professional standards may be taken into account by the courts as a measure of the therapist's competence.

Soft law also includes generally applicable government guidance, some of which may be enforceable by the courts by statutory regulation, e.g. *Working Together to Safeguard Children* (DCSF 2010). Some soft law may be enforced by the courts, e.g. *Provision of Therapy for Child Witnesses Prior to a Criminal Trial: Practice Guidance* (CPS 2005a) and *Provision of Therapy for Vulnerable or Intimidated Adult Witnesses Prior to a Criminal Trial: Practice Guidance* (CPS 2005b).

3.2 Contractual issues

In practice, all therapists might enter into a wide variety of contracts, in their personal and professional life. Even though volunteers are not employees, they may have 'volunteer agreements' with their agency, which may constitute legally enforceable contracts. In order for a contract to be legally enforceable, something (consideration) must be given in return for the goods or services provided. Volunteer counsellors provide their time and services to their agency or organisation, and the organisation in return may provide therapists with experience leading to sufficient hours for accreditation, free supervision, use of rooms and office facilities or services, training, refreshments, etc. Where volunteer counsellors agree in their volunteer contract to comply with agency rules and policies for example, it is our view that this agreement is legally enforceable. For further discussion of contract law and legally enforceability, see Mitchels and Bond (2010: 44–64). Another major contract for most therapists is their professional civil liability insurance, see Mitchels and Bond (2010: 87–92).

In agencies and organisations using volunteer counsellors, the client will usually have an intake session in which agency policies and procedures are explained, along with a risk assessment process and taking a brief client history. This intake session will usually be with experienced agency staff or a senior practitioner, before the client is allocated to a therapist. In many agencies, the salient terms of the therapy (such as donations and payments, confidentiality, records, frequency and timing of sessions, etc.), are agreed at intake with the agency staff, before the client is allocated to a therapist. We are aware of some organisations, however, in which salient issues are not discussed in detail at intake, and the client is left to negotiate a therapeutic contract with the allocated therapist in their first session, in which specific issues such as the limits of confidentiality are left by the agency to be 'fine-tuned' and agreed between client and therapist.

In our view it is good practice to establish a clear mutual understanding about the terms of therapy, especially the limits of confidentiality, before therapy begins, and to reflect this, if possible, in a written therapeutic contract, or one recorded in some other format.

3.3 Practice issues

3.3.1 Clarity of role

Agencies sometimes are less clear than they should be about defining the role of volunteers. Some agencies do not provide a written contract of engagement with a description of the role and the boundaries within which the volunteer is expected to work. Volunteers may then have difficulty in knowing the full extent of their role, where for example, issues of record storage, referrals, information sharing within a team, or how far they should maintain confidentiality with others external to the agency. Volunteers may not know the agency's policies, e.g. on sharing information in cases where information is requested about clients by external agencies for child protection or other aspects of client safety. Organisations and agencies should have a clear policy on these issues, preferably in written form, for all their employees and volunteers to follow.

A volunteer may have a written contract for their services (see 3.2 above) and this is likely to be legally enforceable in situations where the volunteer needs to clarify their working conditions or terms of work, or where the agency needs to enforce disciplinary measures against the volunteer, e.g. for malpractice, or for failure to comply with government or agency policies or with professional supervision requirements etc.

3.3.2 Issues of internal supervision

Some organisations may use supervisors directly employed or funded by them, either in one-to-one supervision or through internal peer-supervision groups, facilitated by a supervisor employed or funded by the agency. If that supervisor is employed and/or line-managed by the agency, then we refer to this as 'internal supervision'.

Supervision is expensive and trainee therapists and/or volunteers may not be able to afford to pay for supervision whilst they are working free of charge. Many agencies that rely on volunteers working in trainee placements therefore offer free supervision as an incentive to their volunteers. Some agencies feel the need to maintain an element of oversight and if necessary, control over the work of all staff and volunteers, and especially over their less experienced therapists. In order for the administrators or directors responsible for the running of organisations to be regularly informed about how their therapists are working and their skill levels, some agencies therefore insist on some form of internal supervision, and/or offer it as a free service for their staff.

If both the volunteer and their supervisor are line-managed by the agency, then there is the potential here for a conflict of interests to arise, and even more so if the supervisor is the therapist's direct line manager. The same comment applies equally to an employed therapist. The line manager has the power to discipline or even sack the therapist, and so the therapist may be reluctant to admit their doubts, mistakes or difficulties in therapy practice – the very issues that an inexperienced practitioner (or any therapist) may need to take freely to supervision. Equally the supervisor may experience conflicts of interest in trying to maintain their supervisee's confidentiality and yet also to report concerns and other administrative issues within the organisation. These matters require clarification by each therapist and supervisor at the outset of their work with the organisation.

BACP is very clear in the *Ethical Framework* (BACP 2010a) that practitioners need to have access to an independent external supervisor. There is a very good reason for this. Some organisations (for perceived benefits of management control), insist on internal supervision, which is tempting for volunteers, because it may also be provided free of charge. If this is the sole source of supervision, it has concomitant risks, especially where an internal supervisor also has a management role in relation to the therapist. Imagine a situation where a person in a management role in an agency is alleged to be in breach of law and/or has been falling below acceptable professional standards in relation to one of the agency's volunteers, for example, by racial or sexual harassment or bullying. The volunteer therapist may be deterred from making a formal complaint (either internally in the organisation or externally to their professional body), perhaps through fear of reprisals from the authority figure or the organisation and/or possibly also losing their placement, or risking a negative reference on application for employed work or accreditation. If that person is also their therapeutic supervisor, this poses an even more difficult situation, and greater potential for conflicts of interest and failure of appropriate supervision.

Supervision should be a relationship in which the supervisee has enough trust and psychological safety to share any issues affecting their therapeutic work, and receive appropriate help and advice. The volunteer in this situation might wish to disclose the facts to their internal supervisor and would probably want to request confidentiality and receive help and support. However, if that internal supervisor is a manager, the therapist may feel unable to admit mistakes or weaknesses. If the supervisor is also line-managed and supervised by a person in authority in the organisation, and if a problem is experienced with the organisation, or if the person in authority is the cause of (or associated with) the problems, the volunteer (and the supervisor, too) would potentially then face an ethical dilemma and possible conflict of interests. If the supervisee realises this, they may be deterred from sharing important information.

If a therapist withholds from their supervisor important information affecting their practice, the supervisory relationship of mutual trust is compromised and may become untenable. A therapist who has an external supervisior (i.e. who has no relationship with their employing organisation) avoids this difficulty of dual relationships and has the opportunity for objective ethical advice and support. (See also Bond 2010; Jacobs 2010.)

3.3.3 Should volunteers accept gifts or donations?

Therapists should not accept gifts from clients since this may impact on the therapeutic relationship (BACP 2010a).

Donations for the benefit of the organisation may be acceptable, since they are not personally for the therapist.

3.3.4 Volunteers in training

If a trainee has undertaken an unpaid placement as part of their work experience during training, they are volunteers as described in this chapter, and entitled to a contract describing the terms of their work. The placement (and also their supervisor) may agree to a contractual relationship with the training organisation with a responsibility to feed back any problems or issues that might impact on the trainee's progress, or the trainee's ability to work effectively with clients.

The ethical duty and responsibilities of the placement organisation and the supervisor will depend both on the duty of care and the terms of their contract(s) with the supervisee and the training organisation, all of which should be compatible. See 3.3.2 above for potential ethical dilemmas.

Training contracts often contain a '3-way' clause where the trainee agrees that their practice will be monitored by their placement and also in supervision, and the trainee specifically permits feedback (from both) to their training organisation. Training contracts may also state that a trainee can be asked to defer all or part of training or to leave training altogether if they are not making appropriate progress. Training can be lengthy and expensive, causing difficulty for trainees who are required to cease training or leave a placement. Trainees should therefore ask for written contracts (from their training organisation, placement and supervisor) and read them all carefully, noting the terms on which they may be asked to defer or to leave training, or to leave a placement. Obtain legal advice where appropriate.

4 Working with Adults in the Context of Social Care Agencies

In this chapter we focus on therapeutic work with adults in the context of social care agencies, by which we mean to include all those agencies providing community care or working with adult clients who are elderly, vulnerable or with special needs, mental illness or disability. We include therapists working with clients with specific conditions such as addictions or eating disorders, or those who are vulnerable for any other reason – this may include those who are refugees or homeless. For ease of reference in this chapter we have subdivided the areas of work into separate categories.

For therapeutic work with children and young people under 18 years of age, including working in the context of social care, see Chapter 9. For adoption support services, see Chapter 10, and Chapter 8 looks at therapeutic work with and for the police and the Home Office, which also includes working with offenders, ex-offenders and probation services in liaison with social services. Chapter 6 looks at therapeutic work within the context of health care, and includes a perspective of therapy in the context of medical social work.

4.1 Law and regulation of health and social care

4.1.1 Background legal context of health and social care provision

The Health and Social Care Acts 2001 and 2008, and the Health and Social Care (Reform) Act (Northern Ireland) 2009, with subsequent subsidiary legislation address, among other things, funding for health authorities and primary care trusts, local authority scrutiny of health services, public involvement, consultation and patient advisory groups. The Health and Social Care (Community Health and Standards) Act 2003 established the *Commission for Healthcare Audit and Inspection* (CHAI). We wonder if they saw the humour of the acronym sounding like the word for 'tea' in several languages! The Act also established the *Commission for Social Care Inspection* (CSCI, often pronounced as 'sea sky'), which had the role of registering social care services under the Care Standards Act 2000 and encouraging improvement in the provision of local authority social services. CSCI ceased to exist on 31 March 2009. At the time of writing, the present coalition government in England is considering further reforms, including a radical revision of health care funding, so watch for additional changes to health and social care provision, funding, standards and inspection.

The structure in Northern Ireland is slightly different. The DHSSPS is responsible for creating policy and legislation for primary, secondary, community and social care. The Health and Personal Social Services Act (Northern Ireland) 2001 addressed funding for health and social services in Northern Ireland. It also established the Northern Ireland Social Care Council (NISCC), whose duty is to provide high standards of conduct, practice and training among social workers. It is responsible for regulating and registering the social care workforce in Northern Ireland.

Registration with the NISCC demonstrates that a particular social worker is suitably trained, professional in their practice and accountable for the work they do. Registered workers must meet the agreed standards in their conduct and practice set out in the NISCC Code of Practice. The NISCC has also developed Registration Rules and Conduct Rules. All three documents are available at www.niscc.info.

The Health and Personal Social Services (Quality Improvement and Regulation) (Northern Ireland) Order 2003 established the Northern Ireland Health and Personal Social Services Regulation and Improvement Authority. The Order also established the Care Tribunal to hear appeals against decisions relating to the regulation of care services and to the employment and registration of social workers in Northern Ireland.

4.1.2 Summary of the new law regarding standards and regulation in health and social care

The Health and Social Care Act 2008 brought in a new, single registration system that applies to both health and adult social care, replacing the earlier system of the Care Standards Act 2000. The new essential standards of quality and safety now consist of 28 regulations (and associated outcomes) that are set out in two pieces of legislation: the Health and Social Care Act 2008 (Regulated Activities) Regulations 2010 and the Care Quality Commission (Registration) Regulations 2009.

The General Social Care Council sets standards of conduct and practice for social care workers and their employers in England and is responsible for the codes of practice, the Social Care Register and social work education and training – see www.gscc.org.uk.

The Care Quality Commission (CQC) is the new health and social care regulator for England. The CQC has the power to require registration of health and social care professionals. Details are available on its website at www.cqc.org.uk, where guidance about registration and compliance can be found. The CQC has established *Essential Standards of Quality and Safety*, published on its website at www.cqc.org.uk/usingcareservices/essentialstandardsofqualityandsafety.cfm. The inspectors will use the *Judgement Framework* to assess compliance with the regulations, and the framework also refers to *Setting the Bar*, a guidance document that helps CQC assessors to make consistent decisions about the registration status of a provider and about the overall level of compliance or concern. Both publications are available as pdfs at www.cqc.org/_db/_documents.

From April 2010, all NHS trusts must be registered with CQC, and all health and adult social care providers are required by law to be registered with CQC if they provide 'regulated activities'. From 1 October 2010, they apply also to independent health care and adult social care providers. From April 2012 they apply to primary medical care services (including GP practices and out-of-hours services). Therapists working for a registered provider in the context of health or social care may therefore find themselves subject to the new regulations. Guidance on standards, implementation and the registration process in adult social care can be found at www.cqc.org.uk.

In Scotland, the Care Commission fulfils a similar function to the Care Quality Commission in England. Further information can be found at www.carecommission.com.

New regulations of particular relevance to therapists

All of the regulations are perhaps relevant in some way, but Part 4 of the Health and Social Care Act 2008 (Regulated Activities) Regulations 2010 contains provisions that may be of particular interest to therapists working in social care contexts, i.e.

- Reg. 9 Care and welfare of people who use services
  - People experience effective, safe and appropriate care, treatment and support that meets their needs and protects their rights.

- Reg. 10 Assessing and monitoring the quality of service provision
  - People benefit from safe, quality care because effective decisions are made and because of the management of risks to people's health, welfare and safety.

- Reg. 11 Safeguarding people who use services from abuse
  - People are safeguarded from abuse, or the risk of abuse, and their human rights are respected and upheld.

- Reg. 18 Consent to care and treatment
  - People give consent to their care and treatment, and understand and know how to change decisions about things that have been agreed previously

- Reg. 20 Records
  - People's personal records are accurate, fit for purpose, held securely and remain confidential. The same applies to other records that are needed to protect their safety and well-being.

- Reg. 23 Supporting workers
  - People are kept safe, and their health and welfare needs are met, because staff are competent to carry out their work and are properly trained, supervised and appraised

In Northern Ireland, the law was reformed by the Health and Social Care (Northern Ireland) Act 2009. This act dissolved the Health and Social Services Boards, the

Mental Health Commission, the Central Services Agency and the Health and Social Services Council. The Northern Ireland Health and Personal Social Services Regulation and Improvement Authority was renamed as the Health and Social Care Regulation and Quality Improvement Authority (RQIA) and took on the functions of the Mental Health Commission in addition to its existing functions. The Act also established the Regional Health and Social Care Board, the Regional Agency for Public Health and Social Well-Being, the Regional Business Services Organisation and the Patient and Client Council.

4.2 Mental illness

There are many issues for therapists in the context of working with clients who have a diagnosed mental illness. Perhaps the most noticeable challenges are posed by the operation of the Mental Health Acts, in particular the Mental Health Act 1983 (MHA 1983) and provisions for compulsory detention for assessment or treatment, and compulsory treatment. Therapists may also be involved with social care in the provision of patient after-care following discharge from hospital and in provision of client care in the community.

The assessment of mental capacity is also an important issue for decision making, for which the Mental Capacity Act 2005 applies in England and Wales. The Bamford Committee has recommended that similar legislation be implemented in Northern Ireland, see www.dhsspsni.gov.uk/bamford.htm/ and for the work of the Bamford Monitoring Group see www.patientclientcouncil.hscni.net/ bamford-monitoring-group (both accessed 8 March 2011). Currently, in Northern Ireland, see also the Mental Health (Northern Ireland) Order 1986.

Under s. 117 of the MHA 1983, the provision of after-care following discharge from compulsory detention in hospital is the duty of the Local Health Board, the Primary Trust and local social services, whilst the person remains under supervision or until they are satisfied that the client is no longer in need of those services. In Northern Ireland, Article 7(1) of the Health Services (Northern Ireland) Order 1972 imposes a duty on local authorities to make arrangements, to such extent as the Department of Health and Social Services and Public Safety considers necessary, for the after-care of a person suffering from illness (the term illness includes mental disorder for the purposes of this Order).

The Care Programme approach (see 4.3 below) comes into play, with similar provisions, when any other mentally ill person is discharged from hospital. There is guidance in the form of a Code of Practice and government circulars (see 4.3 below). See also *Building Bridges – A Guide to Arrangements for Inter-agency Working for the Care and Protection of Severely Mentally Ill People* (DH 1995).

The law with regard to the respective duties of health professionals and social care needs is complex. Authorities may get into a 'who should do what' argument, particularly in cases where clients may deteriorate, e.g. in dementia. There is a clear and useful exposition of the relevant law in Chapter 7 of the *Community Care Law and Local Authority Handbook* (Butler 2008).

The law in the area of community care is rapidly developing, partly due to the demographic of the section of the population to which it applies, i.e. generally older adults. The case of *R v Ealing District Health Authority, ex parte Fox* [1993] 3 All ER 170 established that health authorities and local authority social services must take reasonable steps to identify appropriate after-care facilities for a patient before discharge from hospital. Discussion should therefore take place before the Mental Health Review Tribunal hearing or hospital managers' meeting takes place. (For discussion of the law, see Butler 2008: 6–27.)

As we have seen, the law with regard to the respective duties of health professionals and social care in meeting clients' after-care needs is complex, and the House of Lords views in the case of *R v Manchester CC ex parte Stennett and two other actions* [2002] 2CCLR 500; [2002] UKHL 34 are relevant.

Soft law includes government guidance, some of which may be enforceable by the courts by statutory regulation, e.g. the Code of Practice issued by the Secretary of State for the provision of after-care for those discharged from compulsory detention in hospital under s. 117 of the MHA 1983.

The Care Programme Approach (CPA) for all patients receiving treatment and care from specialist psychiatric services is set out in the Circular HC(90) 23/LASSL(90)11 (see http://cpaa.co.uk/thecareprogrammeapproach) and in the Welsh Office Mental Illness Strategy (WHC(95)40). The key elements of the CPA are:

- Systematic arrangements for assessing health and social care needs
- Formulation of a care plan addressing identified needs
- Appointment of a key worker to keep in close touch with the patient and monitor care
- Regular review and make/implement agreed changes to the care plan

As to funding, see the report from the Health Service Ombudsman (2003), see http://www.ombudsman.org.uk/_data/assets/pdf_file/0013/1075/NHS-funding-for-long-term-care.pdf

4.3 Clients with special needs, including disability, the elderly and vulnerable adults

The National Health Service and Community Care Act 1990 s. 46, established the duty of local authorities to plan, provide and publish community care services in their area. Assessment is mandatory where it appears to the local authority that community care services may be required for an individual. Assessment should be followed by evaluation for provision of services, within the principles of reasonableness discussed in 4.1.2 above. Any of the client groups with special needs, disability or mental illness may qualify for assessment, also those who are elderly or otherwise vulnerable. The Community Care Assessment Directions 2004 added the requirement to consult the person being assessed, to give information about any payment required, and to agree the services to be provided with the recipient. Where appropriate, this also applies to that person's carers.

In Northern Ireland, the Health and Personal Social Services (Northern Ireland) Order 1977 contains a duty for local authorities to 'make arrangements to such extent the Department of Health, Social Services and Public Safety considers necessary for the presentation of the prevention of illness and the care and aftercare of a person suffering from an illness'. While the Order does not explicitly require local authorities to make a care assessment, the *People First: Care Management Guidance on Assessment and the Provision of Community Care, 1993* guidance makes it clear that local authorities should carry out an assessment of anyone who appears in need of community care services, including residential care. The Disabled Persons (Northern Ireland) Act 1989 also places a duty on local authorities to make a care assessment of people who are defined as 'chronically ill or disabled'.

The term 'disabled' is defined in law in s. 16 of the National Assistance Act 1948. Not necessarily the best definition, it has to be said! For children under 18 years, see Part III of the Children Act 1989. If a person is disabled, then under s. 4 of the Disabled Persons (Services Consultations and Representations) Act 1986 assessment is triggered, even without a request.

Since then, additional legislation has been passed, including the Community Care and Health (Scotland) Act 2002, dealing with assessments, payment and joint working of health and local authorities, and the Community Care (Delayed Discharges etc.) Act 2003, which made provision for delayed discharge payments in respect of qualifying hospital patients who will need community care services on discharge from hospital.

Politics and law often run together. An old case, *Associated Provincial Picture Houses Ltd v Wednesbury Corpn* [1948] 1 KB 223, concerned the requirement that films could only be shown on a Sunday if all children under the age of 15 were excluded. The cinemas challenged this draconian condition. In deciding in favour of the cinemas, the court established the firm principle of the need for 'reasonableness' in the exercise of the discretion of a local authority when carrying out its duties. Courts and lawyers will now refer to a 'Wednesbury unreasonable' decision.

The concept of reasonableness (or 'Wednesbury unreasonableness') may apply when they are considering the allocation of local authority resources to meet an individual's needs. The leading case on this is *R v Gloucestershire County Council ex parte Barry* [1997] 1 CCLR 40; [1997] 2 WLR 459 HL. In this case a disabled man was assessed as needing cleaning and laundry services at home, but the local authority withdrew the services, on the basis of a lack of resources. The House of Lords held that the local authority should have regard to the relationship between the cost of providing the service, balanced against the benefit to the client and their need for that benefit, but that the local authority must carry out its responsibilities in a responsible fashion. If the local authority is acting with Wednesbury unreasonableness, then a disabled person would have a remedy.

Lord Browne-Wilkinson followed this reasoning in the later case of *R v East Sussex County Council ex parte Tandy* [1998] 2 All ER 769; *Re T (A Minor)* [1998] 1 CCLR 352.

He said that, 'To permit a local authority to avoid performing a statutory duty on the ground that it prefers to spend the money in other ways is to downgrade a statutory duty to a discretionary power.' He added 'Once the reasonableness of the actions of a local authority depends on its decision how to apply scarce financial resources, the local authority's decision becomes extremely difficult to review' (p. 360 para. E-1). In that case, the court held that the local authority should first assess a need, and only then can the matter of resources be considered in deciding whether it is reasonable to provide for that need.

The Department of Health in England and Wales has issued guidance on the eligibility criteria for 'social care': *Fair Access to Care Services – Guidance on Eligibility Criteria for Adult Social Care* (DH 2002a). It carries the force of law, being made under s. 7(1) of the Social Services Act 1970 which makes it compulsory for local authorities and government departments to follow unless there are cogent reasons to depart from the guidance. It is enforceable through local complaints procedures, and in the High Court by judicial review. The enforceability of government guidance made under s. 7(1) of the Social Services Act 1970 by judicial review in the High Court was established in the case of *R v Islington LBC ex parte Rixon (Jonathan)* [1998] 1 CCLR 119, (1996) The Times 17 April. The High Court will, however, expect that before seeking judicial review, local complaints procedures will be followed.

See also, *Care Management and Assessment: Practitioner's Guide* (Department of Health and Social Services Inspectorate, 1991), which provides greater detail supporting the DH (2002a) guidance. In March 2001 the government produced *Modern Standards and Service Models – Older People – National Service Framework for Older People* (DH 2001).

The website states that:

> These documents set out the Government's commitment to improve the quality of services for elderly people. The implementation of the National Service Framework will provide a structure for improving the standards of care to all elderly people, offering integrated services that will allow elderly people to receive appropriate care at home, in residential or nursing homes and in hospitals. The aims are to end age discrimination in the provision of health and social care services, to promote healthy lifestyles and provide support so that elderly people can live independently, but overall to treat older people with respect by providing high quality services.

It remains to be seen how the CQC and the new regulations made under the Health and Social Care Act 2008, Health and Social Care Act 2008 (Regulated Activities) Regulations 2010 and the Care Quality Commission (Registration) Regulations 2009 (described in 4.1.1. above), as well as the corresponding arrangements in Northern Ireland, will impact on work with the elderly.

Significantly, therapy seems to have received very little attention as part of a care package for the elderly. It seems that, unless a specific mental health need is identified in the initial assessment process, counselling or psychotherapy is unlikely to be considered as an option (for example as a supportive or preventive measure) for the elderly during subsequent reviews, unless a clear mental health issue arises or therapy is specifically requested.

For the elderly with dementia or mental health illnesses, the NSF requires the NHS and local councils to work with care homes in their areas to develop a range of services to meet the needs of older people with mental health problems, including specialist residential care places for older people with dementia (DH 2001, para. 7.19). Within residential care, one would expect that therapy should be available to those who need it, but therapeutic interventions will only be requested if this need is identified as part of the assessment and formulation of a care plan for the individual.

In 2001, the NSF statistics about dementia made grim reading ... 'Approximately 600,000 people in the UK have dementia. This represents 5% of the total population aged 65 and over, rising to 20% of the population aged 80 and over. Dementia can also occur before the age of 65; there are about 17,000 people with dementia in younger age groups in the UK'; see DH 2001, para. 7.34. In 2010, the Alzheimer's Research Trust states that there are 820,000 people with dementia in the UK, with their care costing much more than care for those with cancer and heart disease. It predicts that, in the UK, '1 in 3 over 65s will die with some form of dementia'; see www.alzheimers-research.org.uk/info/statistics/ (accessed 6 December 2010).

The NSF was updated in 2007 with the 'single assessment process' see *Modernising Adult Social Care – What's Working* (DH 2007).

In considering the provision of services for an adult, or a child in need, where an assessed need exists, a local authority may take into account its available resources but it may not take decisions on the basis of resources alone and unreasonably refuse to provide a necessary service – its decision is subject to the series of principles established in the cases of *Associated Provincial Picture Houses Ltd v Wednesbury Corpn, R v Gloucestershire County Council ex parte Barry* and *R v East Sussex County Council ex parte Tandy,* discussed in 4.1.3 above. See also the Local Authorities Social Services Letter (97) 13 issued by the DH on 11 December 1997 (LASSL (97) 13).

Therapy practice guidance

Another form of guidance that may be regarded as soft law is the policy and accepted standards of practice in the therapy profession, e.g. the *Ethical Framework* (BACP 2010a) and, where applicable, the current GMC Members Code of Conduct (see www.gmc-uk.org). In cases of alleged breach of duty of care or negligence, accepted professional standards may be taken into account by the courts as a measure of the therapist's competence. If the practice of counselling and psychotherapy is regulated in the future, specific standards and competencies may be adopted. Watch the BACP website and www.hpc-uk. org/ for developments.

4.4 Contractual issues

All therapists working in the context of social care need professional indemnity insurance, which may be funded (or provided) by their employer, or for the self-employed, it is likely to be required as part of their contract for services.

- For discussion of insurance, see Chapter 1 at 1.1.7 and Mitchels and Bond 2010: Chapter 6.
- For contracts of employment (as employer or employee in a business or organisation) see Chapter 2 at 2.2.3 and Mitchels and Bond 2010: Chapter 9. For contracts for work as a volunteer in an agency or organisation, see Chapter 3 at 3.1 and 3.2. and also Mitchels and Bond 2010: Chapters 4 and 9.

A breach of the duty of care by a therapist working in the context of social care may lead to a formal complaint to the local authority, to the therapist's professional body, and/or a legal claim. Any complaint or legal action involving a therapist (whatever their employment status) should be notified to the therapist's own professional liability insurers. Claims may be covered by an employer's professional insurance. In situations where the therapist has acted in the course of their work (e.g. where the therapist has complied with social care agency policies and government guidance), the agency (e.g. the local authority, adoption agency, etc.) may be held vicariously liable for the actions of the therapist; see Mitchels and Bond 2010: Chapters 3 and 9.

Therapeutic contracts with clients will be regulated by the general law relating to the duty of care (see Mitchels and Bond 2010: Chapters 3 and 4), the therapist's professional code of conduct giving the client a right of complaint, and also by general contract law. Agency policies and procedures may place limits on the contractual arrangements between a therapist and client working in social care, e.g. the place where the therapist may see the clients, times of appointments, health and safety procedures, confidentiality in making, keeping and storage of records, fees payable, etc.

4.5 Practice issues

4.5.1 Disclosures of abuse

Therapists working with vulnerable adults in residential care or living with their families may be told of situations where the client is the victim of bullying or direct physical or other form of abuse. The client may be afraid of reprisals as a result of any disclosure, and so they may request the therapist not to say anything to others about the situation. The therapist then is faced with a potential dilemma of whether to make a disclosure to protect the client from future harm and in the public interest, or to keep silent and maintain their duty of confidentiality to the client. The therapist's decision might be influenced by their employment contract, which is likely to require compliance with agency policies or procedures and/or compliance with government guidance. The limits of confidentiality should always be made clear to clients at the outset of therapy as part of the therapeutic contract, and if the situation is regulated by the therapist's agency, clients should be made aware of (and agree to) the terms of work. See 4.3 for considerations in dealing with confidentiality issues, and Mitchels and Bond (2010: Chapter 4) for contractual considerations.

4.5.2 Non-compliance with care plans or contracts for care in residential settings – 'whistle-blowing' on bad practice

Therapists may find themselves aware of organisational or individual failures, e.g. failure to comply with the patient's contract of care, or to fulfil the care plan of a person in residential care. Therapists are then in the difficult position of having to disclose the failures of staff or work colleagues in the best interest of the client. No professional is likely to feel entirely happy about reporting the bad practice or professional misconduct of another person, especially a colleague with whom they work. However, in some situations, 'whistle-blowing' may be necessary to maintain good professional practice, and it may be permitted or even required within agency policy (contractually agreed by all the agency's employees) or it may be required by law (e.g. reporting terrorist activities under the Terrorism Act 2000 or disclosing the identity of a driver when required by the police under the Road Traffic Acts [or, in Northern Ireland, Road Traffic Orders], or by an order of a court).

There are other situations where whistle-blowing may not be specifically required by law or agency policy, but is left to the therapist's discretion. These situations may include the discovery of criminal acts by a colleague, e.g. a therapist taking illegal recreational drugs and placing vulnerable clients at risk, or ethically bad practice leading to the risk of potential harm to a child or vulnerable adult, where therapists feel that preventive action is necessary and that therefore whistle-blowing is morally and ethically justified. The issue for the therapist then is whether whistle-blowing is *legally* defensible, for example, in the public interest (i.e. that the protection of the general public may justifiably outweigh personal or private rights).

Bear in mind that the law prohibits attacks on the reputation of another person and court cases can be brought for slander (untrue verbal allegations damaging the reputation of another) and libel (untrue and damaging allegations about another made in writing). A legal defence to both of these claims would be that the allegations made were true and that disclosures were made in the public interest.

In the case of bad professional practice, where a colleague has been clearly warned about their conduct and has failed to make necessary changes, or where the colleague conceals their conduct from management or their professional organisation, practitioners may feel that whistle-blowing may be the only way left to stop the bad practice continuing.

4.6 Interface and managing movement between social care and other contexts

4.6.1 Confidentiality

Confidentiality is never protected as an absolute right in England and Wales, Northern Ireland or Scotland. The public interest may be paramount in the eyes of the law over an individual's right to confidentiality, and disclosure may be required by statute in certain situations, e.g. acts or threatened acts of terrorism, drug trafficking, in cases of child protection and when specifically required by police under certain road traffic legislation (see Bond and Mitchels 2008: 23–5).

Inter-agency sharing of information is increasing so much that it has now become the norm, and therapists working in the context of education, social care, health care and police may need to share information for the public protection or for the safety and welfare of a client.

Information may be shared with the full explicit consent of the client. In other situations, in the absence of client consent, the public interest may require the exercise by a therapist of their discretion to disclose information, e.g. where there is an imminent risk of serious harm to the client or to others. In these situations, the therapist's discretion to disclose information in the public interest is protected by the courts, in that they will not enforce a client's right to confidentiality (i.e. they will not punish the therapist for disclosure) in cases where the therapist acted in good faith and the public interest was protected by making the disclosure. See the case of *W v Edgell and others* [1990] 1 All ER 835.

The General Medical Council guidance to doctors directs, 'If you remain of the view that disclosure is necessary to protect a third party from death or serious harm, you should disclose information promptly to an appropriate person or authority' (GMC 2004: para. 27). The Department of Health also provided guidance on the type of situations where this may apply:

> Murder, manslaughter, rape, treason, kidnapping, child abuse or other cases where individuals have suffered serious harm may all warrant breaching confidentiality. Serious harm to the security of the state or to public order and crimes that involve substantial financial gain and loss will generally fall within this category. In contrast, theft, fraud or damage to property where loss or damage is less substantial would generally not warrant breach of confidence. (DH 2003: 35)

For discussion of ways to approach decision making when faced with dilemmas about confidentiality and disclosure, and for a checklist of factors to consider, see Chapter 1 at 1.4.1 and Bond and Mitchels (2008).

4.6.2 Information about third parties

Therapists may receive information from a client about a third party, e.g. where a client reports abuse, but requests the therapist not to disclose this information;

or where a therapist hears in the course of work that a third party poses a risk to the health or welfare of others, the therapist may face a dilemma in which they balance public interest against their professional duty of care, which includes confidentiality.

A duty of confidentiality may arise, even where there is no contractual relationship, even in the ever-widening context of exchange of information between agencies:

> A professional (like anyone else) who somehow acquires confidential personal information may be saddled with an obligation of confidentiality toward X, the subject of the information, whether there was a direct, indirect or no contact with X. All that is necessary is that the professional was aware, or a reasonable person in her position would have been aware, that the information is private to X. (Pattenden, 2003: 13)

See also the case of *A v B plc and C ('Flitcroft')* [2002] EWCA Civ 337; 3 WLR 542, reversing [2001] 1WLR 2341.

See 4.3 for considerations in dealing with confidentiality issues, and Bond et al. (2010), Bond and Jenkins (2009) and Bond and Mitchels (2008).

4.6.3 Referrals

Information given by someone about a potential client in the process of making a referral is also covered by a duty of confidentiality even though this is an indirect communication about the person concerned. The knowledge that someone might require or is seeking therapy is a private matter. Similarly, information sent in error about a client to the wrong therapist also creates a duty of confidentiality, even though there has been no contact between the therapist and client nor is any future contact intended. A legally wise response to this situation would be to notify the sender of the error, assuring them that the information is being treated as confidential, and ask their guidance on whether they would like it securely returned or destroyed.

5 Education

Are school counselling services subject to the same government control as the school itself?

How do I find out about the policies and procedures of the school in which I work?

What can I do if I am concerned about the welfare of a child in school?

What if I feel that John needs therapy, but his parents say that they don't want him to have counselling?

Jane's father turned up at school demanding to know what his daughter had said about her parents in her therapy sessions with me. Do I have to give him any information?

The Head asked me what the twins had said in their counselling with me about the bullying in their year group. Do I have to tell him?

Should the Head be allowed to see my records of my therapy with the children in school?

I work for two days a week as a school counsellor, and the remainder of the week at home in private practice. I don't want to keep my school client records at the school, but this is what the school wants me to do. Must I comply?

I work in a University Student Counselling Service. One of the students has told me that they are an illegal immigrant, and asked me to keep this confidential. Do I have to report this to anyone?

This chapter puts the work of therapists into the context of the law as it applies to the education system currently operating in England and Wales. By the terms 'education' and 'education system' we include each of the nursery, school, further education and higher education levels. We regret that we are not able to discuss the relevant law in Scotland and Northern Ireland in detail here, but we have included references for further reading. We are most grateful to Barbara Lawton and to Ruth Caleb and the committee of the AUCC for the practice issues that they have raised with us, and which we have addressed in this chapter.

The education system for the general population has developed in response to social and economic change, and it is only in comparatively recent times that psychotherapy and the use of school, college or university counsellors has become an established part of that system.

In the centuries before 1600, academic learning was considered necessary only for the higher classes, who tended to focus mainly on male education. Although some women were educated, women were mainly encouraged to develop household, creative and cultural skills. The education of the lower classes (and of women) gradually developed as a result of philanthropy, continuing social change and also as a result of the economic need to provide skilled workers. Interestingly, in modern times, gender differentiation seems to lie in subjects: women predominate in arts and social sciences, e.g. nearly three times as many females than males take Psychology and Sociology. *The Gender Agenda – Research and Evidence* (DCSF 2008b) shows that in one year, 230 men and 10 women took Applied Engineering, while Health and Social Care was taken by 4,720 female and just 180 male students (see also Ward and Eden 2009: 132–3).

Education may also be seen politically as a means of national development and also as an instrument of commercial success through marketing schooling and the development of education to feed the requirements of a global marketplace. Higher education in Universities and Colleges in particular is partly dependent on commercial success through the sale of student places and through investment in buildings, staff and resources. This places administration, staff and students under considerable pressure in many ways: to provide 'value for money', to utilise resources wisely and to achieve success in order to justify investment. The assessment, measurement and evaluation of these criteria has therefore become an industry in itself which may be outsourced, e.g. Ofsted (the government organisation for education inspection) has only a few permanent staff in London and outsources its work to private companies who bid for the inspection contracts. It remains to be seen how the role of the Department for Education (DfE) created on 12 May 2010 and the new programme for the creation of Academy freedoms will impact on schools.

However, all these factors and changes inevitably impact on staff and on the counsellors who work with staff and/or students. The pressures at all levels of education of increasing commercialism, assessment and evaluation, with increased state monitoring of education as evidenced by the paperwork of reports, internal examinations and tests, all contribute to the existing stressors for both education staff and students of all ages. Appropriate support for staff and students is necessary, and therapy services are being delivered in an increasingly complex educational and political environment.

5.1 Legal features of education

5.1.1 Legal history of compulsory education

The development of education at national level, alongside the growing economic need for skilled workers, was accompanied by a parallel development of public awareness of child development, children's rights and the need for child protection, as evidenced by the passing of the Factory Act in 1833 and the Poor Law Reform Act in 1834. Under the 1880 Education Act, children's developmental needs were recognised and schooling became compulsory for 5–10-year-old children. The Prevention of Cruelty to and Protection of Children Act became law in 1889. It was not until the 'Fisher' Education Act of 1918 that compulsory schooling was increased until the age of 14, along with nursery education and medical inspections for schoolchildren. Under the Education Act 1944 free secondary education was provided for children aged 11–15, and the Act of 1972 raised the school leaving age to 16. The Education Act 1981 made requirements for provision for children with special educational needs.

5.1.2 State monitoring and control of education

State control of schools gradually developed as governments increasingly sought to make schools and teachers accountable for the good use of state funds invested in education. In 1902, the 'Balfour' Education Act abolished the School Boards and handed the control of education to the Local Education Authorities (LEAs), who continue to retain this role. The Education Act 1944 (now amended by subsequent legislation) first established the structures of primary, secondary and further education and this basic structure remains intact.

Following the recommendations in *Every Child Matters* (DfES 2004), under the Children Act 2004, local authorities are required to co-ordinate education, health and social care for children and young people under the age of 18 (in Northern Ireland, this requirement is contained in the Commissioner for Children and Young People (Northern Ireland) Order 2003). The DfES was then divided into the Department for Innovation, Universities and Skills (DIUS) and the Department for Children, Schools and Families (DCSF). In 2007, the *Children's Plan* (DCSF 2007) set out a vision for the education and well-being of children and young people. On 12 May 2010, the Department for Education (DfE) was formed and is responsible for both education and children's welfare – see www.education.gov.uk.

Northern Ireland, Scotland and Wales do not have equivalent Children's Plans. However, in Northern Ireland the Office of First Minister and Deputy First Minister issued a strategy document called *Our Children and Young People – Our Pledge: A ten year strategy for children and young people in Northern Ireland 2006–2016.* This document sets out a framework to ensure that the children and young people of Northern Ireland are fulfilling their potential. (This is available at www.dardni. gov.uk.) Following this, the Health and Social Services Boards, together with the Children's and Young People's Committees, produced a Northern Ireland Children's Service Plan, based on the six outcomes set out in *Our Children and Young People – Our Pledge.* The plan sets out the regional priorities for the period 2008–2011. (This is available at www.northernchildrensservices.org.)

Education is currently available in a range of learning environments, including:

- Privately funded schools
- County schools maintained by their LEA
- Trust schools, i.e. a state-funded foundation school supported by a charitable trust comprising the school and partners working together for the benefit of the school. Any maintained school can become a trust school – primary, secondary or special schools
- Voluntary schools provided by non-statutory bodies, e.g. religious or charitable organisations
- Academies

Now, following the change of government in 2010, the Department for Education has extended the role of Academies, further decreasing government control of education. The Academies Act 2010 extends the range of schools able to apply to be registered as 'Academies', i.e. they will become publicly funded independent schools, free from many restrictions, including local authority control, the National Curriculum, standard length of school days or terms, and with the freedom to negotiate pay and conditions for staff, collaborate with public and private organisations and with greater control over their budgets. Subject to Parliamentary approval, all maintained schools may apply to become an academy, with schools rated outstanding being fast-tracked for approval by the Secretary of State. Other primary, secondary and special schools will be able to convert at a later stage with the final decision on which schools become academies resting with the Secretary of State.

5.1.3 Teachers' role as being *in loco parentis* to children in school

The Latin term *in loco parentis* means 'in the place of a parent' and is used to describe a number of situations, including where a child is looked after following the death of the child's parent or guardian, where others have parental responsibility (a legal term) for a child, and it also includes situations where teachers have responsibility and a duty of care towards their pupils.

When a child is in a teacher's care, the teacher must assume certain responsibilities and recognise the legal and ethical obligations implicit in that role. The term *in loco parentis* was explained in law in 1888 (referring to the ability for teachers to correct pupils) and later reported in an old case, *Williams v Eady* (1893) 10 TLR. The judge, Mr Justice Cave, explained that the 'duty of a schoolmaster is to take such care of his boys as a careful father would take of his boys'. Teachers are expected to take the same care of their pupils as a 'reasonable' parent. This does not imply a standard of perfection, but of an ordinary person with reasonable common sense. However, the concept of teachers being *in loco parentis* is now being replaced by the concept of a general duty of care of a teacher to their students.

The degree of care required to be exercised depends mainly on the age, ability and the cognitive and emotional maturity of the pupil, along with any particular susceptibilities which ought to be known to the teacher. Older pupils may self-evidently be exposed reasonably to greater risk than younger pupils.

The duty of care of teachers *in loco parentis* to children in school was reiterated by the court in the case of *Hippolyte v Bexley L.B.C.* [1995] PIQR (309) CA. That duty is now supported by section 3(5) of the Children Act 1989, which states that a person who has care of a child may do what is reasonable under all circumstances for the purpose of safeguarding or promoting the child's welfare. The phrase in section 3(5) 'has care of' applies to a wide range of people, including schools and teachers, e.g. in dealing with medical or other emergencies, care within the school and looking after children on school trips.

The roles and risks of school and home are different. Teachers may have 25 or 30 children to control and supervise at any one time, and children at school may be exposed as part of the education process to risks they would not face elsewhere, e.g. scientific experiments, use of equipment for sports, association with other children in the playground, etc. Torbay Council points out in its document 'S101 Loco Parentis' that those teachers who ask themselves 'What would a prudent parent do in this situation?' might give themselves a misleading answer. The Torbay document points out that situations may arise where a teacher cannot or should not act as parent, and gives the examples:

- A parent may send a child to his or her room as punishment but a teacher who detains a small child leaving him or her to walk home through darkened streets may be at fault.
- A parent who instructs his young son to explore the properties of explosive chemicals, of which neither parent nor child has any detailed knowledge, is negligent. A skilled and experienced teacher properly supervising the use of the same substances for sound educational reasons is not negligent.

Teachers have certain authority conferred by their roles and functions in a compulsory education system. They also have a concomitant responsibility to show due care and skill in their work. The reasonable parent test remains useful, alongside government audit and guidance (see 5.1.4 and 5.1.5 below), to assist a court to determine whether a teacher has achieved the expected standard of care in a given set of circumstances.

The duty of care and indirect risks

General

The duty of care extends across the range of work which teachers commonly undertake. Those with responsibility for equipment and machinery are obliged to take reasonable steps to ensure that they are maintained in a condition safe for use by pupils. They should not normally undertake repairs but should make the appropriate arrangements for repairs by experts, taking the equipment out of use until it is repaired.

School administration

Teachers who have administrative responsibilities owe a duty to discharge those responsibilities for the safety of pupils. Timetabling should ensure that pupils of an age or disposition, for which almost constant supervision is needed, are not left unsupervised.

Student teachers and probationers

Teachers who accept responsibility for directing probationary or student teachers must discharge that responsibility for the safety of children. It is conceivable that a court could find that a student had done his or her best as a student to cope with a situation but that the directing teacher was guilty of negligence for failing to exercise proper oversight of the student or to give proper guidance.

School trips

Teachers who organise school trips must make adequate safety arrangements. A teacher who releases a pupil to travel in the car of a volunteer parent may be found negligent if the parent in question is known to have a list of convictions for careless driving.

Delegated organisation

Heads and their deputies, senior teachers and heads of department, have major organisational responsibilities. The system they direct and operate must always show the necessary regard for pupils' safety.

(Extract from 'S101 Loco Parentis', Torbay 2002)

Search at www.torbay.gov.uk for the full document and links for relevant further reading. We would suggest that this duty of care applies equally to school counsellors, in addition to the professional duty of care of a therapist to a client.

5.1.4 Government Inspectorates and audit agencies

- Audit Commission is an independent watchdog, driving economy, efficiency and effectiveness in local public services to deliver better outcomes for everyone. See: www.audit-commission.gov.uk. Tel: 0844 798 2134.
- Education and Training Inspectorate provides inspection service for a number of organisations in Northern Ireland, including the Department of Education. The Inspection Services Branch provides the Education and Training Inspectorate with administrative support in the work it carries out. See: www.etini.gov.uk. Tel: 028 91279726.
- National College for Leadership of Schools and Children's Services works to develop and support great leaders of schools, Early Years settings and children's services. See: www.nationalcollege.org.uk. Tel: 020 7023 4870.
- NI Audit Office is responsible for the external audit of central government bodies in Northern Ireland, including Northern Ireland Departments. The results are reported to the Northern Ireland Assembly (or to Parliament during suspension of devolution). See: www.niauditoffice.gov.uk. Tel: 028 90251000.
- Office of Standards in Education (Ofsted) inspects and regulates to achieve excellence in the care of children and young people, and in education and skills for learners of all ages. See: www.ofsted.gov.uk. Tel: 020 7421 6622.
- Office of the Qualifications and Examinations Regulator (Ofqual) regulates qualifications, exams and tests in England. As an independent regulator it reports directly to Parliament. See: www.ofqual.gov.uk. Tel: 0300 3033342.
- Qualifications and Curriculum Development Agency (QCDA) is responsible for developing and reviewing the national curriculum, improving and delivering assessments, and reviewing and reforming qualifications. The QCA transformed into the QCDA in July 2009. See: www.qcda.org.uk. Tel: 0300 303 3012.
- Training and Development Agency for schools (TDA) is the national agency and recognised sector body responsible for the training and development of the school workforce. See: www.tda.gov.uk. Tel: 0300 065 6763.

- Young People's Learning Agency (YPLA) was established by the Department in April 2010 and is responsible for championing education and training for young people in England. It supports local authorities to commission suitable education and training opportunities for all 16- to 19-year-olds in England, funds and manages the performance of open academies and provides direct support for learners. See: www.ypla.gov. uk. Tel: 020 7904 0945.

5.1.5 Statute, subsidiary legislation, case law and guidance relevant to child welfare in the context of education

The law and guidance which governs education in the UK might broadly be divided into the areas of:

- Setting up, funding and running educational establishments
- The curricula taught in schools
- Monitoring and evaluation of teaching and learning
- Child welfare and child protection.

For the purposes of this book, we are treating the provision of therapy in schools as an aspect of child welfare. The law and guidance relating to the protection of children will also apply to therapy in schools.

Provision of services and resources for children in need

Under the Children Act 1989 (Section 17 and Schedule 2) local authorities have a duty to provide for each 'child in need' in their area. (The equivalent Northern Ireland provisions can be found in Part IV of the Children (Northern Ireland) Order 1995.)

The government 'Quality Protects Programme' was created to 'ensure that referral and assessment processes discriminate effectively between different types and level of need, and produce a timely response' (John Hutton, Minister of State for Social Services, March 2000). Once an assessment of a child's specific needs is complete, an appropriate care plan can be put together.

To facilitate the implementation of the Quality Protects Programme, the Department of Health set up steering and advisory groups and the Departments of Health, Education, Employment and the Home Office issued materials to provide guidance, practice material and training resources. Their emphasis is on evidence based practice, and careful consideration of the needs of the individual child, with an expectation that inter-agency child protection and social work practice is based on analysis, reflection and sound judgment in decision making.

Two major contributions to the Quality Protects Programme materials are the companion volumes, *Framework for the Assessment of Children in Need and their Families* (DH 2000b) and *Assessing Children in Need and Their Families – Practice Guidance* (DH 2000a). Additional resources are the range of Initial and Core Assessment Records (2000) for children of different age groups and the *Family Assessment Pack of Questionnaires and Scales, 2000,* all available at www.dh.gov.uk.

The Family Assessment Pack of Questionnaires and Scales provides a set of measurement scales for different family situations, including questionnaires on:

- Strengths and difficulties (screening for emotional and behavioural problems)
- Parenting daily hassles (screening for parenting stressors)
- Adult well-being (screening for irritability, depression and anxiety)
- Home conditions (family cleanliness etc.)
- Adolescent well-being (for self-rating for depression)
- Family activity (in different age bands, 2–6 and 7–12 years) (child-centredness)
- Recent life events (life events as potential stressors)
- Alcohol scale (screening for alcohol overuse).

Therapists may well be able to assist in the assessment process, particularly in the areas of assessment that examine family stressors, well-being, moods, attitudes and behaviours. For therapists who want to explore more, there is an excellent comprehensive training pack, produced by the NSPCC and the University of Sheffield, called *The Child's World: Assessing Children in Need, Training and Development Pack*. It contains a video, training guide and a reader and is available through both the Department of Health and NSPCC websites.

The Children and Family Court Advisory Service (CAFCASS) has also introduced a plethora of 'tools' for working with both children and adults. These include the *Needs, Wishes and Feelings Pack*, and the *Domestic Violence Tool Kit*, both available through the CAFCASS website.

A child who is at risk of harm is by definition deemed to be 'a child in need'. Therefore all the guidance materials listed above apply to children who are subject to care proceedings, and also apply to many other children who may be assessed for the provision of resources by a local authority under s. 17 and Schedule 2 to the Children Act 1989.

For further reading on provision of service for children in need in Northern Ireland, please see *Care Matters in Northern Ireland – A Bridge to a Better Future*, available at www.dhsspsni.gov.uk.

The key areas of assessment are:

a   the child's developmental needs, which broadly looks at his emotional, social and behavioural development and function including a consideration of his identity. This area also considers the child's physical health, his self-care skills and his educational development;

b   the second limb considers the parenting capacity of the child's carers and as might be expected includes an appraisal of the provision of basic care, nurture, stimulation, guidance and boundaries, stability and emotional warmth;

c   the third domain considers family and environmental factors, including the family history and functioning, the wider family, housing, employment, income, the family's social integration and the availability of community resources.

The structure of the framework has been specifically designed to provide a systematic method for gathering and analysing information about children so that

Figure 5.1   The Child Assessment Framework (from DH 2000b)

Note: a copiable version is available at http://www.dh.gov.uk/prod_consum_dh/groups/dh_digitalas
sets/@dh/@en/documents/digitalasset/dh_4014430.pdf

different types and levels of need can be more effectively identified. It takes into account the needs of children from different cultural and ethnic groups. The Practice Guidance points out that this assessment model is equally applicable to disabled children and their families. However, the needs of their carers should be a particular factor to be taken into account.

Care plans

The courts have confirmed in case law that the care plan formulated following assessment should be in the form set out in Local Authority Circular (99) 29. The circular is issued under section 7 of the Local Authority Social Services Act 1970, which requires local authorities to act under the guidance of the Secretary of State, and it supplements the Children Act Guidance and Regulations Volume 3 Residential Care, and Volume 4 Family Placements of the Children Act 1989. The revised *Care Planning, Placement and Case Review Regulations (England) 2010* and accompanying statutory guidance *Putting Care into Practice* came into force on 1 April 2011.

A care plan may require provision of services and resources, or it may require a court order under the Children Act 1989, or the Children (Northern Ireland) Order, 1995 for the protection of the child. Specialist education and/or therapy for the child or the family may form part of a care plan. A local education authority may make provision for a child in need of its own volition, or special education arrangements may be part of a care plan filed with the court in care proceedings under s. 31 Children Act 1989 or

Part V of the Children (Northern Ireland) Order 1995. There is insufficient space in this book to discuss child protection procedures in detail here, but a comprehensive reference work used by lawyers and the courts is *Children Law and Practice* (Hershman and McFarlane 2010). For a briefer outline , see (Mitchels and James 2009), from which, with permission, we have reproduced Figure 5.2, a flowchart of local authority referral procedures, and Figure 5.3 showing the process of a Child Protection Conference.

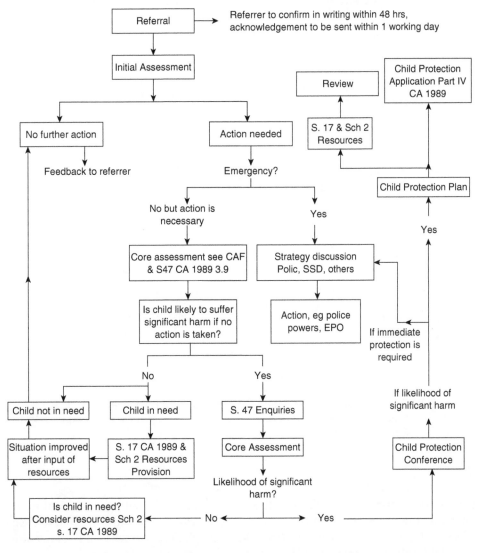

Figure 5.2   Flow chart of Local authority referral procedures (from B. Mitchels and H. James (2009) *Child Care and Protection: Law and Practice*, 4th edn. London, Wildy, Simmonds and Hill)

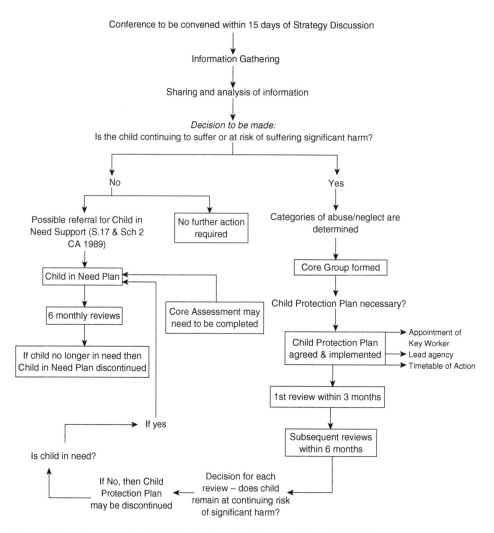

Conference to be convened within 15 days of Strategy Discussion

Information Gathering

Sharing and analysis of information

Decision to be made:
Is the child continuing to suffer or at risk of suffering significant harm?

No

Yes

Possible referral for Child in Need Support (S.17 & Sch 2 CA 1989)

No further action required

Categories of abuse/neglect are determined

Child in Need Plan

Core Group formed

6 monthly reviews

Core Assessment may need to be completed

Child Protection Plan necessary?

If child no longer in need then Child in Need Plan discontinued

Child Protection Plan agreed & implemented

➤ Appointment of Key Worker
➤ Lead agency
➤ Timetable of Action

1st review within 3 months

➤ If yes

Subsequent reviews within 6 months

Is child in need?

If No, then Child Protection Plan may be discontinued

Decision for each review – does child remain at continuing risk of significant harm?

Figure 5.3   Process of a Child Protection Conference (from B. Mitchels and H. James (2009) *Child Care and Protection: Law and Practice*, 4th edn. London, Wildy, Simmonds and Hill)

Government guidance on inter-agency roles in child protection

Schools (and therapists working in them) should comply with government guidance on child protection, enforceable by the courts by statutory regulation, e.g. *Working Together to Safeguard Children* (DCSF 2010). (The former DCSF role is now covered by the Department for Education, see www.education.gov.uk.)

*Government guidance on therapy for child witnesses in
criminal prosecutions*

Giving evidence is stressful. Children in particular may need support through-out a criminal prosecution procedure. For therapists working with children involved as witnesses in criminal prosecutions, see *Provision of Therapy for Child Witnesses Prior to a Criminal Trial: Practice Guidance* (CPS 2005a) available at www.cps.gov.uk.

Professional standards

In cases of alleged breach of duty of care or negligence, accepted professional standards may be taken into account by the courts as a measure of a therapist's competence, therefore policy and accepted standards of practice in the therapy profession are highly important, e.g. the *Ethical Framework* (BACP 2010a) and, where applicable, relevant GMC guidance (GMC 2004; 2006).

5.2 Contractual issues

In education, the services of therapists may be commissioned by the school or education authority, or they may be employed by the local education authority or by the educational organisation. For contracts of employment, see Chapter 1 at 1.2.9.

Therapeutic contracts with child clients in schools, and the child's right to request confidentiality (e.g. to receive therapy without their parents' knowl-edge) will be subject to the child's maturity, level of understanding and ability to make their own decisions – for further details see 5.3. below and Chapter 8 at 8.1.1.

5.3 Capacity, consent and confidentiality

5.3.1 Definitions of 'child' and 'parent'

A child is defined in law as a person under the age of 18 (CA 1989 s. 105, Children (Northern Ireland) Order 1995 art. 2, Children (Scotland) Act 1995, s. 15(1)). 'Parent' is usually interpreted as meaning the biological mother and father or adoptive parents of a child, but in some legislation the term may include other people who are not the biological parents but have parental responsibility for the child.

People may assume that all parents have the power to make decisions for their children. This is emphatically (and perhaps surprisingly) not so. The ability of a parent, or anyone else, to make a decision for their child depends on whether they have 'parental responsibility', which is the legal basis for making decisions about that child, including consent for therapy (see 5.3.2 below).

5.3.2 Parental responsibility

The Children Act 1989 (CA 1989) created the concept of 'parental responsibility', defined in section 3(1) as 'all the rights, duties, powers, responsibilities and authority which by law the parent of a child has in relation to a child and his property'. (See also the Children (Scotland) Act 1995, s. 1 and the Children (Northern Ireland) Order 1995, art. 6.) More than one person can have parental responsibility for a child at the same time. It cannot be transferred or surrendered, but aspects of parental responsibilities can be delegated – see CA 1989 s. 2(9); Children (Northern Ireland) Order 1995, art. 5(8); Children (Scotland) Act 1995, s. 3(5).

5.3.3 Child's capacity to consent to therapy and request confidentiality

Valid consent in law for therapy with a child or young person under the age of 18 includes:

- Consent of a person with parental responsibility for the child, see 5.3.2. above and Chapter 8.
- Consent of the child, if aged over 16, under the Family Law Reform Act 1969 s. 8(1), Age of Legal Capacity (Scotland) Act 1991, s. 1 or Age of Majority Act (Northern Ireland) 1969, art. 4(i).
- Consent of a child aged under 16, if they have sufficient age and understanding of the issues involved and the consequences of consent (i.e. if the child is 'Gillick competent' as defined in the case of *Gillick v West Norfolk and Wisbech Area Health Authority and Another* [1986] 1 AC 1212; [1985] 3 All ER 402 (HL) [1986] 1 FLR 224, or the Age of Legal Capacity (Scotland) Act 1991, s. 2(1) and (4).
- A Direction of the High Court / Court of Session.

Children with capacity (over 16 or 'Gillick competent')
A child who has the capacity to enter into a therapeutic contract can ask for confidentiality, and this should be respected unless there is a legal and ethical justification in the public interest to disclose information to the child's parents or any other agency or organisation. If in any doubt about this, seek legal advice about the specific situation, as such circumstances are rare, and usually complex. A more likely situation is the need to refer, or help the child to refer the child's situation or disclosures to another agency in the public interest or for the protection of the child or others, without telling the parents (see 5.4.5 below).

Children without capacity (under 16 and not 'Gillick competent')
If a child for any reason does not have the capacity to consent, then those with parental responsibility for the child are entitled to information about the child and may make decisions for that child (see 5.3.1 above). This also applies in the case of legally separated or divorced parents with parental responsibility. In the case of children in care under s. 31 of the Children Act 1989, or Part V of the Children

(Northern Ireland) Order 1995, the local authority acquires parental responsibility for the child for the duration of the care order.

Therapists working in primary schools are therefore likely to need the consent of those with parental responsibility for the child before they can provide therapy. Other older children may have the capacity to consent.

5.4 Practice issues

5.4.1 Do parents have to give consent for children in school to have counselling?

Consent for a child to receive counselling or psychotherapy is required either from the child, if the child has the legal capacity to give it (see 5.3 above) or from those with parental responsibility for the child. Those who have parental responsibility for a child should be able to provide documentary proof (if necessary) e.g. by way of their marriage certificate, the child's birth certificate, a parental responsibility agreement or a court order.

5.4.2 What if parents or those with parental responsibility refuse (or cannot agree) to allow their child to have counselling in school?

Someone with parental responsibility for a child, who may or may not be the child's biological parent, can refuse permission for that children to come to counselling. The refusal will be ineffective for children over 16 because children of this age are considered sufficiently competent in family law to make decisions on their own behalf.

The situation is more complex for children under 16. In order to override a refusal by someone with parental responsibility, the counsellor should have conducted an assessment to determine whether the young client is capable of making a decision on his own behalf, see *Gillick v West Norfolk & Wisbech Area Health Authority and Another* [1986]. Children and young people are considered competent to make decisions on their own behalf when they are able to fully understand the situation and can come to an informed decision, having considered all the implications. This has come to be known colloquially as 'Gillick competence' (see 5.3. above). The notes should record that this assessment has taken place and should note the questions and answers and any other significant information on which a decision about the child's competence was reached.

5.4.3 What if a child needs urgent assessment or treatment but those with parental responsibility and/or the child refuse?

If a therapist working in a school considers that a child is in need of therapeutic assessment or treatment, but consent for an appropriate referral to the child's doctor or other agency is not forthcoming from any of those entitled to give it, there are a number of avenues open.

Serious situations needing urgent medical/psychological treatment
If the child needs urgent psychological or medical treatment where the situation is serious or life threatening (e.g. if the child is injured or makes a suicide attempt) and parents are not available to consent, then urgent medical action can be taken under s. 3 of the Children Act 1989, or art. 6 of the Children (Northern Ireland) Order 1995 which empowers those without parental responsibility but responsible for the care of the child to take necessary action for the welfare of the child, for example, for staff to call an ambulance to take a child to hospital following an accident at school in which the child is injured. If such action is taken, those with parental responsibility for the child should be informed immediately. Section 3 (Article 6) is absolutely not intended to be used for general non-urgent situations, e.g. routine vaccinations etc.

Possible 'child in need'
If a child in school may be a child in need (see 5.1.5 above).

5.4.4 Should parents be given information about their child's therapy at school?

The answer to this question will depend upon the child or young person's capacity to make an informed decision about therapy, to enter into a therapeutic contract and to request confidentiality, see 5.3 above. If the child has capacity to request confidentiality then this should be respected unless, in the public interest, the child's wishes should in the opinion of the therapist be overridden, see 5.4.3 above. If there is a referral to another agency, follow the appropriate procedure, see 5.4.5. If, in the context of court proceedings, a court requests a report (e.g. from a counsellor or educational psychologist) giving information about a child's therapy at school, the court may also make directions about who should receive copies of that report.

5.4.5 Referrals to other agencies or organisations

When a therapist wishes to refer a child at school to an external agency or organisation (e.g. specialist therapy services, other schools, social care officers, police, health care services, etc.), the consent of the child or a person with parental responsibility for the child is required. The law set out 5.3 and 5.4.3 above applies to this situation, but please note that in some situations of child protection, urgent action may need to be taken *without* informing the child's parents in cases where any family knowledge could put a child at risk or compromise an investigation, e.g. an allegation of organised child abuse, for example in paedophile rings or satanic child abuse; alleged child abuse by parents or close family; or other investigations into serious concerns involving family members or persons known to the family. See the next paragraph for child protection referral procedures.

5.4.6 Child protection situations – what to do

There is a defined system for collecting and sharing child protection information within schools and referral on to Social Services which is described in *Working Together to Safeguard Children: A Guide to Inter-Agency Working to Safeguard and Promote the Welfare of Children* (DCSF 2010). The outline practice and procedure of inter-agency cooperation in child protection is set out in the first part, issued as statutory guidance, and mandatory in England under s. 7 of the Local Authority Social Services Act 1970. This means that the guidance must be followed, and any departure from it must be justified in respect of any subsequent complaints procedure or judicial review. Part 2 is non-statutory practice guidance. It sets out clearly the levels of cooperation expected from social services, schools, health professionals, police and others, and the inter-agency procedures for child protection. Schools have further specific duties under the Education Act 2002. For Scotland, see the Education (Scotland) Act 1980 and the Education (Support for Learning) (Scotland) Act 2004. For Northern Ireland, see the Education (Northern Ireland) Order 2006 and *Co-operating to Safeguard Children* (DHSSPS 2003); and for Wales, see NAW, 2007.

Working Together to Safeguard Children (DCSF 2010) requires that a person is nominated in each school to be responsible for child protection liaison. The procedures are set up by the local Safeguarding Children Boards (formerly the Area Child Protection Committees) for each county and set out in the local education department's child protection guidelines for schools. Copies should be available in all schools. Chapter 8 and the references at the end of this book contain resources on child protection law, practice and procedure in the UK and in Scotland.

Additional advice and guidance on child protection is usually readily available from the relevant local authority and is also often supported by publicly available policies and procedures on the web. Recent developments in policy and practice to protect vulnerable children are available as non-statutory guidance from www.education.gov.uk. This includes *What to Do If You're Worried a Child Is Being Abused* (DfES 2006) and *Information Sharing: Guidance for Practitioners and Managers* (DCSF 2008a). Further government legislation, e.g. the Safeguarding Vulnerable Groups Act 2006, created safeguards and made provisions for registration with the Independent Safeguarding Authority (ISA), along with CRB checks for those working with children and vulnerable adults. However, the wide scope of that legislation may be radically curtailed by the recent Protection of Freedoms Bill 2010, if it is enacted. See 5.4.7 below for further details.

Where a child makes a disclosure of any form of neglect or physical, sexual or emotional abuse, and the therapist considers that the child is or may be in need of protection, they should follow the procedure set out in *Working Together to Safeguard Children* (DCSF 2010). The therapist should consult with the school designated lead for child protection and the headteacher. They may also need to seek advice from the local authority legal department as to whether a referral is appropriate to the social care department, and any other action to take. Any verbal referral made should be followed up in writing immediately to the local authority, setting out the relevant details.

The therapist and school child protection lead should make a record of the referral details.

The therapist's record of referral details should contain:

- Identity of child
- Details of any disclosure made by the child or others
- Person(s) to whom disclosure made
- Reasons for referral
- Person(s) to whom referral made and date of referral
- Whether consent obtained, and if so from whom
- If no consent, explanation for referral in absence of consent
- If legal advice sought, note of person consulted (and if appropriate, of advice received).

If a referral is made without first obtaining the consent of the child or those with parental responsibility (for example if parents are not available or if close family or friends may present a serious risk to the child or others), the referral record should explain why this was done.

Once a child protection referral is received, the local authority will take appropriate action. This might include: obtaining a court order for emergency protection for the child if necessary, provision of accommodation for the child, other applications to the court as appropriate to protect the child, and provision of services for the child and their family. The local authority will commence an investigation into the child's circumstances, in cooperation with the police and other agencies. (For details see DCSF 2010.) In cases where a child who is suffering or at risk of suffering significant harm has been subject to child protection proceedings, the family court can make a variety of protective orders in the best interests of the child. Under some of these court orders, the court can direct medical or psychiatric examination or assessment of a child. Where there is a care order in force, the local authority shares parental responsibility with the child's parents or carers, and, where necessary, can override their decisions, for example about therapy. Usually, this would involve consultation with the parents and seeking their positive involvement. Exceptions to parental involvement may arise when a child or young person is considered sufficiently competent to insist on confidentiality or it is considered that involving the parents would increase the risk to the child, for example if the parent is suspected of abusing the child. If the professional is involved in assessments and any consultations with other professionals to inform decision-making in child protection, details should be included in their notes.

5.4.7 CRB checks and Independent Safeguarding Agency

The Criminal Records Bureau (CRB) is an executive agency of the Home Office which maintains the records of criminal offenders in England and Wales. Disclosures are available in England and Wales from the CRB, in Scotland by CRBS (see below) or Disclosure Scotland, and in Northern Ireland, by Access Northern Ireland. Once a therapist is convicted of any criminal offence their criminal record will be held, subject to the law. A search of the records is popularly known as a 'CRB check' which can require either 'Standard' or 'Enhanced' disclosure. A signed request for a CRB check contains the signatory's consent for disclosure. The 'Standard' CRB check will show details of convictions. The 'Enhanced' check shows not only convictions, but also acquittals and non-conviction information held on local police records relevant to the position which the person has selected. The police may also send additional information to employers in a separate letter. Further information is available at www.crb.gov.uk. In Scotland, the Central Registered Body in Scotland (CRBS) provides enhanced disclosures in the voluntary sector for those working with children, young people and adults at risk, see www.crbs.org.uk. Disclosure Scotland provides disclosures upon request and payment of a fee, see www. disclosure-scotland.co.uk/apply/. In Northern Ireland, a similar service is provided by Access Northern Ireland, see www.accessni.gov.uk/.

Agencies, including schools, may require a certificated CRB check as a condition of employment. Additional legislation, the Safeguarding Vulnerable Groups Act 2006 (SVGA) and the Safeguarding Vulnerable Groups (Northern Ireland) Order 2007 underpins a new 'Vetting and Barring Scheme', which, in 2010, was gradually being brought into force in England, Wales and Northern Ireland. This created a requirement for people working with vulnerable groups in specified activities (which includes teachers and other people with a specified level of direct contact with children in schools) to register with the Independent Safeguarding Agency (ISA). Registration includes both a CRB check and also relevant enquiries from the lists, from local authorities and the police, etc.

Under that Act, the ISA has the role of maintaining lists of people who are barred from working with children (the 'Child First' list) and with vulnerable adults (the 'Adult First' list). These lists are now in force. Inclusion on a list may happen automatically on caution or conviction for certain 'autobar' offences, or for meeting other specified criteria. Schedule 3 of the SVGA sets out the criteria for determining who is included in these new lists, and the ISA makes the decisions about inclusion. If a school therapist feels that their name has been included in a list wrongly, then they may appeal against a finding of fact or on a point of law to the Care Standards Tribunal.

Some of the Act's provisions (e.g. the lists mentioned above) are already in force, but the new Coalition Government in England that took office in May 2010 considers the additional measures draconian and, following a review, has held back further implementation, with the intention of revising the legislation.

The scope of the SVGA may now be radically curtailed by the recent Protection of Freedoms Bill 2010, if it is enacted. See www.isa.gov.org.uk for updates on the impact of any new legislation.

In Scotland, the Protecting Vulnerable Groups (Scotland) Act 2007 went live on 28 February 2011, and is managed by Disclosure Scotland. Implementation is being phased in to ease the administrative burden on individual organisations. For information call 0870 609 6006 or email PUCorrespondence@scotland.gsi.gov.uk, and for further details of the Scottish provisions, see the PVG Scheme Information Booklet (available online and in hard copy) and also available in BSL as a DVD.

See also the Safeguarding Vulnerable Groups Act 2006 (Commencement No 1) Order 2007 and the Safeguarding Vulnerable Groups (Northern Ireland) Order 2007, see www.dhsspsni.gov.uk. For a copy of the relevant legislation, see www. legislation.gov.uk.

5.4.8 Agreeing length and frequency of sessions in school counselling

School counsellors may see their clients for half-hour sessions rather than the traditional 'counsellor's 50 minutes' and they may see them less frequently than once a week. This may be because children respond better to shorter times for sustained concentration, or perhaps it may fit in more comfortably with school timetables. Counsellors who work in schools also have to try to manage the numbers of clients wanting to access their service.

5.4.9 Finding designated space for counselling in school

We understand that getting a designated room for counselling in a school can sometimes be difficult; often the rooms allocated also contain office equipment and therefore may be subject to interruptions from people coming in to use the photocopier, etc., so clear boundaries are necessary, and maybe a big notice on the door, too!

5.4.10 Boundary issues and dual roles in schools

Ethical and boundary issues such as confidentiality (see 5.5.1 below) and conflicts of interest may present problems for those school counsellors who also have another role in the school, e.g. as a teacher or classroom assistant. See the *Ethical Framework* (BACP 2010a) and *Dual Roles* (Jacobs 2010).

5.5 The interface and managing movement between education and other contexts

5.5.1 Confidentiality in the school setting

Confidentiality can be more difficult within a school where the free exchange of information between staff is routine practice. Confidentiality curtails what a counsellor can communicate. It excludes casually discussing clients with a fellow teacher or staff member, however much the counsellor might want to share information which she feels may be useful to teaching staff and helpful to the child or student in some way.

Where it is helpful for teachers to know the counsellor's concerns, this should normally only be done with the consent of the child or those with parental responsibility for the child, unless it is a child protection issue being reported to the member of staff identified as responsible for this area of work (see 5.3. above).

If a school counsellor unjustifiably discloses confidential information arising from their therapeutic work with a child without consent and (in extreme cases) this disclosure causes quantifiable loss or damage, then if direct causation can be proved, it is possible the counsellor could be sued for damages or other remedies. Complaints might also be made to the school, local education authority or the counsellor's professional body.

5.5.2 Confidentiality in a further education, college or university setting

All counselling services need to attend to managing confidentiality for staff and students within their service. Ethical dilemmas can arise, for example regarding dual roles, boundaries, sharing information with Human Resources or Occupational Health departments. Some services consider it best to separate staff and student counselling services to avoid the ethical dilemma (and potential embarrassment) of a client who is a staff member meeting one of their students in the corridor or waiting room of the counselling service. Irrespective of whether staff and students are separated or not, those services that have a waiting room should inform clients of this in advance so that they are prepared for any possible encounter with other members of staff or students.

A therapist should be careful to avoid conflicts of interest or dual roles, e.g. in counselling a member of staff and another person in the university who may be their student, their boss, or in some other way closely associated with them. It is not easy to check for conflicts of interest without giving away the name of other clients. Unless a client has consented to disclosure of their name, one cannot simply ask 'Do you know or work with Mrs X?' or 'Is Mr Y a student/staff member of your Department or School?' It is therefore best to have separate premises and separate staff for the staff counselling and student counselling services. That does not solve the problem of confidentiality entirely, but it can help. Also make sure that all clients are aware if there is a waiting room in the counselling service, so that if they encounter colleagues or students there, this is not an unwelcome surprise.

As a general rule, information should not be shared with Human Resources or Occupational Health without the explicit consent of the client. It may be that the policies and terms of being a student or staff member of the college or university will include a clause giving consent for such disclosures where necessary. In some cases the public interest may also justify disclosure in the absence of consent, e.g. in situations where a staff member or student may pose a serious risk to themselves or others.

The law regarding confidentiality for sixth form, college and university students is in most respects the same as that for adults, if the students are 'Gillick competent' or over 16 years of age.

As with adults, therapists may breach confidence where:

- the law requires it (e.g. in cases of terrorism, certain road traffic offences, etc.)
- the law permits it (e.g. where it is in the public interest to disclose information)
- the client consents.

An exception to this general rule is where a young person, who is under 16 and 'Gillick competent' or over 16 but under 18 years of age, needs urgent medical or psychiatric assessment or treatment. If that young person refuses treatment, then those with parental responsibility for them may be asked for consent. If there is no consent, or a parental disagreement, the High Court may be asked to step in and make an appropriate order settling the matter and/or making a direction that the necessary treatment may be lawfully carried out. The older and more mature the child, the greater respect the court will have for their wishes, but there have been cases where the court has nevertheless directed that medical treatment may be given. A judge explained to a mature boy of 14 with sickle cell anaemia who had refused a blood transfusion for religious reasons that the High Court would step in to save his life until he reached the age of 18, but after that he could decide for himself.

It may be considered in the public interest to disclose information without the consent of the client in circumstances where the client or others are at imminent risk of serious harm, e.g. attempted suicide, child abuse, or serious assault. For a process of considering such decisions see the disclosure checklist in 1.4.1 above and see BACP 2010a; Bond and Mitchels 2008: 31–41; and Bond et al. 2010.

5.5.3 Keeping records in schools, colleges and universities

It is always professional good practice for therapists to keep careful records unless the therapist can justify not doing so (BACP 2010a).

In schools, colleges and universities, under the Freedom of Information Act 2000, records containing sensitive personal data are subject to the data protection legislation, whether handwritten or stored electronically. All confidential records need to be stored in a secure safe place at all times, i.e. in a locked cabinet with appropriate security measures in place. Leaving a key to the filing cabinet that is freely available to all staff, particularly those outside the circle of confidentiality, breaches the data protection requirement to keep records securely.

Leaving records out (e.g. in the staff room, school office, college or university common room etc.) where they can be seen by others may constitute a breach of the duty of care to the client. If these records are seen by anyone else outside the circle of confidentiality then the counsellor or the school could be sued for negligence.

For school records, it may be helpful to see Kirstie Adamson's examples of a school counsellor's records and the legal commentary in Chapter 8 of *Confidentiality and Record Keeping in Counselling and Psychotherapy* (Bond and Mitchels 2008).

In any educational setting, the therapist's records may become significant evidence in certain legal cases, e.g. child protection, personal injury, or compensation claims. If a client suffers an injury with a lasting effect (e.g. physical injury from a bullying incident, or an accident on the educational premises), he might want to make a personal injuries claim, or seek compensation. In a case of bullying, he would need to prove that the incident had happened as a result of an act of violence and that he was an innocent victim. Alternatively, the victim could claim for negligence against the school if he could prove that the assailant was of known violent character and the school knowingly had placed him in a position where he was likely to be attacked by that person. If a child victim of bullying had been in counselling, his lawyers might seek third party disclosure of any counselling notes there may be. In England and Wales, the Civil Procedure Rules govern the right to apply for disclosure. A judge would have to be convinced that these documents were relevant and their importance was such that it justified them being disclosed. Similar disclosure of records could be sought in Scotland by way of a procedure known as 'commission and diligence'. In Northern Ireland, the client may consent to his notes being disclosed. In absence of this, the lawyers for the opposing party may seek disclosure through a court order.

It is also possible for a claim of negligence to be made against a therapist (or any staff member) where it can be demonstrated that their actions, e.g. making inaccurate records, has resulted in someone suffering a loss (e.g. where a child is wrongly blamed for something and that blame is based solely on an inaccurate record).

Self-employed therapists working in schools

If a counsellor is self-employed, the counsellor may be responsible for all therapy records and their storage, unless otherwise agreed with the school. The counsellor needs to examine her contract for services with the school to see whether (and to what extent) she is bound by the school policies and procedures. Self-employed counsellors working with children and vulnerable adults should make themselves aware of the local procedures for child protection and referral, and ensure that they know how they should be implemented – see 5.4.6 above.

5.6 Protection of vulnerable adults

The committee of the AUCC feel that another area of law most relevant to counselling students and staff in university and college settings is legislation pertaining to the protection of vulnerable adults. While universities tend not to have students below the age of 18 (though some are now admitting younger students, often from overseas, on to foundation courses), colleges certainly do, and therefore the issues of informed consent, reporting abuse and confidentiality are as important in these setting as for younger students.

An increasing number of vulnerable adults are finding their way into further and higher education and therefore presenting as clients. In further education (FE), they tend to be on courses to develop life skills and may have learning difficulties. They are likely to be still living at home or in other accommodation locally, so have support systems and services outside the institution. In universities therapists have seen a significant rise in the numbers of students coming to university with pre-existing mental health problems, physical disabilities and condition such as Asperger's syndrome. These students may be living away from home and may require considerable support within the institution, so issues arise about sharing information between internal support services and with external services such as the NHS.

The right of a vulnerable adult to confidentiality will depend on their mental capacity to make their own decisions, and to enter into a therapeutic contract and request confidentiality or consent to disclosure. The Mental Capacity Act 2005 creates a way of assessing mental capacity which is situation-specific, i.e. the person concerned must have sufficient understanding of the context in which a decision has to be made, the likely consequences of consent or refusal, and also the ability to communicate their decision. If they do not have the capacity to run their own affairs, then the Court of Protection can appoint a public guardian to do so. The law of mental capacity is briefly set out in Chapter 1 at 1.2.5 and for further discussion, also see Bond and Mitchels 2008: Chapter 11; and Mitchels and Bond 2010: 63–8.

See also the legislation for the protection of vulnerable groups and the role of the Independent Safeguarding Agency in 5.4.7 above.

5.7 Fitness to practise

Fitness to practise issues can also arise where counsellors are working with students who are on vocational courses such as medicine, teaching, nursing, social work etc. and undertaking placements with children or vulnerable adults, e.g. judgements may have to be made about breaking confidentiality if the counsellor feels the student client is not fit to undertake a work placement.

Sometimes, therapists find it necessary to report bad professional practice (colloquially called 'whistle-blowing'), or to make referrals to Occupational Health, Human Resources or to other agencies because a client is deemed unfit to practise. These referrals will usually be made with the consent of the client, because in education and training establishments it is usual practice to require (as part of each training contract) the general consent of the student or trainee to make any necessary referrals, and an undertaking by the student/trainee to adhere to relevant government guidance, and to the organisation's policies and procedures.

If such a decision is necessary, check the student/trainee contract, and the policies and procedures of the organisation before taking action. If there is no consent in the contract, and no agreement to adhere to policies etc., then a decision must be made in the public interest, and at the therapist's discretion with the support of supervision. If the decision is truly in the public interest then the therapist is unlikely to be held liable for breach of their duty of care to the client. For a discussion of the law of tort and the duty of care, see Mitchels and Bond (2010: Chapter 2).

It is never easy for a therapist to make these judgements and to decide to refer a client, but the support of supervision and the experience of peers is helpful. The BACP *Ethical Framework* (2010a) recognises the necessary professionalism required in making such referrals.

5.8 Tensions between the educational institution and professional practice guidance

Tensions can arise between the regulations of an educational institution and practice enshrined by a particular therapeutic model or the BACP *Ethical Framework*. We heard about a situation a few years ago when a student attending a therapy group in a university made a complaint about the facilitator's behaviour. The university counselling service was BACP Accredited, and wanted to handle this complaint according to group therapy principles and the BACP *Ethical Framework*, but the regulations of the university had to take precedence. The result was that the action the counselling service wanted to take (in what they felt were the best interests of the client and of the group) could not happen – the formal procedures of the institution had to be adhered to, even though they were not designed for therapy situations and were arguably not appropriate in that particular context.

We cannot offer much useful advice here, save to suggest that university counselling services try to forestall these tensions by agreeing (if they can) a policy with the university which includes a suitable method of dealing with complaints related to the activities of the counselling service which satisfies the counselling service's perception of the best interests of clients and of the people or groups concerned. It might be argued in favour of such a policy that the counselling service is separate from the academic side of the university and can therefore run along different lines. However, we are aware that such an argument may in some universities have consequent implications for the funding of the counselling service.

Practice guidance

For useful guidance see the new edition of the *AUCC Guidelines for University and College Counselling Services* (Lawton et al. 2010). In it, the AUCC outlines the main legal, ethical and professional considerations of which counsellors working in Further and Higher Education need to be aware. It contains an appendix of printed and Web based resources relevant to counselling university and college students and staff.

6 The National Health Service (NHS) and Private Health Care

I work part time in the local GP surgery. Who do my clients have a therapeutic contract with – the general practice, or me?

The doctors in the GP practice want me to keep my notes at the surgery with their health records. I want to take them home. Can I insist on this?

I am self-employed and I work for two days a week as a play therapist in a hospital children's ward. The medical records in our hospital are available on the hospital computer network to administration, ward staff and health care teams. Our hospital manager wants me to make my notes part of the computer-held hospital medical records. I want to protect the children's confidentiality and keep them manually in a locked cabinet. Can I insist on separate records?

Where there is a conflict between the NHS policy and procedures and those of my own professional organisation, which takes precedence?

I work in a hospital. In the event of a complaint, would I be subject to the hospital disciplinary procedures, or to my own professional body, or both?

If my clients tell me about bad practice by doctors or nursing staff, should I report this?

There has been a spate of burglaries on the estate served by the GP surgery in which I work. My client told me who the thief is, and she knows where most of the stuff is. Should I tell the police?

I work in a hospital as a counsellor for staff support. John has been depressed, and told me this morning that he knew that he was HIV positive, but now thinks he may have AIDS. He is going home to Eire for his diagnostic tests during his holiday this summer, so that he can keep it quiet here. He wants me to keep his worries confidential. If he loses his career here, his depression will worsen, and he may even become suicidal – what should I do?

One of the paramedics has symptoms of severe anxiety and stress. Last week, she told me she is being bullied and sexually harassed by her manager and she feels that she cannot cope with it much longer. She has also admitted that she has made some mistakes recently through not concentrating, but others on her shift covered for her. The manager knows this. Now she is afraid to make a complaint about him as he could report her as incompetent and she risks losing her job. How can I help her?

I am a hospital staff counsellor. Recently I heard gossip about drugs being stolen from the pharmacy. The person allegedly taking them is my client. What should I do?

Counselling within the NHS or private health care may involve work with patients or staff in hospitals, clinics, doctor's surgeries, or other health care settings. For options in counselling careers within the NHS, see the websites www. nhscareers.nhs.uk and www.hscrecruit.com. These are changing times in the NHS, in which general practitioners may have greater control over commissioned services, and we advise therapists to watch for news of developments in funding and in the organisation and provision of services in the NHS, and particularly in the context of primary care. Information may be found on www.bacp. co.uk; www.nhs.gov.uk, www.wired-gov.net, and other relevant websites and publications.

In a hospital, therapy might take place with a medical social work team, for example, advising patients about the services available to them, and assisting them to make effective use of what is available. Sometimes patients are not making the best use of available facilities, or they are not benefiting from their treatment as much as they might be expected to do. Helping patients and relatives to understand hospital procedures and to adjust and comply with necessary hospital regimes, or to appropriately challenge those that appear unnecessary or intrusive is all part of the work.

Some patients need help to adjust to a new situation caused by their illness or accident, e.g. to loss of bodily movement or functions, loss of limbs, or to disfigurement. Other patients may need treatment for the trauma of life events, or for bereavement. Often recent trauma may bring up earlier traumatic experiences, all of which benefit from therapeutic intervention. Group support for patients is helpful in many situations within the NHS, e.g. in the care of the in-patient elderly, in post-surgical support (for example the excellent 'zipper club' founded in Norfolk for post heart-surgery patients) or self-help groups for specific illnesses such as diabetes, cancer and multiple sclerosis, or for specific psychological conditions such as eating disorders, addictions and substance abuse.

Therapists may sometimes find themselves in a dilemma in which they wish, or are requested by a client, to agree to terms in a therapeutic contract which may run counter to their terms of employment or their agency policy. This may be particularly relevant, for example, regarding issues of confidentiality, making, storing and retaining client records, or when making referrals.

Therapists should bear in mind that the courts may enforce explicit contractual agreements including their own contract of service (a contract of employment) or contract for services (self-employed contract) with the NHS or private health care body. There are two possible exceptions: agreements which conflict with statutory law and those which would be contrary to the public interest, e.g. by preventing the investigation or detection of serious crime. Health care agency policy should therefore be compatible with the law, government guidance and the public interest, and in order to avoid conflict, clients should be offered terms which accord with the relevant agency policy.

Therapists who disagree with any aspect of their health care organisation's policy may need to consider their position carefully and then address and resolve outstanding issues. High compatibility of client contracts with law and organisational policy creates the best chance of providing a professional service that clients can trust and protection for therapists and others from legal liabilities.

6.1 Legal features of working in health care settings

6.1.1 The Care Quality Commission (CQC)

The Care Quality Commission, set up in 2010, is the independent regulator of health care and adult social care services in England. It also protects the interests of people whose rights are restricted under the Mental Health Acts. The CQC is responsible for driving improvement and taking action if providers and commissioners of care do not meet essential standards of quality and safety. It will also ensure that people have the power to make informed choices about the care services they receive and access to the services they need. The Care Commission fulfils a similar function in Scotland. For further information see www.carecommission.com.

In 2010, in response to the Department of Health (DH) publication *New Horizons* (2009c) and taking into account national policy, guidance and research findings, the CQC published a five-year action plan, which covers the provision and commissioning of health and adult social care services for all people with mental health needs, including people subject to mental health legislation (CQC 2010). This includes the range of health care sectors (primary, secondary and specialist care) and settings (provider trusts, local authorities, independent sector). The plan encompasses children and young people in contact with specialist child and adolescent mental health services (CAMHS) to services for adults and older adults with mental health needs. CQC recognises the importance of taking a whole systems view of the provision (and commissioning) of services for people with mental health needs. See the website www.cqc.org.uk for details.

The CQC is also concerned with the improvement of transition between child and adolescent mental health facilities and interventions with young offenders (see Chapter 8).

CQC's *Position Statement and Action Plan for Mental Health 2010–2015* (CQC 2010) provides a description of its role in relation to mental health including improving:

- Access to services – in particular evidence-based psychological therapies, good physical health care, early intervention, out-of-hours support and easier access to consultants.
- Quality of inpatient care and inpatient environments.

- Primary care, prevention and mental health promotion – including the need for better recognition and support of mental health problems in primary care and a greater emphasis on mental health promotion and prevention.

The CQC's core statutory functions include:

- The registration of health and social care providers to a common set of quality and safety standards, and checking ongoing compliance with these registration requirements
- Powers of escalation and enforcement where services fall below essential quality standards
- Visiting patients whose rights are restricted under mental health legislation to ensure their rights are protected
- Carrying out periodic reviews of the performance of providers and commissioners
- Undertaking special reviews and studies of particular aspects of care
- Publishing information to drive choice, change and improvement.

Of particular interest to therapists working in the NHS, may be the following paragraph:

> For the first time, we will be able to use a common set of requirements when regulating the quality and safety of health and social care providers. We have ensured that the detail of our system for registration is focused on the outcomes for people using services, that it promotes their rights and ensures that care is delivered in a person-centred way. (CQC 2010: 10)

Rachel Freeth, in her challenging book *Humanising Psychiatry and Mental Health Care: The Challenge of the Person Centred Approach* (Freeth 2007), pointed out that the present NHS system, particularly in psychiatry and psychological services, contains little in it that is person-centred. We might assume that private mental health care may be similar in approach to that of the NHS in this respect.

The CQC's action plan was developed in the context of existing national policy and the government's *New Horizons* strategy (DH 2009c) to improve the mental health and well-being of the population and to improve the quality and accessibility of services for people with poor mental health. However, CQC points out that financial constraints mean that service improvements will need to be 'self-financing, soundly evidence-based, and clearly related to local commissioning intentions, as informed by Joint Strategic Needs Assessments (JSNAs)' (2009c: 10). CQC sees effective multi-agency and specialist commissioning as the key to better quality services and better value for money, and is concerned that current commissioning of services to meet the mental health needs of local populations is not sufficiently mature and sophisticated to drive this change. Although it recognises the challenge of a potential increase in the need for mental health services in response to recession and also the increase in cases of dementia (CQC 2010: 11), it remains to see whether any of the present Improving Access to Psychological Therapies (IAPT) system will change.

Quality control is partly governed by the Health and Social Care Act 2008. Under this, the Health and Social Care Act 2008 (Regulated Activities) Regulations 2010 will be important, particularly:

- Regulation 9 (Outcome 4): care and welfare of people who use services
- Regulation 11 (Outcome 7): safeguarding people who use services from abuse
- Regulation 17 (Outcome 1): respecting and involving people who use services
- Regulation 18 (Outcome 2): consent to care and treatment
- Regulation 23 (Outcome 14): supporting workers.

These regulations do not apply in Scotland.

The CQC will insist on compliance with the National Institute for Clinical Excellence (NICE) guidelines, and will encourage registration of the health professions. It is committed to the identification and treatment of mental health problems within primary care, which may require some attention to the implementation of IAPT as it is currently structured, given the rather daunting statistics quoted below.

There are many interesting statistics in the CQC five-year plan, but one in particular stands out:

In 2007, around a quarter (24%) of the general population with common mental health problems received treatment for their condition, mostly in the form of medication. The level and nature of treatment very much varied by mental health problem: over half of adults (57%) with a phobia were receiving treatment compared with only 15% of those with depression and anxiety. Half of those (48%) with two or more disorders were receiving treatment. For those with more enduring mental health problems, four in every five people were receiving some form of treatment (medication and/or counselling). (CQC 2010: 24)

It goes on to analyse the various forms of treatment provided. One wonders what happened to the other 76% of the general population also identified as having 'common mental health problems' and to the remaining 85% of people identified with depression and anxiety.

The CQC plan goes on to say that:

Most of the people treated by the NHS for a mental health problem are treated by their GP and do not need referral on to more specialist services, although some may be offered additional treatment in the form of talking therapies such as cognitive-behavioural therapy. Nine out of 10 people with a mental health need have their condition managed entirely in primary care, including around a quarter of people with severe mental health problems. It is thought that a third of all consultations with GPs at least in part relate to a mental health issue. (CQC 2010: 25)

So it seems to us that out of all those who suffer from common mental health problems/depression and anxiety, only a very small proportion receive treatment. Most of these will receive treatment from their GP (i.e. medication), and some may be offered counselling. The vast majority of the others, it seems, are currently receiving no help at all within the NHS system. The evolution of the scheme of *Improving Access to Psychological Therapies* (IAPT) indicates a level of aspiration, but the scale of need means that there is much work remaining to be done.

See the case of *YL (by her litigation friend, the Official Solicitor) v. Birmingham City Council* [2007] 1MHLR 85, in which the provision of accommodation and care by a private company operating on a commercial basis was held by the House of Lords not to be a public function for the purposes of s. 6 Human Rights Act 1998. It was considered a contractual arrangement, even if paid from public funds, and so residents had no Convention rights as against the private care home. However, the regulation and supervision of care homes are all public functions of the local authority, so residents will have public law rights, including Convention rights, against the local authority involved.

6.1.2 Range of mental health services

Mental health services now include:

- **Early intervention services** for young people at the onset of their illness.
- **Crisis resolution/home treatment teams**, which provide a direct alternative to hospital admission for people with acute mental health problems and can facilitate early discharge for people whilst still in an acute phase of their illness.
- **Assertive outreach teams**, which provide treatment and support to people who mental health services have found hard to engage – usually people with severe mental health problems and often additional needs relating to substance misuse, offending and social relationships.
- **Community mental health teams**, which are the mainstay of community based provision, often providing long term support to people with enduring mental health problems.
- **Child and adolescent mental health services (CAMHS)**, which provide both community and inpatient services for children and young people.

6.1.3 Law and guidance within health care settings

Relevant law includes:

- Mental Health Act 1983 (amended in 2007 to include supervised community treatment, and the introduction of *Community Treatment Orders* in 2008)
- Mental Capacity Act 2005 (amended by the Mental Health Act 2007 which introduced the *Mental Capacity Act Deprivation of Liberty Safeguards*)
- Optional Protocol of the United Nations' Convention Against Torture (OPCAT)
- Equal opportunities legislation.

Policy and guidance relevant to work within the NHS includes:

- *Refocusing the Care Programme Approach: Policy and Positive Practice* (DH 2008)
- Independent Mental Health Advocacy
- *New Horizons: A Shared Vision for Mental Health* (DH 2009c)

- IAPT programme (to support primary care trusts in implementing the National Institute for Health and Clinical Excellence (NICE) guidelines for people with depression and anxiety disorders)
- The NICE guidelines (for the Quality and Outcomes Framework, NICE Guidance and contact information, search at www.nice.org.uk)
- *Living Well with Dementia* (DH 2009b)
- *Improving Health, Supporting Justice* (DH 2009a)
- Mental health standard contract: covering agreements between Primary Care Trusts (PCTs) and providers for the delivery of NHS-funded services
- GMC guidance on health care issues, including confidentiality, see www.gmc-uk.org.

All mental health care work is subject to the relevant government guidance, some of which may be enforceable by the courts by statutory regulation, e.g. the NICE guidelines and the guidance of the Local Safeguarding Boards (watch for new names under any revised legislation) in child protection and *Working Together to Safeguard Children* (DCSF 2010) – see www.education.gov.uk.

Counselling and psychotherapy in the context of mental health provision is also subject to the policy and accepted standards of practice in the therapy profession, e.g. the *Ethical Framework* (BACP 2010a) and, where applicable, relevant guidance from professional associations including the Royal College of Psychiatrists (RCP) www.rcpsych.ac.uk/; British Medical Association (BMA) www.bma.org.uk; and the General Medical Council (GMC) www.gmc-uk.org, e.g. (GMC 2004, 2006). In addition, there are many professional associations for counsellors and psychotherapists, e.g. BACP, BPS, UKCP, ACC etc. In cases of alleged breach of duty of care or negligence, accepted professional standards may be taken into account by the courts as a measure of competence.

Other guidance may be noted by the courts, e.g. *Provision of Therapy for Child Witnesses Prior to a Criminal Trial: Practice Guidance* (CPS 2005a) and *Provision of Therapy for Vulnerable or Intimidated Adult Witnesses Prior to a Criminal Trial: Practice Guidance* (CPS 2005b); both are available at www.cps.gov.uk. Please note that these two guidance documents are currently being updated and amalgamated, so watch for a new version soon.

6.2 Contractual and workplace issues

For counselling careers within the NHS, see www.nhscareers.nhs.uk.

Therapists may be employed by the health care provider under a contract of service. Other self-employed therapists may be running their own therapy business and work under a contract for services with health care providers. In either case, the contract might be made in various possible ways in the reorganised NHS, but will require compliance with government health care policies and guidance in force at the time. It is important therefore to be clear about what these policies and guidance documents contain.

Particular policies which may cause therapists problems relate to confidentiality and disclosure issues. Some typical situations are discussed below.

6.2.1 I work part time in the local GP surgery. Who do my clients have a therapeutic contract with – the general practice or me?

This may depend on whether the therapist has a contract of employment with the GP practice, or is self-employed. See Chapter 1 for self-employment and also Mitchels and Bond (2010: Chapters 8 and 9).

If the therapist is an employee of the GP practice, then the therapist (and therefore their client, too, as a patient of the practice) is likely to be contractually bound by the policies of the GP practice. This also has implications for insurance and professional liability, e.g. the nature and levels of the duty of care. An employer is vicariously liable in some circumstances for the actions of its employees in the course of their work (see Mitchels and Bond 2010: Chapters 2 and 9).

If the therapist is self-employed and providing services to a GP practice, they will usually have a written agreement with the health care provider which binds them to comply with government policies and guidance. In the absence of such an agreement, the therapist's professional ethics and responsibilities apply. Aspects of the law relating to various business contracts relevant to the private provision of therapy are set out in Chapter 1 of this book, and also in Mitchels and Bond (2010). References to the relevant chapters of that book are included here, should further information be required:

- For the lease or purchase of premises from which to work (Chapter 7)
- For professional indemnity insurance (Chapter 6)
- For goods and services relating to their therapy practice (e.g. photocopier rental, purchase of office goods and computer equipment, cleaning services, etc) (Chapter 4)
- Commissioning services (e.g. of an accountant or a lawyer) (Chapter 4)
- Contracts of employment (as employer in a business or organisation) (Chapter 9)
- Contracts of work as a volunteer in an agency or organisation (Chapters 4 and 9)
- Therapeutic contracts with clients (Mitchels and Bond 2010: Chapter 4), and for confidentiality (Bond and Mitchels 2008)
- Dealing with legal claims (Chapter 10)

6.2.2 The doctors in the GP practice want me to keep my notes at the surgery with their health records. I want to take them home. Can I insist on this?

If the therapist is employed, then they will be bound by the terms of their employment contract, which may include the storage of records. If they are self-employed, then their contract with the practice will indicate the extent of their duty to comply with the prevailing practice procedures. See 6.2.1 above.

Counselling records held with health records, and part of health records will be subject to the Freedom of Information Act 2000.

6.2.3 Can a therapist working part time in a hospital setting insist on keeping separate records?

One of the questions we had in a workshop was this: 'I am self-employed and I work for two days a week as a play therapist in a hospital children's ward. The medical records in our hospital are available on the hospital computer network to administration, ward staff and health care teams. Our hospital manager wants me to make my notes part of the computer-held hospital medical records. I want to protect the children's confidentiality and keep them manually in a locked cabinet. Can I insist on keeping my own separate records?'

Hospital policies and systems of record keeping vary across the country at the moment. Some have computer records which can be accessed by a wide range of staff and others have restricted access on a 'need to know' basis. It might help to bear in mind the 'Caldicott Principles'. These are six principles for testing whether to disclose patient-identifiable information. They were made by a committee chaired by Dame Fiona Caldicott in 1997 (the Caldicott Committee), in the Report on the Review of Patient-Identifiable Information, as part of a review of information sharing within the NHS and between NHS and non-NHS organisations. The 'Caldicott Guardians' appointed to oversee the system should be existing members of the management board or senior management team, senior professionals, or hold responsibility for promoting clinical governance or equivalent functions within organisations providing health or social care. The Department of Health has produced the *Caldicott Guardian Manual* (DH 2010b) for their guidance, available from www.dh.gov.uk.

Again, in this situation, if the therapist is employed, then they will be bound by the terms of their employment contract, which may include compliance with all hospital policies and procedures, including the making and storage of records.

If the therapist is self-employed, then their contract with the hospital will indicate the extent of their duty to comply with the prevailing hospital procedures.

It may be possible to re-negotiate a contract if the therapist feels strongly about the issue and can convince the hospital managers that their proposal is compatible with government guidance and is also in the best interests of patients. If the situation cannot be changed, then patients should be informed and fully understand the procedures and the possible consequences of the sharing of information.

6.2.4 Where there is a conflict between NHS policy and procedures and those of a professional organisation, which takes precedence? In the event of a complaint, would a practitioner be subject to the hospital disciplinary procedures, their professional body, or both?

One of the frequent issues raised in our workshops is that of how to address and resolve potential conflicts that may arise between agency policy and the client's wishes or between agency policy and the therapist's ethical framework. We don't have an easy answer to this, because each situation is different, but we would first recommend that practitioners working in an NHS setting should make themselves fully aware of all the agency policies and procedures relevant to their work.

Any therapist who is employed or otherwise contractually bound to comply with NHS policies and procedures will potentially be in breach of their employment contract if they fail to comply. This may justify the employer ending the contract by dismissal or by the use of internal complaints procedures. The therapist may feel that they need to take a stand against a particular policy or procedure that they feel is wrong. However, although perhaps a stand of this sort may be justifiable morally and ethically, that action may still constitute a breach of contract which would have to be evaluated by a court if a claim is made, or by a tribunal in the event of a complaint.

Breach of law or government guidance may also lead to external legal claims against the therapist or their employer (or both) by an injured party, e.g. a claim in tort on the basis of a breach of the duty of care, brought against the hospital or medical practice by an aggrieved client who has suffered damage.

Breach of the therapist's own ethical framework or code of practice may also lead to disciplinary proceedings by their professional organisation if the matter is a breach of sufficient seriousness. However, since professional ethical frameworks usually allow a degree of discretion, it seems unlikely in most circumstances that compliance with government guidance would also constitute a serious breach of professional ethics.

6.2.5 If clients tell therapists about bad practice by doctors or nursing staff, should this be reported?

Bear in mind that if the report has come from a client or third person (as opposed to the therapist's own observations), the report may (or may not) be true, or the account given may not be accurate or complete. Whatever clients say should of course always be taken seriously and considered carefully. However, if there is additional corroborative evidence for the matter reported (i.e. others have said the same thing, or there is some other physical corroborative evidence of the conduct reported, for example the presence of bruises, supporting an allegation of rough handling or assault), then the client's report will carry greater evidential value.

Making an untrue allegation that damages another professional's work or reputation can possibly lead to a legal claim for damages for libel (written allegations) or slander (verbal allegations). A straightforward defence to such a claim is, of course, that the allegation made is true, and is made in good faith.

In this situation where allegations are made on which a therapist is asked to act, it is always worth seeking professional advice, e.g. in supervision, and carefully considering the client's issues and personality, taking into account their mental state of health at the time, whether they are usually truthful, or whether they may be seeking attention, are being punitive, exaggerating, or are in any other way motivated to make an unfounded allegation.

'Whistle-blowing' or reporting bad professional practice in health care is sometimes a statutory requirement (e.g. acts that amount to terrorism or criminal acts that have led (or could lead) to death or serious harm to a patient). An example would be the deliberate administration of an overdose of drugs, with the purpose of ending a patient's life. Dr Harold Shipman was the first medical doctor in England to be convicted of murdering many of his patients, in several medical practices, over a period of time. His case was heard in the Preston Crown Court and on 31 January 2000, he was convicted of 15 murders. The Shipman Inquiry (www.the-shipman-inquiry.org.uk) later concluded that he was probably responsible for around 250 deaths. Earlier, Dr John Bodkin Adams had been accused of multiple murders of elderly patients, many of whom had left him money in their wills. Despite the designation of over 160 of his patients' deaths as 'suspicious' by Dr Camps, a Home Office pathologist, Dr Adams was acquitted of all murder charges at his subsequent trial at the Old Bailey. A hospital nurse, Beverly Allitt, was convicted in 1993 of the murder of four children in hospital care, attempting to murder another three, and grievously wounding a further six children. From these criminal cases alone, one can see that, in certain circumstances, whistle-blowing may be necessary in health care where there is a reasonable suspicion of bad (or criminal) practice which puts patients or others at risk of serious harm. If a failure to report bad practice might put patients at risk, then the therapist may feel that they have no option but to discuss the matter with line management or other appropriate authority.

Examples of cases involving complaints relating to expert witness errors in evidence include: *Council for the Regulation of Healthcare Professionals v General Medical Council and Southall* [2005] EWHC 579 (Admin); *Meadow v General Medical Council* [2006] EWHC 146 (Admin)[2006] 1 WLR 1452; *R v Clark* [2003] EWCA Crim 1020, CA; *X (Minors) v Bedfordshire County Council* ELR WLR [1995] 2 AC 633; [1995] 3 WLR 152; [1995] 3 All ER 353, HL(E).

In other situations, where there is no immediate risk of serious harm, but the practice issue remains of concern to the therapist, the usual course would be to first speak to the person concerned, and if no change is evident, then there is a discretion as to whether the matter should be reported. These are issues which it would be helpful to discuss confidentially in supervision, provided that there is no close relationship or conflict of interest between the roles of supervision and line management.

Checklist: Issues to be considered in dilemmas over confidentiality

With all clients, including those who have refused consent, discuss with the client if appropriate, consider and ideally also discuss in supervision these issues:

- What is the likelihood of serious harm in this case?
  - How serious is this harm?
  - How imminent is this harm?

- If I refer, what is likely to happen?
- If I do not refer, what is likely to happen?
- Do the likely consequences of non-referral include any serious harm to the client or others?

- If so, are the likely consequences of non-referral preventable?
- What would have to happen to prevent serious harm to client or others?
- Is there anything I (or anyone else) can do to assist in preventing this harm to my client or others?
- What steps would need to be taken to implement such assistance?
- How could the client be helped to accept assistance/the proposed action?
- Does my client have the mental capacity to give explicit informed consent (or refusal of consent) at this moment in time?
- If the client does not have mental capacity, then what are my professional responsibilities to the client and in the public interest?
- If the client has mental capacity but does not consent to my proposed action (for example referral to a GP), what would be my legal and professional situation if I went ahead and did it anyway?

(See Bond and Mitchels 2008: 41)

6.2.6 Workplace bullying, harassment and discrimination

Workplace bullying, harassment and workplace discrimination is contrary to the policies of the NHS and also it may be illegal (see Mitchels and Bond 2010: 115–16).

Unlawful discrimination

Unlawful discrimination in the workplace includes:

Disability discrimination – see Disability Discrimination Acts 1995 and 2005, and search at www.direct.gov.uk for disability rights and obligations.

Discrimination on the grounds of sex, sexual orientation or gender reassignment – see the Sex Discrimination Act 1975, the Sex Discrimination (Northern Ireland) Order 1976, the Equal Treatment Directive (76/207/EEC) and the Equal Opportunities Directive 2006/54/EC implementing equal opportunities, e.g. equal pay. See also the provisions relating to sexual orientation and sexual discrimination in the Employment Equality (Sex Discrimination) Regulations 2005, the Employment Equality (Sex Discrimination) Regulations (Northern Ireland) 2005, Employment Equality (Sexual Orientation) Regulations 2003 and the Employment Equality (Sexual Orientation) Regulations (Northern Ireland) 2003, the Employment Equality (Sexual Orientation) Regulations 2003 (Amendment) Regulations 2004 and the Sex Discrimination Order 1976 (Amendment) Regulations (Northern Ireland) 2004.

Age discrimination – see the Employment Equality (Age) Regulations 2006, which have been in force since 1 October 2006, and the Employment Equality (Age) Regulations (Northern Ireland) 2006.

Discrimination on the grounds of religion or belief – see the Employment Equality (Religion or Belief) Regulations 2003 and the Fair Employment Treatment (Northern Ireland) Order 1998 as well as the Fair Employment Treatment Order Regulations (Northern Ireland) 2003.

Discrimination on the grounds of race – see the Race Relations Act 1976 and the Race Relations (Northern Ireland) Order 1997.

In addition, it is unlawful to discriminate on the grounds of:

- pregnancy, maternity leave or paternity leave
- marital or civil partnership status: see the Sex Discrimination Act 1975, and the Sex Discrimination (Northern Ireland) Order 1976, as amended by the Civil Partnership Act 2004, s. 251(1)–(2).

Part-time workers are protected in relation to pay and other potential detriments by the Part-time Workers (Prevention of Less Favourable Treatment) Regulations 2000 and the Part-Time Workers (Prevention of Less Favourable Treatment) Regulations (Northern Ireland) 2000.

Harassment

The Protection from Harassment Act 1997 and the Protection from Harassment (Northern Ireland) Order 1997 were designed to protect victims of harassment, whatever form it takes, wherever it occurs, and whatever its motivation. Harassment is unlawful and may occur in the context of any of the forms of discrimination listed above. In the workplace, harassment can take various forms, depending on the context in which it happens, and it may involve the violation of dignity or the creation of a hostile working environment.

Breaches of the Protection from Harassment Act 1997 of the Northern Ireland Order may constitute a criminal offence, or may give rise to civil liability, or both. The legislation (as amended by subsequent legislation), with specified exceptions, states in s. 1 (or art. 3 as the case may be):

1   A person may not pursue a course of conduct
     a   which amounts to harassment of another and
     b   which he knows or ought to know amounts to harassment of the other.

A 'course of conduct' implies an action on at least two occasions, section 7(2),(3) (or art. 2(3)) and 'conduct' includes speech, s. 7(1),(2). If the actions are separated by several months with no causal link between them, the court finding a 'course of conduct' is less likely than when actions are close together, e.g. within three months of each other, see *Pratt v DPP* [2001] EWHC 483. The test applied by the courts as to whether the potential offender 'ought to know' that the actions amounted to harassment, is what a reasonable person with the same information might think, in a similar situation. Clearly, physical violence or threats of violence are likely to constitute criminal harassment, and repeated verbal aggression may also constitute harassment.

In the workplace, harassment might take the form of a criminal offence if the actions taken amounted to a sufficient level, causing the victim 'alarm' or 'distress' s. 7(2) (art. 2(2)). Three threatening or abusive phone calls may constitute harassment, as in the case of *Kelly v DPP* [2002] EWHC Admin 1428 166 JP 621.

It is our view that threatening email and Internet communications may also constitute harassment if they cause alarm and distress to the recipient, see *S v DPP* [2008] EWHC (Admin) 438.

An interesting and leading case on this topic relevant to NHS work is the House of Lords decision in *Majrowski v Guy's and St Thomas's NHS Trust* [2006] UKHL 34. In this case, an employee, a clinical auditor, was subjected to criticism and bullying by his departmental manager, who was rude, abusive and critical to him in front of other staff, imposing unrealistic targets and threatening disciplinary action if these targets were not met. In this case, the court supported the concept of the 'vicarious liability' of employers for acts of their employees in the course of their employment, and reiterated that imposing this strict liability on employers encourages them to maintain standards of good practice by their employees. For those reasons, where one employee harasses another, the employer may be held liable. Employers can cover their potential liability with appropriate insurance, etc. For a detailed discussion of the relevant law, see the judgment in the *Majrowski* case and Slade 2008: Chapter 12. Whilst *Majrowski* is an English case, it is a decision of the House of Lords and therefore highly persuasive in the Scottish courts.

Where issues in the workplace come to the attention of a therapist because incidents are reported by a client, it is our view that the therapist should do their best to empower and support the client, and should the client wish to make a complaint or to report the matter, the therapist should then support them within the context of therapy.

Therapists may find themselves in a difficult position if a client requests them to report incidents of harassment etc. In law, reporting what another person has told us is called 'hearsay' and is not admissible evidence in criminal cases. Witnesses of fact can give evidence only of matters they have personally seen or experienced.

In therapy we are rarely in objective possession of all the facts, since our clients' accounts of events are usually influenced by reliance on memory and an individual perspective of a situation. If possible, therefore, it is better practically and therapeutically to empower a client to take action on their own behalf.

In one of the questions posed at the beginning of this chapter, a NHS employee is in therapy for symptoms of severe anxiety and stress, as a result of bullying and sexual harassment by her manager and she feels that she cannot cope with it much longer. She has also admitted that she has made some mistakes recently through not concentrating, but others on her shift have covered for her, and the bullying manager is aware of this. The client is afraid to make a complaint about her manager as he could act punitively and cause her to risk losing her job. In this situation, we would recommend that the therapist may help best by working with the client and empowering her to do whatever she feels right for her. Referral to appropriate confidential professional advice (for example legal advice on harassment, bullying and employment rights) may be helpful to assist the client to evaluate her situation and decide what it is best to do. Therapy can assist to reduce anxiety, and promote self-esteem and confidence. If the client makes a complaint, therapy can support her through the process.

6.3 Practice issues, the interface and managing information sharing between the NHS or private health care work and other professionals, agencies and organisations

6.3.1 How do agency policies affect therapy clients, e.g. records, confidentiality and disclosure?

Therapists need to be aware of the agency policies when negotiating an employment contract of service or a self-employed contract for services, and ensure that they can practise comfortably within the required framework. When starting client work, practitioners should make clients aware of any requirements of agency policies that may affect them. Practitioners should explain relevant policies and procedures where necessary and it is advisable to elicit clients' explicit agreement to comply with them.

Often GPs do not explain their policies in detail to patients but instead they provide an information leaflet in which they state the policies in simple language. There is usually a form for the patient to complete and sign when joining a practice, which includes reference to the policies and asks the patient to confirm their agreement to abide by them.

We advise that therapists should ensure that clients fully understand what these policies may entail, for example, where there is a medical or psychiatric report that forms part of a patient's records, patients should know that this report is likely to stay on their record permanently, and it may then influence how a doctor or therapist subsequently approaches them. We often hear about situations where a client feels haunted by old reports from the past, e.g. about past abuse, suicide attempts, or mental illness. Such earlier reports may have to be disclosed in medical assessments for work or possibly for life and health insurance purposes. Old reports are unlikely to reflect subsequent changes in the client's life and/or their psychological development, in which the client may have moved on to a completely new situation. Changes may not be automatically reflected in the patient records (and this may hamper the client's job opportunities etc.) but therapists may be able to encourage the practice to update records or where necessary help the client to obtain fresh, revised psychological or psychiatric reports or updates.

If the therapist is self-employed, then their contract with the practice will indicate the extent of their duty to comply with the practice procedures. The therapist should then explain this to clients and obtain agreement at the outset of their work.

6.3.2 Clients' accounts of others' crimes or confessions of their own criminal acts: Should they be reported?

Clients may carry feelings of shame or guilt about criminal acts that they have committed, and wish to talk about this in therapy. They may also talk in therapy about the criminal acts of others, e.g. when clients are victims of abuse, assault or harassment. Therapists then may have a legal and ethical dilemma about whether these crimes should be reported, if so, whether client consent is required, and to whom should the report be made and how?

Therapists do not have a general legal duty to report crimes of which they have knowledge, unless the law specifically requires it. In certain cases, we are legally obliged to disclose information, e.g. in certain crimes related to terrorism, police enquiries following road traffic incidents about the driver of a vehicle, and drug money laundering (see Mitchels and Bond 2010: 71–5). Also, in the context of working with children and young people, the family court can make a recovery order under s. 50 of the Children Act 1989, or art. 69 of the Children (Northern Ireland) Order 2005, in relation to a child who is in care, under police protection or subject to an emergency protection order, if the child is abducted, has run away or is otherwise missing. When a recovery order is made, the court may require any person who has information as to the child's whereabouts to disclose that information, when asked to do so by a constable or the court, see s. 50(3)(c), 51, or art. 69 (3)(c). Failure to comply with the order may constitute the offence of contempt of court.

Clients' confessions of their own criminal acts

A client may feel the need to confess and talk about past criminal acts. Healing from overwhelming guilt and shame may be an important part of their therapy. Therapists have a duty of confidentiality regarding sensitive personal information, and should only breach it:

- where the law requires (see the statutory requirements for disclosure above)
- where the law permits (i.e. disclosure without consent may be justified in the public interest, for example, see the DH guidelines below)
- where the client consents.

The Department of Health has offered the following guidance about reporting serious crime:

> Murder, manslaughter, rape, treason, kidnapping, child abuse or other cases where individuals have suffered serious harm may all warrant breaching confidentiality. Serious harm to the security of the state or to public order and crimes that involve substantial financial gain and loss will generally fall within this category. In contrast, theft, fraud or damage to property where loss or damage is less substantial would generally not warrant breach of confidence. (DH 2003: 35)

However, there is no general duty to report a crime except for the statutory exceptions described above. The therapist does have discretion to disclose criminal acts, but if this is done *without* the consent of the client, then disclosure should only be made if it is lawful or justifiable in the public interest. If a disclosure is unlawful, untrue and/or made in bad faith, the client (or a third party who is the subject of a disclosure) may make a claim for damages resulting from the breach of the duty of care if damage results from it. A defence to such a claim may be established if the court rules that the facts reported were lawful, true, and/or that the therapist reasonably believed them to be true and the disclosure was made in the public interest.

We feel that unless the crime clearly falls within the statutory requirements for disclosure, or a person is at imminent risk of serious harm, or if it clearly falls within the definitions of the serious crimes set out in the DH (2003) guidance above, the therapist is well advised to take legal or other professional advice or at least to discuss the matter in supervision, before they decide to breach the client's confidentiality without appropriate consent.

Referring to the DH guidelines, therapists may take the view that serious financial gain or loss is far less important as an issue for disclosure than an imminent risk of serious harm to a person, and we recommend giving very careful consideration indeed before breaching confidentiality for theft or other property offences.

Client reports of others' crimes

There was a question at the beginning of this chapter from a therapist about whether it is ethical and lawful to disclose information to the police about crimes reported by her client. In that case, the crimes were a spate of burglaries on an estate served by a GP surgery in which the therapist works. Her client told her who the thief is and where the goods stolen were being kept.

The duty of care (and confidentiality) is to the client. Third parties may also expect confidentiality from a professional about sensitive information which they might reasonably expect a professional to keep confidential (see A *v* B *plc and C* (*'Flitcroft'*) [2002] EWCA Civ 337; 3 WLR 542, reversing [2001] 1WLR 2341). The same rationale described earlier in this section regarding clients' reports of others' crimes and confessions of their own crimes applies equally here.

In addition, bear in mind that the client's report may be untrue, inaccurately reported or biased, and a disclosure based on information from a client may be at best inaccurate, or at worst, it might be slanderous or libellous. A third party suffering damage to their reputation or livelihood may then bring a legal claim against the therapist if the disclosure was not lawful or justifiable in the public interest and the chain of causation could be proved in relation to damage suffered (see Mitchels and Bond 2010: Chapter 2). See pages 107–8 above.

Reports received from others about criminal acts by the therapist's client

Therapists (especially those working for employee assistance providers in large organisations like the NHS) may well hear about alleged criminal or anti-social activities of their clients, e.g. thefts from work, harassment, discrimination, bully-ing, substance misuse, etc. In one situation, a hospital staff counsellor heard gossip about drugs being stolen from the pharmacy for personal use, and the description of the thief seemed to point to one of her clients.

There are a number of issues to consider here:

- the accuracy and reliability of the information received
- whether it is right to challenge the client directly in therapy about the allegations made
- the nature and seriousness of the criminal act
- the duty of the therapist to their employer (as an employee under a contract of service or as a self-employed person under a contract for services)
- the duty of care of the therapist to their client (the risk to the client)
- the therapist's responsibility to protect other staff and patients in the hospital (i.e. the risk to others)
- the legal duty (if any) to report the crime
- is the disclosure defensible in law in the public interest, if the client refuses consent to disclose?

Consideration of the nature and seriousness of the criminal act may depend on a number of factors including the type of drug; the circumstances of the client (is the client unwell, taking prescription drugs, or addicted to illegal drugs?), and whether the theft was a 'one-off' (e.g. the client felt ill at work one day and just helped themselves to an analgesic), or was it planned, long-term, systematic theft from the pharmacy to support addiction or for financial gain? Was the therapist already aware of the client's drug taking (i.e. is the client actively addressing an addiction)? Was the client taking drugs for others, or to sell? If so, this may be the serious criminal offence of dealing in illegal drugs. Is the phar-macy (or the hospital) already aware that the client is the thief? Are the police already investigating the thefts?

All these factors will impact on the therapist's decision making about disclo-sure. Usually, unless statute forbids 'tipping off' (warning a person that they will be reported), it is best to talk to a client about the issues and to empower them to stop the offending behaviour and to comply with what the law requires, support-ing them through the process.

6.3.3 How can I balance my client's well-being against the safety of others?

We had a question from a therapist working in a hospital as a counsellor for staff support, concerning a depressed client who thinks that he may have developed Acquired Immune Deficiency Syndrome (AIDS). The client is awaiting diagnostic test results (from a different hospital) and wants his therapist to keep his worries confidential. The therapist is concerned that, if disclosure is made, the client may lose his job and he may then become actively suicidal.

The hospital must abide by government guidance and current legislation. It will therefore have a Health and Safety policy for the protection of patients, which contractually binds staff. If that policy covers disclosure of communicable diseases (e.g. blood-borne disease, for example, Hepatitis B, Hepatitis C and HIV, and other contagious diseases such as TB), then if the diagnosis of AIDS is confirmed, the client could be in breach of his employment contract if he continues working without necessary safety procedures and patients are put at risk. NHS staff with such diseases may be allocated to duties that do not involve exposure-prone procedures. See the report of the committee set up to consider the risk to patients of being exposed to health care workers with serious communicable diseases, *Health Clearance for Serious Communicable Diseases* (DH 2002b). The General Medical Council provides clear guidance in *Good Medical Practice* for doctors and health care staff who have a communicable disease:

> 77. You should be registered with a general practitioner outside your family to ensure that you have access to independent and objective medical care. You should not treat yourself.
>
> 78. You should protect your patients, your colleagues and yourself by being immunised against common serious communicable diseases where vaccines are available.
>
> 79. If you know that you have, or think that you might have, a serious condition that you could pass on to patients, or if your judgement or performance could be affected by a condition or its treatment, you must consult a suitably qualified colleague. You must ask for and follow their advice about investigations, treatment and changes to your practice that they consider necessary. You must not rely on your own assessment of the risk you pose to patients.
>
> (GMC 2006: Health)

See also the additional legislation in the UK available at www.gmc-uk.org regarding health clearance and communicable diseases, from the UK Advisory Panel for Health Care Workers Infected with Blood-borne Viruses. The NHS Trusts and Primary Care Trusts (Sexually Transmitted Diseases) Directions 2000, with earlier Regulations, requires NHS bodies in England and Wales to 'take all necessary steps to secure that any information capable of identifying an individual … with respect to persons examined or treated for any sexually transmitted disease shall not be disclosed except – (a) for the purpose of communicating that information to a medical practitioner, or to a person employed under the direction of a medical practitioner in connection with the treatment of persons suffering from such disease or the prevention of the spread thereof, and (b) for the purpose of such treatment and prevention.' In its *Confidentiality: Supplementary Guidance*, the GMC comments that:

> In particular, there have been concerns that a strict interpretation would prevent the disclosure of relevant information, except to other doctors or those working under their supervision, even with the patient's consent or to known sexual contacts in the public interest. Our view is that the Regulations and Directions do not preclude disclosure if it would otherwise be lawful at common law, for example with the patient's consent or in the public interest without consent. (GMC 2009: 21)

Where staff are at risk of infection after a needle-stick or other injury caused by a patient with mental incapacity, the GMC website www.gmc-uk.org states that staff considering testing that patient must take account of the current legal framework governing capacity issues and the use of human tissue. See the Human Tissue Act 2004 (E&W & NI) and the Mental Capacity Act 2005 (E&W only). In Scotland, see the Adults with Incapacity (Scotland) Act 2000 and the Human Tissue (Scotland) Act 2006. The GMC states:

> As we understand it, current law does not permit testing the infection status of an incapacitated patient solely for the benefit of a healthcare worker involved in the patient's care. Concerns about how best to care for healthcare workers who may have had high risk exposure to a serious communicable disease, where the patient's infection status is not known, should be raised with local occupational health advisers, and legal advice should be sought where necessary. (www.gmc-uk.org/guidance/update_serious_communicable_diseases.asp accessed 16 July 2010)

The other considerations discussed earlier in this book regarding consent and disclosure of sensitive client information versus the protection of the public apply here. In the context of sharing information in the context of NHS and private health care, we recommend consideration of the issues on the Disclosure Checklist in 1.4.1 above and the 'Caldicott Principles' (see 1.4.3 above).

7 Counselling in Spiritual or Pastoral Settings

What is the difference between pastoral care and counselling?

When 'Christian counselling' and 'prayer counselling' are mentioned in church, do these have the same meaning as in secular use, e.g. 'counselling and psychotherapy'?

What should I do if a penitent admits to child abuse during their confession?

My church has its own Canon law – does that take precedence over the law in the UK?

Can I promise confidentiality when (apart from formally taking confessions) I provide counselling and pastoral care in the course of my ministry?

I am a Minister, and also a qualified counsellor/psychotherapist. Can I provide professional counselling for parishioners within the BACP Ethical Framework, or will there be issues of dual boundaries for me and those in the church with whom I work?

I am a Minister and concerned that, potentially, issues of power and hierarchy might adversely affect my counselling relationships.

Is it ethical for me to provide counselling for members of my religious community and also continue to see them regularly in other roles in our meetings?

There are so many possible ways in which counselling may be provided in a spiritual or pastoral context, that we felt that we should write about counselling in a spiritual or pastoral setting, rather than simply refer to spiritual or pastoral counselling.

We have tried here to offer as many reflections as we can in the space available for discussion and exploration, and to provide general legal and ethical information wherever appropriate to this context. For a further perspective, see also the useful BACP Information Sheet *Working with Issues of Spirituality, Faith or Religion* (Harborne 2009). Lynette Harborne points out that whilst numbers released by the Church of England (see also www.churchofengland.org/about-us) show that Sunday Anglican church attendance is in decline, the number of mosques and Sikh, Buddhist and Hindu temples is increasing, paganism claims to be the fastest growing religion in the UK, and new religious movements and new age spirituality are increasingly popular (West 2004: 18). Therapists may therefore encounter clients with a wide variety of faiths, spirituality and religious backgrounds and experiences.

We make no assumptions here about any of the many faith contexts in which counselling may be provided. We intend to be inclusive, and therefore write in general terms, but inevitably, there are occasions in this chapter where we mention an example from a specific religious perspective, but we do not intend these examples to maximise or minimise the importance of that faith, or to exclude any other religion or spiritual belief system.

By 'spiritual' we use the *New Oxford Dictionary of English* (2001) definition of the spirit as both the 'rational or intelligent being not connected to the material body' and 'the animating and vital principle ...' The word originates from the Latin *spiritus* meaning 'the breath of life'. Those working in pastoral care may meet with people who profess personal spirituality without an affiliation to any particular religion or belief system. They may have no allegiance at all to a faith community, but nevertheless wish to explore their spirituality.

We adopt the *Oxford Dictionary* (2001) definition of 'religion' as

1. The belief in and worship of a superhuman controlling power, especially of a personal god or gods, a particular system of faith and worship;
2. A pursuit or interest followed with devotion.

and the use of the word 'faith' here refers to a strong belief in such a religion or a system of religious belief. Explicit and implicit issues that might be brought to spiritual or pastoral counselling might include:

1. Explicit issues of belief or experiencing which are causing distress or difficulty, e.g. events which have led to loss or questioning of faith.
2. Explicit issues arising from within a belief-sharing community, e.g. relationships within that community.
3. Implicit issues, e.g. bereavement, relationship, sexuality, depression, seen with a specific spiritual perspective.
4. Explicit issues arising from outside a belief-sharing community, e.g. family or peer pressure not to join, or to leave, the community.

(See Harborne 2009)

We have also taken on board the comments of a senior practitioner who told us that 'pastoral counselling' can be seen as a specific discipline in itself and it is a term that emanated from the USA a long time ago. He added that 'It assumes that there are three people in the room, the counsellor, client and God!' In the light of this, we have not written about 'pastoral counselling' specifically, but included generic issues which we feel are relevant.

7.1 Legal and ethical features of the context

7.1.1 Confidentiality

It is important here to make a clear distinction between pastoral care in ordained ministry and the specific activity of counselling. Confidentiality of sensitive information in a faith context is usually protected by a mixture of the law specifically relevant to that faith, i.e. ecclesiastical and Canon (Church) law, Sharia law, etc. and the law of the state. The Anglican and the Roman Catholic Churches each have their own respective Canon law. In addition to the relevant Canon law, confidentiality in the context of a counselling or psychotherapy relationship is governed in the UK by a complex mix of guidance, case law and statute (Bond and Sandhu 2005).

It is our view that counselling and psychotherapy, when provided in the context of spiritual and religious practice or pastoral care, are ultimately subject to the law of the state when matters such as professional liability, duty of care, contracts, health and safety, equality, confidentiality, public interest, etc. are in issue. Tensions may therefore potentially arise on occasions between religious law and practice and the law of the state.

Confessions and the 'seal of the confessional'

Some faiths have developed a code of conduct for those who work within their organisation. One particularly complex aspect of faith vs. state in the context of confidentiality is the religious concept of the 'seal of the confessional' where, in certain faiths, confessions to an ordained minister and absolution for sins are held within the faith to be totally confidential. In the Church of England (the Anglican Church), the *Guidelines for the Professional Conduct of the Clergy* (C of E, 2003 at sections 7.2–7.4) state that a priest who discloses any information from the confessional, to anyone, without the explicit consent of the penitent, commits an ecclesiastical offence under Canon 113 in the Canons of 1604. This remains unrepealed by the subsequent Canons of 1969. There may be a possible exception in relation to acts of treason (Litchfield 2006: 25).

The Church of England guidance regarding the confidentiality of confession makes no exemption for disclosure of abuse of children or vulnerable adults, even where a penitent's behaviour gravely threatens his or her well-being or that of others, although

> the priest should urge the person to report his or her behaviour to the police or social services, and should also make this a condition of absolution, or withhold absolution until this evidence of repentance has been demonstrated.

But

> If a penitent's behaviour gravely threatens his or her well-being or that of others, the priest, while advising action on the penitent's part, must still keep the confidence. (Church of England 2003: 7.3–7.4)

The Guidance notes that 'Whether the civil courts will always respect this principle of absolute confidentiality remains uncertain' (2003: 7.4), but interestingly, there is no mention here of the criminal courts, who also have power to order disclosure. Where a person is aware of serious criminal acts, e.g. knows material facts related to terrorism, child abuse, etc, the courts may expect disclosure in the public interest. For specific guidance relating to child protection issues, see 7.3.1 below.

The Catholic Code of Canon law is available online from the Vatican Archive at www.vatican.va/archive. The Canons govern guidance and policy on confidentiality, and assert that 'The sacramental seal is inviolable; therefore it is absolutely forbidden for a confessor to betray in any way a penitent in words or in any manner and for any reason' (Canon 983). A confessor is also 'prohibited completely from using knowledge acquired from confession to the detriment of the penitent even when any danger of revelation is excluded' (Canon 984–1) and adds that 'A person who has been placed in authority cannot use in any manner for external governance the knowledge about sins which he has received in confession at any time' (Canon 984–2).

The website www.catholicculture.org sets out the historical details of the norms relevant to the clerical abuse of minors, amendments and references, and the current text of the Norms on *delicta graviora* (exceptionally serious crimes) currently in force as approved by Pope Benedict XVI on 21 May 2010.

The Catholic and Anglican Canons are not relevant to other religions and they do not govern secular contexts. In the UK, other religions may have their internal law and practice (e.g. halacha, the Jewish legal system based on biblical legislation), and as a result, conflicts of interest may arise between the criminal and civil law of the state, and faith-based law. In issues of confidentiality, the courts would probably do their best to respect the faith system, as far as possible, but it is likely that if a statute or a court requires disclosure of information in the public interest, failure to comply may risk legal sanctions. We believe that the courts do generally respect the privacy of confession in so far as the law allows, but we would warn counsellors that canon law and the law of any other faith may well provide neither exemption nor defence against the statutory duties of compulsory disclosure or orders of the courts in the UK.

7.1.2 Counselling in the context of general pastoral care

The term 'counselling' seems widely used, with an even wider variety of meanings attributed to it. Our use of the term 'counselling' here includes the provision of counselling or psychotherapy in or out of the context of pastoral care, i.e. it is therapy provided by a person who is a qualified counsellor or psychotherapist (we mean here a 'qualified professional' as defined in 7.1.3 below). The therapist may provide that service in the context of pastoral care, and in that context, appropriate professional codes of ethics and conduct, e.g. BACP's *Ethical Framework* (BACP 2010a) will apply alongside state law, and ecclesiastical and Canon law or other faith law will apply where relevant.

Therapy in the context of pastoral care involves the duty of care owed by a counsellor to their client, both in the law of contract and in common law (Mitchels and Bond 2010: Chapter 2). The duty of care includes an expectation of confidentiality, subject to disclosures made with client consent or in accordance with the requirements of the law. The therapist and client may negotiate and agree, i.e. 'fine tune', the terms of confidentiality, which then forms part of their therapeutic contract.

7.1.3 Advice and listening skills used in the context of pastoral care

Where an ordained minister or person employed by or working in any other capacity for the church or other religious organisation uses active listening skills or provides spiritual or other advice to parishioners, this may be part of pastoral care. It is only the provision of counselling or psychotherapy by a qualified professional, however, that is likely to constitute a formal therapeutic (counselling) relationship. By the term 'a qualified professional' here, we mean a trained counsellor or psychotherapist working under professional supervision, and who is a member of a counselling organisation abiding by its ethical and code of conduct, and who is professionally accredited or working towards professional accreditation. As an informal relationship, the codes of practice for counselling and psychotherapy may not necessarily apply. Canon law (e.g. that relating to confessions) does not apply to informal pastoral conversations, but state law certainly does.

7.2 Practice issues

7.2.1 Keeping appropriate physical, sexual, emotional and psychological boundaries in pastoral care

In all pastoral work, where many forms of power (or perceived power) may be attributed to those in the organisation, there is a risk of abuse of power or privilege, competitiveness or manipulation, whether it is intentional or unintentional on the part of those involved.

The Church of England guidance (2003) clearly recognises this risk and advises that attention should be given to dress, places of meetings, furniture, lighting, and making night visits. It warns that inappropriate touching or gestures of affection should be avoided. See also 7.3.1 for child protection.

7.2.2 Meeting the personal needs of clergy and those involved in ministry

Clergy are encouraged to recognise the importance of knowing themselves and their own emotional needs, and to be aware of the dangers of dependency in pastoral relationships, e.g. Church of England, 2003: 2.8, 2.10.

Some churches and faith communities provide support for the spiritual, psychological and physical needs of candidates, priests, ministers and others involved in serving their church or faith community, e.g. St Luke's Centre in Manchester, which supports those serving in the Catholic Church, see www.stlukescentre.org.uk. This centre also complies with national and international standards for specialised risk assessments and provides a range of other psychological assessments.

We understand that in the Anglican Church, ministers are soon to be subject to terms of service, and that Human Resources departments are being set up to look after their needs. This will include the provision of counselling. It is likely that other churches may follow this route. Many Anglican dioceses employ a Diocesan pastoral Care and Counselling Adviser. These will generally see clients them-selves or refer on to a network of qualified counsellors. They may belong to the Anglican Association of Advisers in Pastoral Care and Counselling (AAAPCC).

Where the church or faith community supports (or pays for) counselling for its staff or ministers, contractual issues may arise. The client may be the church, the individual, or both. Confidentiality may be limited by custom and practice in that faith community, with an expectation of 'reporting back' or information sharing. Clients may feel obliged to work hard, to improve quickly, or to achieve therapeutic goals. They may find it difficult to express feelings and thoughts that seem disloyal, or that question their faith, yet need to explore these. Clergy may have family hous-ing and income entirely dependent on their role. They may then fear to discuss events which could jeopardise their vocation (and their livelihood) if disclosed.

One major issue on some faith communities is sexuality and sexual orientation. See the Association for Pastoral and Spiritual Care and Counselling's *Guidelines for the Pastoral Care of Lesbian, Gay and Bisexual People in Faith Communities* (APSCC 2002). Information may be obtained by contacting the Chair and Vice-Chair, through the website www.apscc.org.uk.

7.2.3 Dual roles

4. Dual relationships arise when the practitioner has two or more kinds of relationship concurrently with a client, for example client and trainee, acquaintance and client, col-league and supervisee. The existence of a dual relationship with a client is seldom neutral and can have a powerful beneficial or detrimental impact that may not always be easily foreseeable. For these reasons practitioners are required to consider the implications of entering into dual relationships with clients, to avoid entering into relationships that are likely to be detrimental to clients, and to be readily accountable to clients and colleagues for any dual relationships that occur. (BACP 2010: 5)

One of the difficulties that may face a priest, minister or other religious or spiritual leader who is also a professional counsellor is how best to provide an effective and efficient service to the community, whilst at the same time managing their dual roles. Dual roles carry with them potential implications for the balance of power, e.g. the Catholic priest who has power derived from ordination to give blessing, absolution or penance also being a therapist, see 7.2.4 below. Dual roles may be positive, for example allowing a client to see their therapist in a wider context and reflect on this.

Dual roles may indirectly impact negatively on clients, perhaps by the use of certain premises for therapy, e.g. where a minister/therapist uses his home (which may be church property), or church premises, for therapy.

A room in the church hall, or in the local church, chapel or Quaker Meeting House etc., may be available for use for therapeutic purposes. However, use of these church or other premises may risk triggering for a client unwanted past memories associated with the venue, creating a risk of transference, or simply removing the ability of the client to feel empowered in therapy and free from demands being made on them. Even in a simple situation, e.g. where a client is a warden or on a cleaning rota, they may come to therapy and on entering the religious premises, realise that they have been neglecting their role, and then feel guilty and apologetic, and perhaps even feeling blamed by their therapist.

Dual roles may result in clients attributing to the therapist/minister/elder/imam/rabbi, etc. unrealistic wisdom or perspicacity. Clients may also fear perceived power or authority, perhaps to 'hire and fire' staff, volunteers and church officers.

The BACP *Ethical Framework* (BACP, 2010a: 4) explicitly requires practitioners to consider how to provide a good quality of care to clients, and in particular draws attention to the potential negative impact of dual roles.

Where a member of the clergy or person with pastoral responsibility wants to provide counselling, a wise precaution is to avoid seeing clients from their own local area of responsibility. It may not always be possible to entirely avoid this, if pastoral responsibility is held over a very wide geographical area.

A further way to avoid (or at least minimise) the potential harm from dual role dilemmas is to check carefully with clients, when negotiating the therapeutic contract, whether there will be any potential negative impact arising from:

- the identity of the therapist
- the use of church or other faith premises for therapy
- the issues of roles and power and
- to address any concerns that the client may have about the therapy before commencing the work.

Opportunities should be given to re-visit these issues from time to time as therapy progresses.

The use of supervision is helpful here to assist the therapist to stand back from the situation and reflect on process objectively, and in identifying danger areas and applying relevant ethical principles to the client/therapist relationship.

7.2.4 Appropriate use of power in pastoral relationships

Decision making in the context of organised religion is often complex and takes place in a hierarchical power structure, e.g. the Anglican Church has a structure of authority requiring obedience by the clergy, who have also taken public oaths of allegiance and loyalty. Structures include the Canons of the Church of England, the Bishop's Regulations, and Ordination vows (Litchfield 2006: 67). Quakers and some other faiths have no ministerial or other authority structure and form use meetings and committees to make decisions and to fulfil necessary administrative functions.

Even within an apparently non-hierarchical faith system, however, there are hidden influences which may exert pressure on decision making, i.e. local culture, tradition, family and community influences, etc. These factors may influence how counselling or pastoral care is provided, and give rise to potential conflicts of interest. Provision of counselling, whether on a voluntary or paid basis, amongst members of the same local faith community, may result in dilemmas over dual roles, conflicts of interest or tensions about information sharing. Jacobs (2010) explores dual roles, and the *Ethical Framework* (BACP 2010a) points out that 'a dual relationship with a client is seldom neutral and can have a powerful beneficial or detrimental impact that may not always be easily foreseeable'. In a pastoral relationship, there may be real authority vested in the faith leader, e.g. arising from ordination or appointment and that power can be perceived as all the stronger if it is understood to come from God or other divine authority. Often there may also be elements of perceived power attributed to the minister or faith leader. They might then have to work at balancing this power in counselling, e.g. through their own humility and by empowering others. Perhaps it is difficult to appreciate sometimes the full impact that the power of the role has on others, and where a faith leader has insecurities or lack of self-esteem, there may be a temptation to use that power to enhance their own sense of self-worth.

It takes courage for the less powerful to take the risk of offering honest criticism to a person who is in a role of authority, especially if they are liked or admired, or if their approval is wanted. It also requires some humility to recognise that the criticisms we wish to make might in some way be misjudged or unfair.

7.2.5 Sharing information in shared ministry, or a pastoral care team

Pastoral care (including counselling) may be shared by a ministry team, who therefore might wish to share information among those in the team on a 'need to know' basis. In this situation it is advisable to create an agreement of corporate confidentiality and to obtain the consent of the people with whom the team works for information to be shared within the team. This avoids potential manipulation and conflicts of interest, e.g. where one person in a ministry team is given information with a request 'not to tell' others in the team (Litchfield 2006: 27). Data protection legislation will apply to any sensitive personal data stored electronically, or manually in a 'relevant filing system' (see Chapter 1 at 1.1.9).

7.2.6 Risk of misinterpretations, giving undue weight to therapeutic interventions, or inadvertent manipulation in the context of pastoral care

When pastoral counselling is given in the context of a hierarchical structure, it may carry undue weight because of the perceived authority of the person offering it.

Actions that may be entirely unintentional, e.g. being late for a meeting or delay in responding to a telephone call or a letter, may be perceived as lack of care or even a snub, and in the context of a power structure the offended person may not feel able to challenge the action. In the context of counselling and psychotherapy, the equality of client and therapist in terms of their respective ability to challenge or change the terms of a therapeutic contract is ethically important (BACP 2010a).

Where exchanges occur in the context of therapy in a non faith-based environment, clients may be unlikely to infer a deep spiritual meaning in the therapist's normal therapeutic interventions. However, in the context of a church or faith setting, particularly where power is attributed to the person providing pastoral care, this sort of inference in therapy is, perhaps, more of a risk. This situation may potentially be exacerbated in situations where the client has a spiritual concern about demonic possession, oppression, etc. It is important for clients to have sufficient self-esteem and emotional freedom to challenge their therapist's interventions whenever appropriate.

Where the therapist has a firm belief system, it is important to reflect and be self-aware, to ensure that responses to the client's material are therapeutic. Therapists may have difficulty in offering acceptance and empathy to clients expressing very different core values. Unempathic or dogmatic responses from a counsellor could adversely affect the client or influence the client's decision making process. If sufficiently serious, this may constitute grounds for complaint.

Clergy are not immune from liability in the general law of tort (for discussion of the duty of care and negligence, see Mitchels and Bond 2010: Chapter 2). A report by Rabbi Mark Dratch, *Suing Your Rabbi: Clergy Malpractice in Jewish Law* at www.jlaw. com (accessed 3 August 2010) describes what may be the first legal case against a pastor in the USA for negligent counselling. See also the article by Robert Reinhold, 'Justices Dismiss Suit Over Clergy', in *The New York Times*, 24 November 1988, p. A20.

In *Nally v. Grace Community Church of the Valley (1980)* No NCC 15668-B, L.A. County Super. Ct, Cal. filed March 31, 1980; 157 Cal. App. 3d 912, 204 Cal. Rptr. 303 (1984) the parents of Kenneth Nally sued California's Grace Community Church of the Valley and its pastors, alleging that negligent counselling resulted in the suicide of their son. Rabbi Dratch writes that 'The California Supreme Court found that clergymen have no legal responsibility for suicide prevention, holding that such a duty may have deleterious effects upon the relationship between the pastoral counselor and the counselee.' He adds (considering the authorities for similar liability in halacha, the Jewish legal system), 'In the absence of such assumed or prescribed liability, the Jewish court would exempt the clergyman from liability in Nally's suicide.'

Be careful of making assumptions about the meanings attributed to words, e.g. 'sin', 'forgiveness', etc. which may have specific meanings for a client which differ from those of the therapist. Shame and guilt may result from a client's inability to fulfil perceived social, cultural or faith-based expectations, and those providing pastoral care may need to empower the client and consider whether expectations which are unrealistic for that client are fostered in the client's church or faith community. This may result in challenges, in which the client may need support, and the therapist may encounter issues of dual roles or conflicts of interest.

Be careful of interpretations and diagnoses based on spiritual or religious experiencing, particularly if the phenomena described are outside the experiencing of the therapist. Clients may describe transcendent experiences during meditation or prayer, near death experiences, paranormal phenomena, psychic abilities, sensing the presence of people objects, or events, e.g. prophets, deities, saints, angels, demons, spirits, mentors, spirit guides, or ancient ancestors. Such experiences may raise questions about the client's mental state. A psychiatric understanding of delusions, for example, would include beliefs with no rational basis, of at least one month's duration, that are inconsistent with the person's culture or religion (APA 2000: 297.1). In this situation, it is important to be familiar with the client's culture, faith and belief system in order to be open and reflect with them on their individual experiencing with empathic understanding, whilst maintaining an objective therapeutic stance.

7.3 Interface and managing movement between spiritual and pastoral care and other contexts

7.3.1 Child protection

Many faiths have produced guidance on child protection, and some have co-operated to produce a wide range of resources and training, e.g. the Churches' Child Protection Advisory Service (CCPAS), at www.ccpas.co.uk, and the Churches Agency for Safeguarding (CAS) at www.cas.methodistchurch.org.uk.

Box 7.1 Child protection guidance issued by different faiths

- *Protecting All God's Children: The Policy for Safeguarding Children in the Church of England*, 4th edn (House of Bishops, London 2010)
- *Child Protection Handbook and Model Policy for Safeguarding Children* (Church of England, Leicester, 2005)
- *Safeguarding with Confidence: Keeping Children and Vulnerable Adults Safe in the Catholic Church* (2007)
- The Cumberlege Commission Report (see www.cathcom.org)
- The Catholic Safeguarding Advisory Service (CSAS) provides a Procedures Manual (see version 3 June 2010), based on the National Policies for Creating a Safe Environment for Vulnerable People in the Catholic Church in England and Wales, see www.csasprocedures.uk.net; see also the work of the National Catholic Safeguarding Commission (NCSC), www.catholicsafeguarding.org.uk, and the National Catholic Safeguarding Service (CSAS), www.csasprocedures. uk.net, and www.csas.uk.net
- The Safeguarding office of the Church of Scotland provides information and resources, see www.churchofscotland.org.uk
- *Child Protection in Faith-Based Environments: Guideline Report* (2006) London, The Muslim Parliament
- *Safe Children, Sound Hearing – Guidance for Madrassas* (2003). Kirklees Education/Social Services
- *Meeting Safety* (2010) Religious Society of Friends (Quakers)
- See also a wide range of booklets and training produced by CCPAS, at www. ccpas.co.uk

---

The child protection law and procedures in England, Wales and Northern Ireland are governed by the Children Act 1989, the Children (Northern Ireland) Order 2005, the Children Act 2002 and the Children Act 2004, along with government guidance, some of which may carry the force of law by subsidiary regulation, e.g. *Working Together to Safeguard Children* (DCSF 2010). Some guidance may be recognised by the courts, e.g. *Provision of Therapy for Child Witnesses Prior to a Criminal Trial: Practice Guidance* (CPS 2005a) and *Provision of Therapy for Vulnerable or Intimidated Adult Witnesses Prior to a Criminal Trial: Practice Guidance* (CPS 2005b) both of these are available at www.cps.gov.uk. Currently, these are both being updated and revised, so watch out for a new amalgamated version soon.

In Northern Ireland, the Department of Justice has provided guidance in *Achieving Best Evidence in Criminal Proceedings: guidance on interviewing victims and witnesses, the use of special measures and the provision of pre-trial therapy.* This is available at www.dojni.gov.uk.

In child protection situations, it is advisable to check with the current codes of practice of the faith, and with local and national child protection guidance. Many faith organisations have a designated child protection officer and some also have a responsibility for training. The NSPCC, local authorities' legal departments and the police may be approached for advice, without necessarily disclosing names. The Churches' Child Protection Advisory Service (CCPAS) and the Churches Agency for Safeguarding may also be approached for advice and resources. The NSPCC has also produced *Faith, Religion and Safeguarding* (available at www. nspcc.org.uk). Intended as an internal briefing paper for NSPCC staff, it provides an overview of the key factors relating to faith, religion and safeguarding children, with useful information, case examples, contacts and resources. We think that this briefing paper is useful for therapists because it presents questions for reflection and challenges to our personal views and beliefs, which may influence our ability to be objective in our work.

When child protection is an issue, the best course is to assist and encourage the perpetrator to allow disclosure of the incidents to the appropriate agencies (e.g. police, social care, etc.) and to clearly address the risk. An exception to seeking consent for disclosure or requiring the penitent to disclose, is where the abuse is of such a nature that warning the abuser might result in risk of further serious harm to a child or to others or to destruction of evidence, compromising a police investigation.

Sometimes, in the context of admissions of abuse made in confession, disclosure may be required by clergy as evidence of penitence before absolution can be given (Litchfield 2006: 25).

When the perpetrator has refused consent for disclosure, consideration should be given to whether disclosure should be made, without consent, in the public interest. Issues to be considered will include the gravity of the situation, the imminence and degree of risk involved to a child or children, whether disclosure will be helpful in preventing further abuse, and the wishes and feelings of the child concerned, if these are known, particularly where the child is over 16 or of sufficient maturity to make their own decisions, i.e. 'Gillick competent'. When disclosure is made, a note should be made of what was disclosed, when, to whom, and how the disclosure was made. For further discussion see Chapter 8 below, and also Bond and Jenkins 2009; Bond and Mitchels 2008; and Bond et al. 2010.

8 Working with Children and Young People

My client is too young to consent to therapy. He lives with his grandparents. How do I know if they have the necessary authority to give consent?

My client is a girl of 14 with an eating disorder, who is also clinically depressed. She may need in-patient psychiatric treatment. Who decides whether she has the mental capacity to accept or refuse in-patient care?

I am a school counsellor. How should I respond if my client's father demands to see her therapy notes?

A solicitor has asked for my 13-year-old client's therapy notes to use in a fact finding hearing in care proceedings. She does not want her parents to see them. Should I refuse to hand them over?

My 15-year-old client has just told me that she was abused by one of the care staff when she was in residential care, three years ago. She is not sure at the moment whether she wants to tell the police and local authority about it. Do I have to tell them now, even if she refuses? If I do that, it might damage our work together.

I work from home. One of my young clients is in secure accommodation and I have been asked to visit her once a week. Who will fund the work and whose consent will I need before I start?

My client, aged 15, committed several local burglaries. At court, he agreed to assessment for a course of CBT for behavioural problems and was referred to me by the youth justice team. We got on well, and he also admitted to me that he has been using recreational drugs, and the court is not aware of this. Do I have to tell the youth worker, or include this information in my report to the court?

I have been working privately with a girl of 8 years for anxiety and panic attacks. Her mother pays for her therapy. Mother now wants a divorce and has accused her husband of sexually abusing their daughter. The little girl loves her father and has not told me of any abuse. The father wants me to go to court and confirm that the girl has not mentioned these allegations in her therapy. He says that the mother is inventing stories to damage his reputation. How should I respond?

I work as a play therapist in a local hospital. They want me to keep my records on the hospital computer system on-site, but I would prefer to make my own records and take them home. Can I insist on what I want?

This chapter covers a very wide range of counselling and psychotherapy situations, and it is helpful at the outset to define our terms. By the generic term 'children', we take the legal meaning under the Children Act 1989, i.e. all who are under 18 years of age. When we refer to 'young people', we mean simply children from the age of 13 upwards. Writing about children and young people, we refer occasionally in the chapter to babies, toddlers, pre-schoolers and school-age children, because we feel comfortable referring to commonly used language to imply various age groups. We will, however, be specific about children's ages where the law applies to certain age groups, e.g. the age of 16, where a child may give valid legal consent for medical treatment.

By 'youth work' and 'youth worker', we mean those who work with young people. The 'Youth Court' is the branch of the Magistrates Court in England and Wales that deals with children and young people aged 10–17 years. In Northern Ireland, the Magistrates Court also has a Youth Court dealing with young people, and in Scotland, the Sheriff's Court has a youth division.

See *Child Care and Protection: Law and Practice* (Mitchels and James 2009) for an explanation of the relevant law and see *Children Law and Practice* (Hershman and McFarlane 2010) for a comprehensive, three-volume, legal encyclopaedia of child law in the UK.

8.1 Legal features of the context

8.1.1 Capacity of children to consent (or refuse) therapy, and to enter into valid and enforceable therapeutic contracts

Working with young people requires specific ethical awareness and competence. The practitioner is required to consider and assess the balance between young people's dependence on adults and carers and their progressive development towards acting independently. Working with children and young people requires careful consideration of issues concerning their capacity to give consent to receiving any service independently of someone with parental responsibilities and the management of confidences disclosed by clients. BACP 2010a:15

The concept of children and young people under the age of 18 making a therapeutic contract involves two separate areas of law. The first is the general law of contract, under which 'minors' (children under the age of majority, i.e. under 18) are allowed, because of their age, to back out of certain types of contract for 'non-necessary' goods and services. The other is the separate line of law about the capacity of children of different ages, maturity and understanding to give their consent (or refusal) for medical treatment, medical asessment/advice and therapy and therefore also their capacity to enter into a therapeutic contract and request confidentiality. The law on children's capacity to make decisions and on other people making decisions for children is complex – see children and contracts in Mitchels and Bond (2010: Chapter 4 at s. 4.7), and decision making about confidentiality in Bond and Mitchels (2008: Chapter 11).

Children and young people under the age of 18 are collectively referred to in English law as 'minors.' Minors may make valid and enforceable contracts in law for 'necessary goods and services,' which includes legal advice. If therapy also counts as 'necessary services' then therapy contracts are legally enforceable.

Children under the age of 16 in Scotland do not have contractual capacity. However, there is an exception to this general rule where the contract in question is one of a kind commonly entered into by young people, and where the terms are not unreasonable. The general rule in relation to 16- and 17-year-olds in Scotland is that they do have the capacity to contract on their own behalf. However, as with under 16s, there is an exception to the general rule. Where a 16- or 17-year-old has entered into a 'prejudicial transaction', then the transaction can be challenged. A transaction will be deemed to be prejudicial where the following two criteria are met:

1   An adult exercising reasonable prudence would not have entered into the transaction.
2   The transaction has caused or is likely to cause substantial prejudice to a young person.

An application to set aside a prejudicial transaction can be made in the Court of Session or in the Sheriff Court.

In practice, enforcement of a therapeutic contract against a young person who is unwilling to continue with it raises ethical and therapeutic issues. Contractual disputes are often about payment or confidentiality, so in relation to children, a more positive and ethical approach would be a review and renegotiation of the therapeutic alliance.

Law and therapy meet when there is a need to assess a child's mental capacity to make an informed decision and consent to any medical, psychiatric or therapeutic assessment or treatment.

Box 8.1 Ability of children under the age of 18 to give legal consent to therapy and/or to make an informed decision to enter into a therapeutic contract

Children aged 16–18, with mental capacity

Children over the age of 16, with mental capacity, will be treated in law for certain (not all) decision making purposes as though they were adults. This stems from s. 8(1) of the Family Law Reform Act 1969, art 4(1) of the Age of Majority Act (Northern Ireland) 1969 and s. 1 of the Age of Legal Capacity (Scotland) Act 1991, which confer on a person of 16 the right to give informed consent to surgical, medical or dental treatment, and therefore they may also make therapeutic contracts. Their decisions are then subject to the same criteria as for an adult, e.g. their mental capacity.

Mental capacity is a legal conceptual framework for the assessment of a person's ability to make rational, informed decisions, and for adults, this is now governed by the Mental Capacity Act 2005, the Mental Health Act 2007 and the Mental Capacity

(Continued)

(Continued)

Act 2005 (Appropriate Body) (England) Regulations 2006. In Scotland, see the Adults with Incapacity (Scotland) Act 2000 and the Mental Health (Care and Treatment) (Scotland) Act 2003. For details, see Chapter 1 at 1.2.5.

In Northern Ireland, there is currently no statute law on mental capacity as this area is governed by common law. Please see the Northern Ireland Executive website www.northernireland.gov.uk and also see www.dhsspsni.gov.uk for the recommendations of the Bamford Committee Review on Mental Health, and watch for new NI legislation.

Children aged 16–18 who do not have mental capacity

Where a child over 16 years of age lacks mental capacity to make their own decisions as a result of mental illness, infirmity or disability etc. (whether temporary or permanent), then any necessary decisions may be made for them by the High Court in England or Northern Ireland (or in Scotland, the Court of Session) or by those who have parental responsibility for them (see 8.1.2 below). Their capacity to make decisions about medical treatment or therapy is likely to be assessed by a doctor, psychiatrist or the therapist. The assessment of the child's mental capacity for other tasks may be made by others, e.g. a lawyer might assess their capacity to make a will, etc.

Children under the age of 16 and competent, according to the 'Gillick' case

Children under the age of 16 may be legally competent to make certain decisions. This principle of law was settled by the House of Lords in the leading case of *Gillick v West Norfolk and Wisbech Area Health Authority and Another* [1986] 1 AC 1212; [1985] 3 All ER 402 (HL) [1986] 1 FLR 224. See also s. 2(1) and (4) of the Age of Legal Capacity (Scotland) Act 1991.

8.1.2 Parental responsibility

People may assume that all parents have the power to make decisions for their children. This is emphatically (and perhaps surprisingly) not so. The ability of an adult to make a decision for a child depends on whether the adult has 'parental responsibility' for that child and also whether the child has capacity to make their own decisions (see 8.1.1 above).

Parental responsibility (PR) is the legal basis for making decisions about a child, including consent for therapy. It was created by the Children Act 1989, and defined in s. 3(1) as 'all the rights, duties, powers, responsibilities and authority which by law the parent of a child has in relation to a child and his property'. There may be new legislation which will further define the concept of parental responsibility, so watch for changes in the law. See also the Children (Scotland) Act 1995, s. 1 and the Children (Northern Ireland) Order 1995, art. 6.

Parental responsibility usually lasts for the duration of childhood, i.e. until the age of 18, with certain exceptions. If the father of a child acquires it by joint registration of the birth, a parental responsibilty agreement or an order of the court, it will last until the child reaches 18, unless a court orders otherwise. Parental responsibility acquired by others, e.g. to a grandparent along with a court order for residence, or to a local authority with a care order, subsists only for the duration of that order.

Parental responsibility may be held by several people at the same time. It cannot be transferred or surrendered, but elements may be delegated, see the Children Act 1989 s. 2(9), Children (Scotland) Act 1995, s. 3(5) and Children (Northern Ireland) Order 1995, art. 5(8).

Note that, as more than one person can have parental responsibility for a child at the same time, there may be disputes about how to use it. For example, where a child is born to a married couple, but after their separation the child lives with the maternal grandparents under a residence order, the mother, father and grandparents may all have parental responsibility for that child. They may disagree about how to bring the child up. If the disagreement is serious and cannot be resolved by discussion, the Family Court may make a ruling under a specific issue order or a prohibited steps order, under s. 8 of the Children Act 1989 or art. 8 of the Children (Northern Ireland) Order 1995.

Who has parental responsibility?

Bond and Mitchels (2008: Chapter 11) discuss the complex law of parental responsibility in detail. Here is a brief summary.

Mothers and married fathers of a child

Every mother (whether she is married or not) has parental responsibility for each child born to her. If the child's father is married to the mother at the time of the conception of the child or marries her subsequently, he will automatically acquire parental responsibility for their child, which will cease only with death or adoption.

Box 8.2 Abbreviations for legislation relating to parental responsibility

- Adoption and Children Act 2002 (ACA 2002)
- Adoption (Northern Ireland) Order 1987 (A(NI)O 1987)
- Children Act 1989 (CA 1989)
- Children (Northern Ireland) Order 1995 (C(NI)O 1995)
- Children (Scotland) Act 1995 (C(S)A 1995)
- Family Law (Scotland) Act 2006 (FL(S)A 2006)
- Family Law Act (Northern Ireland) 2001 (FLA(NI) 2001)
- Human Fertilisation and Embryology Act 1990 (HFEA 1990)

Unmarried father of a child

An unmarried father may acquire parental responsibility (PR) for his biological child in one of several ways, the first three of which can only be removed by order of the court:

- In England, from 1 December 2003, an unmarried father automatically acquires parental responsibility for his child if, with his consent, he is named as the child's father on the registration of the child's birth. This law does not operate retrospectively. (For similar provisions in Scotland, see the FL(S)A 2006 s. 23 and art. 7 C(NI)O 1995, amended by s. 1 FLA (NI) 2001.)
- By a formal *Parental Responsibility Agreement* signed by the mother and father, witnessed by an officer at court, and then registered. Copies may be obtained for a fee, in a similar way to obtaining a birth certificate – see Parental Responsibility Agreement Regulations 1991 and the C(S)A 1995, s. 4.
- The court can make an order under s. 4 (1)(a) of the CA 1989, awarding parental responsibility to the father, consistent with the interests of the child.

Parental responsibility can also be acquired by a child's biological father under the following circumstances:

- A residence order made under s. 8 of the CA 1989, directing the child to live with the father, and PR is awarded along with it (see also art. 12(1) of C(NI)O 1995).
- Appointment as the child's guardian made under s. 5 of the CA 1989 or art. 159 or 160 of C(NI)O 1995.
- Subsequent marriage to the child's mother.
- Certain placement or adoption orders under the ACA 2002 or the A(NI)O 1987.

Acquisition of parental responsibility by stepparents, civil partners and others

Parental responsibility may be acquired by others, including civil partners, in a variety of ways. 'Husband' below infers a married partner who is *not* the father of the child.

- Adoption. In this case, the parental responsibility held by all others prior to the adoption will be lost.
- The child's mother may enter into a Parental Responsibility Agreement with her husband of civil partner (subject to the agreement of the father if he has parental responsibility) (CA 1989 s. 4A(1) as inserted by ACA 2002 s. 112 and amended by CPA 2004 s. 75(1). This is not possible in Northern Ireland).
- The husband or civil partner of a mother may seek a parental responsibility order from the court (CA 1989 s. 4A(1) as inserted by ACA 2002 s 112 and amended by CPA 2004 s. 75(1). In Scotland, the civil partner may seek an order under Section 11 of the C(S)A 1995. In Northern Ireland, the step-parent (whether he/she is married to the civil partner of the child's mother who has parental responsibility) may seek an order under art. 7 (1A) of C(NI)O 1995).
- The child's father (if he has parental responsibility), may enter into a parental responsibility agreement with his wife or civil partner (subject to the agreement of the child's mother) (CA 1989 s. 4A(1) as inserted by ACA 2002 s. 112 and amended by CPA 2004 s. 75(1)). This is not possible in Northern Ireland.
- The wife or civil partner of a father with parental responsibility may seek a parental responsibility order from the court (CA 1989 s. 4A(1) as inserted by ACA 2002 s. 112 and amended

by CPA 2004 s. 75(1)). In Scotland, the civil partner may seek an order under s. 11 of the C(S)A 1995. In Northern Ireland, the step-parent (whether he/she is married to the civil partner of the child's father who has parental responsibility) may seek an order under art. 7 (1A) of C(NI) O 1995.

- Step-parent adoption by the husband or civil partner of the mother of a child born through assisted reproduction (HFEA 1990 was not amended by CPA 2004).
- A parental order under s. 30 HFEA 1990 declaring a married couple to be the parents of a child born through surrogacy arrangements. This order operates like adoption, and the child's surrogate birth mother loses her parental responsibility.

In the additional situations listed below, parental responsibility may also be acquired. It will then be shared with those who already have it in relation to the child, and the exercise of parental responsibility may be limited by the court in various ways:

- Residence order awarded by the court (ss. 8 and 12 CA 1989, s. 11 C(S)A 1995, art. 8 C(NI) O 1995)
- Guardianship Order (CA 1989 s. 5, s. 7 C(S)A 1995, art. 159 and 160 C(NI)O 1995)
- Care order made under s. 31 CA 1989 (parental responsibility is acquired by the local authority), see CA 1989 s. 33 (3), s. 86 C(S)A 1995, art. 50 and 57 C(NI)O 1995
- Emergency Protection Order under ss. 44-46 CA 1989 or art. 63-64 C(NI)O 1995 (but note that the duration and exercise of PR is limited)
- Special guardianship.

What if there is nobody with parental responsibility for a child?

Some children may have nobody with legal parental responsibility for them, for example the child of a single mother (biological father unknown), who then dies without appointing a guardian to take over after her death. Relatives or others wishing to care for the child will then have to apply for parental responsibility under one of the applications listed above or, failing this, the local authority has a responsibility to provide necessary care for a 'child in need,' and can seek an appropriate order.

There is an additional provision in s. 3(5) of the CA 1989 that those without parental responsibility may 'do what is reasonable in all the circumstances to safeguard and promote the welfare' of a child in their care. This provision is useful in day-to-day situations, e.g. allowing a babysitter, neighbour or relative who is temporarily looking after a child, to take that child for medical help in an emergency. See also s. 5 of the C(S)A 1995 and art. 6 (S) of C(NI)O 1995. This provision is unlikely to apply to counselling, unless in the context of an emergency.

8.1.3 Consent to therapy and/or sharing information between professionals working with children and young people

Where the child consents to therapy and/or disclosure

Where a child is able to give their consent, i.e. if they are over 16 with mental capacity or competent to give consent in accordance with the principles in the *Gillick* case (see 8.1.1 above), this consent is acceptable. Practitioners should make a record of the consent given, any information provided to the child (and on which the consent is based) and any limitations placed on the consent. The additional consent of those with parental responsibility for the child is not necessary.

Where the child refuses therapy and/or disclosure

If the child is over 16 and has mental capacity or is competent to give consent in accordance with the principles in the *Gillick* case (see 8.1.1 above), their refusal of therapy or of disclosure should be taken seriously by the court. However, even if the child has mental capacity, the court may overrule the wishes of the child for their own protection, e.g. the High Court may give a 'declaration of lawfulness' enabling medical staff to carry out medical or psychiatric treatment necessary to save the child's life.

In relation to sharing information between professionals, despite the refusal of consent of the child, if disclosure is justifiable in the public interest and/or for the child's protection or that of others, disclosure of necessary facts may be made to other professionals in accordance with child protection law and guidance (see 8.1.4). Issues may arise which challenge the inter-relationship between the therapist's duty of confidentiality to the child, their responsibility to the court, and their ethical and legal duty to act for the best interests of the child and in the public interest.

A child may wish to maintain confidentiality, but the therapist may feel that the child's best interests would be served by careful disclosure. In the case of older children, the best way forward here is to gain the trust of the child, address their fears, and then to work with the child to make the disclosure together, supporting the child to do this in the best way for the child, and to commit to continue supporting the child through the impact of the results of the disclosure.

If the child will not agree to careful joint disclosure, then, with the help of supervision as a reference point and as support, the therapist must make their own decision, having considered issues including:

- the *Ethical Framework* (BACP 2010a)
- the needs and welfare of the child client
- the protection of the child client
- protection of other children who may be at risk
- the requirements of the law, including any orders made by the court
- any available consents.

See also Bond and Mitchels (2008), Bond and Sandhu (2005) and the Disclosure Checklist at 1.4.1. For child protection law, policy and procedures, see 8.1.4 below.

Note: disclosure of information about a child may also be made with consent of those with parental responsibility for the child, but in some child protection situations, it may be inadvisable to seek the consent of family or carers, if to do so would place that child or other children at risk of harm, or prejudice the investigation of a serious offence, e.g. in a police investigation of organised child abuse in which family members, carers or close family friends are implicated.

Where the child consents to treatment or disclosure but those with parental responsibility refuse

In this situation, the therapist is justified in proceeding with therapy or disclosure if the child is able to give their consent, i.e. if they are over 16 with mental capacity or competent to give consent in accordance with the principles in the *Gillick* case (see 8.1.1 above).

If the child does not have the capacity to consent, then the consent of a person with parental responsibility for them will suffice. If parents or carers with parental responsibility cannot agree among themselves, an appropriate court order may be sought, i.e. a High Court declaration of lawfulness for therapeutic or medical treatment, an order for disclosure in court proceedings, or a specific issue or prohibited steps order made by the Family Court under s. 8 of the CA 1989 or art. 8 of C(NI)O 1995.

8.1.4 Child protection legislation, policies and procedures

Over the years, governments have issued a huge raft of statutes, subsidiary legislation and guidance to protect the interests of children and vulnerable adults. It is far too complex to set out in detail here, but the main current provisions in child protection law, policy and practice are listed in www.everychildmatters.gov.uk and www.legislation.gov.uk. See also Hershman and McFarlane 2010; and Mitchels and James 2009 for discussion of current child care and protection law and practice.

Current provisions include:

- United Nations Convention on the Rights of the Child
- Human Rights Act 1998
- Children and Young Persons Act 1933 (Schedule 1 offences)
- Children Act 1989 (covers England and Wales)
- Children Act 2004 (integrating children's services, implementing the *Every Child Matters Programme* created following the *Victoria Climbié Inquiry Report*, 2002)
- Children (Northern Ireland) Order 1995
- Children (Scotland) Act 1995
- Children and Adoption Act 2002
- Serious Organised Crime and Police Act 2005
- Safeguarding Vulnerable Groups Act 2006
- Protection of Vulnerable Groups (Scotland) Act 2007
- Care Planning, Placement and Case Review Regulations (England) 2010

Guidance includes:

- *Working Together to Safeguard Children: A Guide to Inter-agency Working to Safeguard and Promote the Welfare of Children* (DSCF 2010)

- *Framework for the Assessment of Children in Need and Their Families* (DH 2000b)
- *What To Do If You're Worried a Child Is Being Abused* (DfES 2006)
- *Co-operating to Safeguard Children* (DHSSPS(NI) 2003)
- *Putting Care into Practice* (which will come into force on 1 April 2011)

All these are listed in the Government Guidance section at the end of the book.
The role of Children's Commissioners was created by:

- Children Act 2004 (England), see www.childrenscommissioner.gov.uk
- Children's Commissioner for Wales Act 2001
- Commissioner for Children and Young People (Northern Ireland) Order 2003
- Protection of Children and Vulnerable Adults (Northern Ireland) Order 2003

The Children Act 2004 places a duty on local authorities to appoint a director of children's services and an elected lead member for children's services, with accountability for the delivery of children's services. It created local Safeguarding Children Boards (replacing the non-statutory Area Child Protection Committees) and places a duty on local authorities and other agencies, i.e. the police, health service providers and the youth justice system, to cooperate in promoting the well-being of children and young people and to make arrangements to safeguard and promote the welfare of children. It also paved the way for the setting up of information sharing databases, although these have not flourished – 'contact point' has now been abandoned.

Section 58 of the 2004 Act creates the offence of hitting a child, if it causes mental harm or leaves a mark on the skin, and removing the old defence (in the Children and Young Persons Act 1933) of 'reasonable chastisement', along with all the ancient historical (and rather dubious) implications of the legality of chastisement by beating wives, children and servants with 'rods no thicker than the thumb'.

The Sex Offenders Act 1997 requires sex offenders convicted or cautioned on or after 1 September 1997 to notify the police of their names and addresses and of any subsequent changes. The Sexual Offences Act 2003 and Sexual Offences (Northern Ireland) Order 2008 updated the Sex Offenders Act 1997 to strengthen the monitoring of sex offenders and created the offences of grooming, abuse of position of trust and trafficking. Notification under Part 2 of the Sexual Offences Act 2003 (known as the *Sex Offenders Register*) is an automatic requirement on offenders who receive a conviction or caution for certain sexual offences. The notification requirements are intended to ensure that the police are informed of the whereabouts of offenders in the community. Offenders must notify the police of certain personal details within three days of their conviction or caution for a relevant sexual offence (or, if they are in prison on this date, within three days of their release). All offenders must reconfirm their details at least once every 12 months, and notify the police seven days in advance of any travel overseas for a period of three days or more. The period of time for which an offender must comply with these requirements depends on whether they received a conviction or caution for their offence and, where appropriate, the sentence they received. Failure to comply with these requirements is a criminal offence, with a maximum penalty of five years' imprisonment. British citizens or residents, as well as foreign nationals, can be placed on the Sex Offenders Register in the UK if they receive convictions or cautions for sexual offences overseas.

Also introduced by the Sexual Offences Act 2003, *Risk of Sexual Harm Orders* are used to protect children from the risks posed by individuals who do not necessarily have a previous conviction for a sexual or violent offence but who have, on at least two occasions, engaged in sexually explicit conduct or communication with a child or children, and who pose a risk of further such harm. They may, for example, prohibit the person from using certain Internet chat rooms.

The Domestic Violence, Crime and Victims Act 2004 closed a legal loophole by creating a new offence of causing or allowing the death of a child or vulnerable adult. The offence established a new criminal responsibility for members of a household where they know that a child or vulnerable adult is at significant risk of serious harm.

In 2005, the Home Office published a circular *Guidance on Offences Against Children* (HO.16/2005) which contained a consolidated list of offences for all agencies to use in identifying 'a person identified as presenting a risk, or potential risk, to children'. This concept of various levels of 'risk to children' replaces the former use of the terms 'Schedule One' offenders and offences, see www.homeoffice.gov.uk/circulars, and para 12.5 at DCSF 2010: 323.

The Serious Organised Crime and Police Act 2005 set up the framework for the Child Exploitation and Online Protection (CEOP) Centre, and recently, the Children's Commissioner in England celebrated the agreement of Facebook to include a CEOP button on the site (see press release, 12 July 2010 at www.child-renscommissioner.gov.uk).

There is still no specific legislation that covers the minimum age at which a child may be left alone, and how old a babysitter should be. For guidance on these issues, see the NSPCC leaflet *Home Alone* at www.nspcc.org.uk.

In many areas of government-controlled work, e.g. the NHS, schools and residential homes, staff must comply with detailed child protection guidance and regulations, some of which carry the force of law. Failure to comply (without reasonable excuse) may justify complaint or legal action against an individual or an authority. In other areas of work, compliance with guidance is discretionary, but in relation to good practice, the BACP's *Ethical Framework* (BACP 2010a: 10) anticipates compliance with the law. Part 1 of *Working Together to Safeguard Children* (DCSF 2010) is statutory guidance issued under s. 7 of the Local Authority Social Services Act 1970 and must be complied with by local authorities carrying out their social services functions. Part 2 is non-statutory practice guidance. For Wales see NAW 2007 and for Northern Ireland see DHSSPS 2003.

Vetting and safeguarding procedures: where are we now?

Following the murders of Jessica Chapman and Holly Wells, the *Bichard Inquiry* (2004, see www.bichardinquiry.org) made recommendations resulting in the Safeguarding Vulnerable Groups Act 2006. In England and Wales, it got off to a flying start on 12 October 2009 with the creation of the *Child First* and *Adult First* barring lists, which are now in force. People who are included on these lists are prohibited from engaging in any 'regulated activity' which brings them into close contact with children or vulnerable adults respectively. Beyond the level of regulated activity falls a further extended range of 'controlled activity' (defined in s. 21). This is a wide sub-category covering those people who have 'an opportunity to have any form of contact with children' or to 'have access to the health records of children'. Note that 'any form' would include direct and indirect contact. If not falling within the regulated activities range, 'controlled activity' includes any form of health care, treatment or therapy which is carried out frequently or on three or more days in any 30-day period. This section gives a long list of controlled situations (including supervision and management). These include situations where individuals have access to sensitive records about children and vulnerable adults, for example, education and social services records, etc. It also includes any health care, treatment or therapy provided under statutory arrangements. In Wales, a person barred as a result of an autobar conviction or caution will not be able to work or volunteer in controlled activity in Wales. In other areas covered by the legislation, i.e. England and Northern Ireland, barred people may be able to undertake controlled activities with tough safeguards, such as stringent supervision.

From October 2009, there is a duty imposed on employers and managers of volunteers in agencies and organisations working with vulnerable groups, to ensure referral to the Independent Safeguarding Authority (ISA) of all dismissals for conduct that harmed or poses a risk of harm to children or vulnerable adults, with criminal penalties for non-compliance. This requirement also applies to BACP and to other professional organisations. The details of the legislation can be found at www.isa-gov.org. For enquiries, contact the Independent Safeguarding Authority at info@vbs-info.org.uk or call the ISA Contact Centre on tel. no. 0300 1231111. See also www.legislation.gov.uk. The Safeguarding Vulnerable Groups (Northern Ireland) Order 2007 No 1351/2007 can be found at www.dhsspsni.gov.uk. In Scotland, the Protection of Vulnerable Groups (Scotland) Act 2007 went live on 28 February 2010 and is operated by Disclosure Scotland. See www.legislation.gov.uk/legislation/scotland/acts2007, and for the *PVG Scheme Information Booklet* and news of the PVG scheme as it unfolds, see www.scotland.gsi.gov.uk.

However, all these safeguards are potentially costly to run, so any further implementation of the safeguarding legislation in England, Wales and Northern Ireland was halted mid-year 2010 by the Coalition Government. The Freedoms Bill 2010 will, if enacted, limit the role of the Independent Safeguarding Authority and the requirement for registration. See www.isa-gov.org.uk for details as the new legislation unfolds. The requirements for criminal records still apply. In England, refer to the Criminal Records Bureau, for information and enquiries at www.crb. homeoffice.gov.uk. In Scotland, the Central Registered Body in Scotland (CRBS) provides enhanced disclosures in the voluntary sector for those working with children, young people and adults at risk, see www.crbs.org.uk. Disclosure Scotland provides criminal records disclosures upon request and payment of a fee, see www.disclosure-scotland.co.uk/apply/. In Northern Ireland, a similar service is provided by Access Northern Ireland, see www.accessni.gov.uk/.

8.2 Working with children and young people 'in care' or subject to care proceedings

A child may be referred to as 'in care' for a number of reasons. They may be subject to a formal care order (see 8.2.1), in voluntary care (see 8.2.2) or in residential accommodation under mental health provisions (see 8.2.3). The position with regard to parental responsibility, and therefore to who can give consent, and for what, is different in these situations. We have therefore addressed each situation separately.

8.2.1 Working in the context of a care order or care proceedings

Where a child is subject to a care order made by one of the levels of the Family Court under s. 31 of the CA 1989, or art. 50 of the C(NI)O 1995, the child is placed by the court into the care of a local authority. One or more interim care orders may be made for a specified period of time. A full care order will remain in force until the child reaches 18, or until it is discharged at an earlier time. The court must approve a general 'care plan' for the child before making a care order, but the local authority has parental responsibility for the child after the care order is made, and should then fulfil the terms of the care plan, with statutory safeguards (e.g. regular reviews) to ensure the best possible continuing care for the child.

If a child is identified as in need of therapy, and therapy is proposed as part of the child's care plan in care proceedings, then the local authority should do its best to meet the child's need, e.g. by finding a suitable therapist (perhaps in liaison with the NHS), by providing transport to get the child to and from therapy and by funding the therapy. If therapy is not provided, and if the child in care is then at risk of suffering significant harm without the necessary therapy, a formal complaint may be made to the local authority and, if unsuccessful, the failure to provide necessary services may be challenged in the courts by judicial review, or an application can be made to the court to revoke the care order, so that the care plan and the care order may be reconsidered. For procedures and local authority duties, see Mitchels and James (2009) and Hershman and McFarlane (2010).

Under a care order, the local authority gains parental responsibility for the child and shares it with those who had it before the care order was made. The local authority can limit the exercise of parental responsibility by others, e.g. by refusing to permit removal of the child from foster care or a residential home or changes to the child's school, restricting contact with family, etc. The local authority will provide the necessary consents for therapy, disclosures, etc. It may also ask for copies of the child's medical notes, school or therapy records, and has the same right of access to information as a parent with parental responsibility.

Therapists working in the context of care proceedings should expect that their notes, or a report of their work with the child may be requested, and that their evidence may be required by the family court. The family court wants to have all relevant information to facilitate an informed decision in the best interests of the child. A court report should be in the appropriate format and use the Welfare Checklist in s. 1 CA 1989 or art. 3 C(NI)O 1995 as a reference point for the best interests of the child (see Bond and Mitchels 2008; Bond and Sandhu 2005).

If the child is concerned that certain parts of the therapy sessions should not be shared with other parties in the proceedings (e.g. parents, etc) then the court may be asked to make directions to limit the disclosure of the therapist's report or notes to certain people, e.g. to the Children's Guardian, local authority and solicitors. Cases may move up or down the tiers of the Family Court as appropriate, and in serious cases, limitations on disclosure are governed at High Court level. (See also 8.1.3 above.)

When a child leaves care, they are entitled to a number of services from the local authority, see the Children (Leaving Care) (England) Regulations 2001 and the Children (Leaving Care) Act (Northern Ireland) 2002. Under the English regulations, any social work records of assessments, pathway plans and reviews should be kept until the 75th birthday of the child or 15 years after their death, if they die before they reach the age of 18. Social work records may include therapy records.

8.2.2 Working in the context of voluntary care

Sometimes a parent or carer cannot manage to look after a child on a temporary basis, perhaps through illness or infirmity. They may ask the local authority to accept the child into care on a voluntary basis, under s. 20 of the CA 1989 or art. 2 of the C(NI)O 1995. In this situation, a person with parental responsibility for the child may ask for the return of that child, and the local authority should comply. If the parent insists that a child should be returned, but the local authority does not feel that it is safe for the child to return home, then it would have to apply for an emergency protection order or a care order.

When in voluntary care, the local authority does not have formal parental responsibility for the child, as there is no court order in place, and so any necessary consent for therapy, disclosure, etc. should be sought from those with parental responsibility.

8.2.3 Working in the context of residential mental health care

When a child is admitted to a residential unit for medical or mental health reasons, they may be admitted for treatment whilst subject to a full care order as part of a care plan. A child may be admitted to a residential unit for medical treatment or psychiatric treatment on a voluntary basis, or they may be compulsorily admitted to in-patient care under the mental health legislation. It is important, therefore, if consent for therapy is sought, to check the legal basis on which a child is resident.

If the child is subject to the care of the NHS, then all the government regulations and safeguards for patient welfare will apply (see Chapter 6). The child or those with parental responsibility for them will have been asked to provide consent for treatment etc., which will include disclosure of notes and relevant information to other members of the health care team responsible for the child's in-patient care. If counselling or psychotherapy is provided as part of the child's in-patient care, the therapy notes, or a summary of treatment provided, may well be requested to form part of the child's health record.

8.3 Working with young people in the 'secure estate'

The 'secure estate' for children and young people includes: Young Offender Institutions (run by the Prison Service), Secure Training Centres (run by private operators under contracts), and Secure Children's Homes (run by local authority children's social care). See DCSF 2010: 74–5. At the end of September 2010 there were 2,070 children under 18 in 'the secure estate' in the UK: 1,637 in young offender institutions, 273 in secure training centres and 160 in secure children's homes, (report of the Prison Reform Trust December 2010 at www.prisonreformtrust.org. uk). The report of the Prison Reform Trust (2010: 29–33) makes disturbing reading, particularly in relation to the treatment of children in the criminal system. For therapists, some of the cited research findings may cause particular concern: '71% of children in custody have been involved with, or in the care of, social services before entering custody. 75% of children in custody have lived with someone other than a parent at some time (compared with only 1.5% of children in the general population)' (Youth Justice Board 2008); 'Prison Reform Trust research has found that one in eight children in prison had experienced the death of a parent or sibling. 76% had an absent father and 33% an absent mother. 39% had been on the child protection register or had experienced neglect or abuse' (Jacobson et al. 2010); and 'Research commissioned by the YJB in 2006 found that 19% of 13-18 year olds in custody had depression, 11% anxiety, 11% post-traumatic stress disorder and 5% psychotic symptoms' (Inspectorate of Prisons, Chitsabesan et al. 2006).

Here, however, we are specifically concerned with 'secure accommodation' as a legal term, defined in s. 25(1) CA 1989 and art. 44(1) of C(NI)O 1995 as 'accommodation provided for the purpose of restricting liberty'. Children aged between 13 and 18 can be placed in secure accommodation for a variety of reasons. They may have committed a criminal offence and need to have their liberty restricted for their own safety or that of others. Orders made in these circumstances are called 'secure orders', to distinguish them from the orders made in civil cases.

A child who is looked after by a local authority, or subject to a care order, may be kept in secure accommodation by the power given by a court order under s. 25 CA 1989 or art. 44(1) C(NI)O 1995. In certain circumstances, a child may be kept in secure accommodation with the consent of those with parental responsibility. This includes children accommodated in residential care homes, nursing homes, mental nursing homes, or accommodated by health authorities or NHS Trusts (under Section 25 CA 1989). The legislation provides that if:

a   (i) the child has a history of absconding and is likely to abscond from any other description of accommodation; and (ii) if he absconds he is likely to suffer significant harm; or
b   that if he is kept in any other description of accommodation, he is likely to injure himself or others, the child can be placed in local authority accommodation by the court.

Secure accommodation is currently governed by s. 25 CA 1989 (the above legislation), by the Children (Secure Accommodation) Regulations 1991 SI 1991/1505, the Children (Secure Accommodation) Regulations (Northern Ireland) 1996 (the 'Secure Accommodation Regulations'), the Children (Secure Accommodation) (No 2) Regulations 1991 SI 1991/2034, the Children Act 1989 Regulations and Guidance Vol 4 Residential Care, Chapter 8, pp. 118–29, the Children Act 1989 Regulations and Guidance Vol 1 Court Orders (2008), and Children (NI) Order 1995: Regulations and Guidance Vol 4: Residential Care.

Secure accommodation should be based on the needs of the child, never because of inadequacies of staffing or resources in residential accommodation, nor because a child is being a nuisance. It may never be used as a punishment, see Children Act 1989 Regulations and Guidance Vol 1 Court Orders (2008) at paras 5.1–5.3, Children Act 1989 Regulations and Guidance Vol 4 Residential Care para 8.5, and Children (NI) Order 1995 Regulations and Guidance Vol 4: Residential Care para. 15.5. A child below the age of 13 years may not be kept in secure accommodation without authority of the Secretary of State. The courts must ensure that any secure accommodation order makes educational provision. Failure to do so would be in breach of the ECHR, see *Re K (Secure Accommodation Order: Right to Liberty)* [2001] 1 FLR 526.

The local authority keeping a child in a secure unit must appoint at least three people, one of whom must not be a local authority employee, to review the placement within one month, and thereafter at three-monthly intervals. The task of these three is to ensure that the criteria justifying secure accommodation still applies, that the placement is necessary, and no other description of accommodation is appropriate. The local authority must keep good case records.

Without the authority of the court, a child may only have his liberty restricted for up to 72 hours, either consecutively or in aggregate within any period of 28 consecutive days, reg. 10(1) (or reg. 6(1) in Northern Ireland) Secure Accommodation Regulations.

Where a child has been placed in local authority accommodation on a voluntary basis under s. 20 CA 1989 (or art. 21 C(NI)O 1995), a person with parental responsibility can remove the child at any time, unless certain exceptions in s. 20(9) (or art. 22(3)) apply. This includes removal from secure accommodation. Where the child has been remanded by a criminal court, the duration is for the period of the remand, with (subject to some exceptions) a maximum order of 28 days.

Under the Secure Accommodation Regulations 1991 SI 1991/1505, the child has the right to education whilst in secure accommodation and to receive therapy if necessary.

If the child is subject to a care order, consent may be given by the local authority. If the child is accommodated on a voluntary basis consent must come from those with parental responsibility for the child.

8.4 Working with young people under a supervision order or an education supervision order

A supervision order places the child under the supervision of a local authority or a probation officer. The supervising officer has a duty 'to advise, assist and befriend' the child, see s. 35 and Sch. 3 of the CA 1989, also art. 54 and Sch. 3 of the C(NI)O 1995. The supervising officer does not acquire parental responsibility for the child. The sanction for failure to cooperate with supervision is an application to discharge the order and to substitute something else, possibly a care order. Directions may be made within supervision orders binding those responsible for the child and also the child, to attend activities or live at specified places.

A supervision order is possible within criminal proceedings on a finding of guilt against a juvenile offender, under s. 7(7) of the Children and Young Persons Act 1969. Those orders may contain a direction that a child lives in local authority accommodation for a period of up to six months, but note that the criteria in s. 31 do not have to be met before a 'criminal supervision order' is made, and also that a criminal court cannot make a care order.

An education supervision order, made under s. 36 CA 1989 or art. 55 C(NI)O 1995 places the child under the supervision of a local education authority. These differ from supervision orders made under s. 31 and art. 50. School refusal is no longer by itself a ground for care, but it may be evidence of neglect, lack of parental control, underlying emotional problems, or that the education system may be failing to meet the needs of the child. School refusal may, therefore, form part of the s. 31 grounds, see *Re O (A Minor) (Care Order: Education Procedure)* [1992] 2 FLR 7. The supervisor's duty is to 'advise, assist and befriend and give directions to the supervised child and to his parents', 'in such as way as will ... secure that he is properly educated', see Sch. 3 to the CA 1989 and the C(NI)O 1995. The supervisor should take into account the wishes and feelings of the child and parents, and directions made should be reasonable, and such that the parents and child are able to comply with them. Directions might require the child to attend meetings with the supervisor or with teachers at the school to discuss progress, or to see a doctor, clinical psychologist or therapist. Directions should be confirmed in writing, and the parents informed. Children Act 1989 Regulations and Guidance (Vol 7) discusses directions in paras 3.31–3.35. Persistent failure to comply with directions may lead to prosecution.

8.5 Working with young people in the context of criminal proceedings

The age of criminal responsibility in England, Wales and Northern Ireland is very young – 10 years, well below the age limits of some of our European neighbours. In Scotland the age of criminal responsibility is 12 years, and the legal system for young offenders is different, for details of the Scottish law, see www.scotland.gov. uk, www.scottish.parliament.uk and www.scottishlaw.org.uk.

In England, Wales and Northern Ireland, the Youth Court is a specialised form of magistrates' court, which deals with young people aged between 10 and 17 who have committed criminal offences. As in the magistrates' court, the case will be heard by magistrates or by a single District Judge (magistrates' courts). The Youth Court is not open to the general public and only those directly involved in the case will normally be in court. If a young person is charged with a very serious offence, which in the case of an adult would be punishable with 14 years' imprisonment or more, the youth court can commit them for trial at the Crown Court. See www.hmcourts-service.gov.uk and www.courtsni.gov.uk for further details.

The Youth Court has power to make a wide variety of orders, which may include treatment for mental illness, remedial work and/or counselling or psychotherapy for problems such as substance abuse, traumatic stress, behavioural problems, etc.

Compliance with the court order is required and failure to do so may result in a further penalty for the young person. Therapists may be required to keep records of the child's attendance, and may also be asked to share information about the progress of therapy with the court and with the Youth Offending Team, who work with the court towards rehabilitation of the young offender.

8.6 Working with young people in the context of family proceedings

The family court has three tiers, the highest being the High Court, then the County Court and the lower level is the Magistrates' Family Proceedings Court. Each tier has similar procedures, and the system is designed so that cases may be moved up or down the levels according to their seriousness.

The Family Court hears private law cases that involve the welfare, property and maintenance of children and their families. If there is concern for a child's welfare, the court has the power under s. 47 CA 1989 (or art. 66 C(NI)O 1995 if in Northern Ireland) to require a local authority to investigate the child's circumstances and to report back to the court. The local authority must consider whether the child is at risk of significant harm, whether an application for a care order (or other order) should be made, and whether the child is 'a child in need' of services from the local authority, which should be provided. A 'child in need' as defined in s. 17 and Sch. 2 of the CA 1989 (and art. 17 C(NI)O 1995), may require services including counselling and psychotherapy. (See Mitchels and James 2009: Chapters 4, 8 and 16 for further details.)

8.7 Working with children and young people in hospital

In Chapter 6, we address the generic issues of counselling and psychotherapy within the NHS and in private medical care. Here we explore the specific legal issues which relate to working with children and young people in medical care.

8.7.1 Consent to hospital treatment

One of the main issues that concern therapists who are working with children in hospital is that of the child's informed consent to treatment, and issues of parental responsibility. See 8.1.1 and 8.1.2 above for a general discussion of the relevant issues. However, when a child is ill in hospital and perhaps distressed by periods of separation from their parents, family and carers, their capacity to think through their situation and to make informed decisions is likely to be less straightforward. This may be further complicated by the effects of medication which may impact on cognitive and emotional processing. Therapists may therefore need to consider consent issues carefully, with the help of experts and supervision.

In particular, consent and capacity issues may be important where therapists are asked to assist the hospital in tasks such as:

- assessment of a child's ability to make decisions, in the context of illness and the possible psychological effects of medication
- assisting a child to reach an age-appropriate understanding of their medical treatment
- helping a child to make necessary psychological adjustments to cope with the impact of medical procedures and medication.

Note that capacity to consent does not imply the absolute power to refuse treatment. Where a child refuses medical treatment which may be necessary to save their life, for example where a child with sickle cell anaemia refuses a blood transfusion on religious grounds, in modern situations, therapists may be asked to assist the child to think through all the relevant issues carefully. Whilst a child's wishes are taken seriously and respected by doctors and the courts, the High Court has the power to overrule the refusal of treatment by a child under 18, if necessary to save their life, even if that child is over 16 or has capacity in the context of 'Gillick' (see 8.1.1). For examples of court rulings, see the cases of *Re O (a Minor) (Medical Treatment)*, 19 March 1993 The Times Law Reports, *Re W (A Minor) (Medical Treatment: Court's Jurisdiction)* [1992] 3 WLR 758, and *Re C (a Minor) (Medical Treatment: Court's Jurisdiction)*, 21 March 1997 The Times Law Reports. In such a situation, the child may well need therapy to adjust to the imposition of treatment against their wishes. From the cases for adults as well as children, it also seems easier for the courts to question capacity to consent when the illness requiring treatment is wholly or partly psychological, e.g. anorexia nervosa.

The High Court may also go against parents' wishes and make a declaratory order in the best interests of the child, allowing doctors not to treat. See *Portsmouth Hospitals NHS Trust v. Wyatt and another* [2005] EWCA Civ 1181, [2005] 1 WLR 3995. In this case, a baby with brain damage and severe respiratory and kidney problems was held to be at risk of emotional and physical harm if her life were to be prolonged by artificial ventilation.

8.7.2 Record keeping in hospital settings

The *Ethical Framework* expects that records will be kept, unless there are justifiable reasons not to do so:

> Practitioners are advised to keep appropriate records of their work with clients unless there are good and sufficient reasons for not keeping any records. All records should be accurate, respectful of clients and colleagues and protected from unauthorised disclosure. Any records should be kept securely and adequately protected from unauthorised intrusion or disclosure. Practitioners should take into account their responsibilities and their clients' rights under data protection legislation and any other legal requirements. (BACP 2010a: 5)

Play therapists, counsellors and psychotherapists working in a hospital are usually expected to keep adequate records of their work, within the expectations of the Health Professions Council. Although not yet regulated by the HPC, counsellors and psychotherapists are working within the general guidance applicable to the NHS (see Chapter 6) and so record keeping is expected. The 'contract of service' (employment) or 'contract for services' (self-employment) that the therapist has with the hospital will determine the policies and procedures with which they are required to comply. Those policies may cover making, keeping and storage of client records. In the absence of a specific contractual requirement, the therapist may negotiate with the hospital administration.

Therapists should explain to their client (in age-appropriate language) the terms on which they work, and obtain the agreement of their child client or those with parental responsibility as part of the therapeutic contract.

9 Adoption Support Services

What exactly is adoption?

What are adoption support services?

What is an adoption support agency?

I am in private practice and want to provide therapy for couples who would like to adopt, and for adopted children and their families. Must I register as an adoption support agency?

I am in private practice and I am commissioned to work from time to time by a local authority to work with adoptive families – what legal regulations and guidance will apply to me?

How do I register as an adoption support agency? What will it cost me to do this?

Adoption means the creation of a new and permanent legal relationship between a child and his adoptive family. A court order for adoption legally severs all the parental rights and ties of the child's birth family and of all those who may have had parental responsibility for the child. This severance of all previous family ties will stop all automatic inheritance rights. The adopted child may, however, be named as a beneficiary in a will of a person from their former birth family.

The legal process of placement and adoption may be psychologically challenging for the child and their birth family, and also stressful for the adoptive family, too. There may be anxious periods of waiting for agencies to make decisions and for court hearings. Some adoptions may present challenges, for example resolving questions of post-adoption contact between an adopted child and their birth family. Adoption support services may be asked to assist in this and other aspects of the welfare of the child, both before and after adoption. For a very readable explanation of adoption law, see *Adoption Law for Adopters* (Lane 2006) and *Making Sense of the New Adoption Law* (Allen 2007), and for greater legal detail, see *Children Law and Practice* (Hershman and McFarlane 2010).

9.1 Legal context of adoption, adoption agencies and adoption support services

The legal framework for domestic adoption in England, Wales and Northern Ireland and for inter-country adoption was modernised and reformed by the Adoption and Children Act 2002 (ACA) and the Children and Adoption Act 2006 (CAA) (although only certain of these provisions apply to Northern Ireland). In Scotland, similar reform was created by the Adoption and Children (Scotland) Act 2007. These Acts were followed rapidly by a raft of legislation dealing with many adoption-related issues including statutory maternity, paternity and adoption pay and appropriate leave; establishment of rules and contact registers; review of determinations, and child maintenance. The main Acts and subordinate legislation are listed at the end of this book. The background policy for the legislation was set out in a government explanatory memorandum written in 2005 and available at www.legislation.gov.uk.

Local authorities have a statutory duty under the Adoption and Children Act 2002 to provide a range of post-adoption support services for adopting families and for children being placed for adoption, including financial support, advice and information, therapeutic services for adopted children, support groups for both children and parents and support to maintain the relationship between children and their birth parents. They also have a general duty to provide assistance to a child in need under s. 17 and Sch. 2 of the Children Act 1989 (or the equivalent Northern Ireland legislation). Some of these adoption support services may be provided by local authorities themselves, or by independent agencies and practitioners, commissioned by local authorities to undertake any necessary work. Independent specialist agencies and therapists in private practice may also provide privately funded work for parents, children and adoptive families, and they may need to register with Ofsted as adoption support agencies – see 9.4 below.

Adoption Support Agencies (whether local authority or independent) are strictly regulated as providers of social care under the Care Standards Act 2000 and may now also be regulated, where relevant, by the Health and Social Care Act 2008.

All this legislation can be found at www.legislation.gov.uk. The adoption legislation is available at www.education.gov.uk. The British Association for Adoption and Fostering (BAAF) also has helpful information on its website www.baaf.org.uk.

From 12 May 2010, the Department for Education (DfE) is responsible for both education and children's welfare, see www.education.gov.uk. Responsible to the DfE is the government Office of Standards in Education (Ofsted), which inspects and regulates many aspects of childcare and children's social care, including the Children and Family Court Advisory Service (CAFCASS), schools, colleges, council children's services and services for looked after children, safeguarding and child protection. Ofsted's aim is to achieve excellence in the care of children and young people, and in education and skills for learners of all ages. Ofsted is responsible for the registration and inspection of adoption agencies and adoption support agencies; for its functions and guidance, see its website www. ofsted.gov.uk. See the new guidance on adoption support services, *Adoption guidance: Provision of Adoption Support Services* (2011). For the full document, see dfe.gov.uk/b0072314/guidance/ch9/providing-support. Further information and comment can be found on other sites, e.g. www.communitycare.co.uk.

Box 9.1 Adoption and adoption support services legislation

Legislation relevant to adoption and adoption support services includes:

- Adoption: National Minimum Standards (Ref DFE 00028–2011, issued March 2011)
- Adoption (Northern Ireland) Order 1987
- Adoption and Children Act 2002
- Adoption and Children (Scotland) Act 2007
- Adoption and Children Act 2002 Statutory Guidance
- Adoption Agencies Regulations 2005
- Adoption Agencies Regulations (Northern Ireland) 1989
- Adoption Support Services Regulations 2005
- Adoption Support Agencies (England), Adoption Agencies (Miscellaneous Amendments) Regulations 2005 (No 2750)
- Adoption Support Agencies (England) (Amendment) Regulations 2010 (No 465)
- Care Standards Act 2000
- Care Standards Act 2000 (Establishments and Agencies) (Miscellaneous Amendments) Regulations 2002
- Children (Northern Ireland) Order 1995
- The Local Authority Adoption Service (England) Regulations 2003
- National Care Standards Commission (Registration) Regulations 2001
- Voluntary Adoption Agencies Regulations (Northern Ireland) 2010

9.2 What are adoption support services?

The term 'adoption support services' is defined in section 2(6) of the Adoption and Children Act 2002 which defines the term, in the context of adoption, as including 'counselling, advice, and information, and any other services prescribed by legislation'. See the Adoption Support Agencies: National Minimum Standards (England) and the Adoption and Support Agencies (England) and Adoption Agencies (Miscellaneous Amendments) Regulations 2005. These include:

- assistance to an adoption agency in preparing and training adoptive parents
- support to any child or adult who has been adopted or their birth relatives
- support and help to adoptive parents to enable them to provide stable and permanent homes for children placed with them
- assisting people who have been adopted to have contact with their relatives.

Watch the Department of Education website www.dfe.gov.uk for news of further changes to the law and guidance.

9.3 What is an adoption support agency?

In law, many definitions are circular. Section 8 of the Adoption and Children Act 2002 defines an 'adoption support agency' as an undertaking, the purpose of which, or one of the purposes of which, is the provision of adoption support services.

An undertaking in terms of this legislation might include a local authority, an agency, a partnership, or an individual therapist in private practice. If they are working in the field of adoption, then they are required to register as an adoption support agency under the Adoption and Support Agencies (England) and Adoption Agencies (Miscellaneous Amendments) Regulations 2005, Regulation 3, unless they fall within certain exceptions (see 9.4. below). No services may be provided by an adoption support agency before being registered with Ofsted. Challenges have been made in early 2011 to Ofsted's inspection standards, and so watch the website www.dfe.gov.uk for any changes made to the current standards in response to criticism.

All adoption support agencies are subject to regular inspection by Ofsted, currently within the first seven months of registration (unless no children or adults receive adoption support services in that time) and thereafter at intervals of three years. It remains to be seen whether the new Care Quality Commission (CQC) will take on any significant role in relation to adoption support services. See their website www.cqc.org for details of the CQC's new role, guidance and regulations. Check as implementation unfolds, and for comment see www.communitycare.co.uk and www.baaf.org.uk

In Northern Ireland, part of the adoption support services are provided by the relevant Health and Social Care Trust.

9.4 Should therapists in private practice providing adoption support services register as an adoption support agency?

Therapists who provide adoption support services, e.g. work with birth families to prepare for adoption or any form of post-adoption counselling (see 9.2 and 9.3 above), may have to register their business as an adoption support agency unless they fall within the statutory exceptions (see 9.4.1 below). The law is complex, and each therapist's circumstances will be different. We strongly advise that all therapists providing counselling in the context of any aspect of adoption should check with Ofsted to see whether they need to register as an adoption support agency.

Therapists who do register as an adoption agency will have to comply with considerable paperwork before providing services, and pass strict Ofsted inspections in which their administration, paperwork, safety systems, insurance, professional practice, premises and procedures are assessed. The full requirements are set out in the guidance (see above) and in the relevant law at www.legislation.gov.uk. See the Adoption Support Agencies: National Minimum Standards (England), available at www.webarchive.nationalarchives.gov.uk. They are also available in Welsh.

9.4.1 Exceptions to the requirements for registration

Many practitioners will be pleased to know that there is now a new exception to the potentially onerous requirements for registration. The Adoption Support Agencies (England) (Amendment) Regulations 2010 (No 465) provide that:

> An undertaking is not an adoption support agency if the undertaking is carried out by an individual who only provides adoption support services (otherwise than in a partnership with others) under a contract for services with either –
>
> (a) an agency in respect of which a person is registered under Part 2 of the 2000 Act as the person carrying on the agency, or
> (b) an adoption agency.

A 'contract for services' or a 'contract to provide services' are the types of contract that a self-employed therapist might have with agencies and organisations, as distinguished from a 'contract of service' or contract of employment. This means that independent therapists, e.g. those in private practice who may have non-adoption work and who also undertake work from time to time for local authorities, adoption support agencies, etc., may now have an exemption from having to register, with a specific limitation. Oftsted explains:

> An individual person, who only provides adoption support services under a contract with a registered adoption support agency or an adoption agency, for example a local authority or a registered adoption agency, does not need to register as an adoption support service. Individuals who are part of a partnership must register even where they only provide services to a local authority or registered adoption support agency. (Ofsted 2011)

Some therapists have asked us 'If I work in an adoption agency part-time, am I also automatically covered to work with adoption clients in private practice?' The answer to this is that the question itself implies a misunderstanding of the rules. It is the adoption agency that is registered, not its staff as individuals. The staff of the adoption agency are therefore only exempt from having to register themselves as an adoption support agency whilst they are undertaking their work with or for the adoption agency. Once a therapist takes on private work (i.e. away from their employment or a contract for services with the adoption agency), if that private work is not on a contract with any adoption agency, or with an agency, in respect of which a person is registered under Part 2 of the 2000 Act as the person carrying on the agency, then Ofsted advises that they are not covered by the Adoption Support Agencies (England) (Amendment) Regulations 2010 and they are therefore liable to register personally.

As this legislation moves to keep pace with changing circumstances, the safest option for practitioners is always to check their specific circumstances with Ofsted to ascertain if they are exempt from registration.

9.5 Registration process, inspection, enforcement and professional standards for adoption support services

9.5.1 Registration

The requirements and conditions for registration as an adoption agency are set out in the Adoption Agencies Regulations 2005, the Adoption Support Services Regulations 2005, and various amendment regulations including the Adoption Support Agencies (England), Adoption Agencies (Miscellaneous Amendments) Regulations 2005 as further amended by the Adoption Support Agencies (England) (Amendment) Regulations 2010. The Ofsted website www.ofsted.gov. uk gives details of registration procedure.

Box 9.2 Documents required for registration as an Adoption Support Agency

- Adoption Agencies Dataset (a questionnaire of 22 pages) to be completed
- Statement of Purpose
- Financial records
- Personnel list, and for each person CVs, references, training records and CRB checks (ISA registration may be required)
- Associates training plan
- Staff training plan
- Safeguarding children policy
- Health and safety policy and procedures
- Historical abuse policy
- Protection of vulnerable adults policy
- Feedback from clients
- References from service users
- Referral procedure
- Bills from service users
- Information for service users
- Quality assurance procedure
- Children's Guide
- Children's Rights Director
- Complaints leaflet
- The registration authority
- Recording policy
- Storage of records
- Disaster recovery plan
- Disability access
- Equality policy
- Risk assessment policy
- EAL (English as an additional language) policy
- Assessment frameworks (and where relevant, certificates of qualification to use them)

See Adoption support agencies: National minimum standards (England) 2005 – pdf at webarchive.nationalarchives.gov.uk; in Welsh at www.wales.gov.uk. For the government consultation on revision of these standards, see also www.baaf.org.uk and www.adoptionuk.org.

9.5.2 Ofsted inspections

Ofsted inspections consider compliance with all the regulations and the national minimum standards, as well as quality of leadership and management.

In (Ofsted 2011: 6) there is an explanation of the system:

An inspection of an adoption service usually takes one day depending on the size of the agency. We always want to speak to children and adults who receive services from the agency during our inspection.

We use a four-point scale to make judgements about the overall effectiveness of an adoption service and the quality of the organisation.

The judgements are:

Outstanding: the provision is of exceptionally high quality
Good: the provision is strong
Satisfactory: the provision is sound
Inadequate: the provision is not good enough.

An inspection report of our findings is published on our website. This may include actions an adoption support agency provider must take to comply with the law or recommendations to help them improve. Providers must respond to any actions we set within a timescale. We may check on progress to meet any actions and will follow up recommendations at the next inspection.

For more information on inspection see *Are you Ready for your Inspection? A Guide to Inspections of Children's Services Conducted by Ofsted* available at www.ofsted.gov.uk.

9.5.3 Enforcement

Government guidance may be enforceable by the courts by statutory regulation, e.g. the *Adoption Support: National Minimum Standards (England)*, which are enforceable under the Care Standards Act 2000. For legislation and updated guidance see website www.education.gov.uk.

Failure to meet the required standards is initially followed by a written communication from Ofsted, explaining what needs to be done to put things right. If this is not met, then Ofsted's range of additional powers includes issuing a compliance notice, cancellation of registration or prosecution. To see how Ofsted investigates complaints and brings about compliance, see the *Compliance, Investigation and Enforcement Handbook* available from Ofsted or on website www.education.gov.uk.

9.5.4 Other professional standards

Therapists working with or for adoption support agencies must also, of course, comply with their own professional practice guidance, e.g. the *Ethical Framework* (BACP 2010a) or the UKCP Ethical Principles and *Code of Professional Conduct* (2009) and, where applicable, the GMC guidance available at www.gmc-uk.org (GMC 2004, 2006). In cases of alleged breach of duty of care or negligence, accepted professional standards may be taken into account by the courts as a measure of competence.

Adoption support agencies are working with children and families and so, as part of their compliance with government registration, they must also demonstrate that they follow all relevant government guidance, e.g. *Working Together to Safeguard Children* (DCSF 2010; see www.education.gov.uk).

9.5.5 The Northern Ireland context

The Voluntary Adoption Agency Regulations (Northern Ireland) 2010 and the Health and Personal Social Services (Quality Improvement and Regulations) Order 2003 govern the provision of services by voluntary adoption agencies in Northern Ireland.

To provide adoption support services, therapists would have to register their businesses (which, under regulation 3, must be an incorporated body) with the Department of Health, Social Services and Public Safety (DHSSPS) by applying to the Regulation and Quality Improvement Authority (RQIA).

The registered provider of the agency must work with the manager of the agency to prepare a statement of purpose, which shall contain statements as to:

a   the overall aims and objectives of the agency
b   the name and address of the registered provider, the responsible individual and the manager
c   the relevant qualifications and experience of the manager and staff (including details of registration with any relevant professional regulatory body)
d   the organisational structure of the agency
e   monitoring systems
f   complaints procedures.

All voluntary adoption agencies registered in Northern Ireland will be regulated and inspected by the RQIA.

9.6 Contractual issues

Adoption support agencies may enter into a wide variety of contracts in the course of their work. Mitchels and Bond (2010) address the law relating to various types of business dealings relevant to therapy, and references to the relevant chapters of that book are included below, should further information be required:

- Contracts for the purchase or lease of premises in which to work (Chapter 7)
- Contracts for office supplies, and office services, e.g. telephone, cleaning, etc. (Chapter 4)
- Contracts with insurance companies and professional organisations (Chapter 6)
- Commissioning services (e.g. of an accountant or a lawyer) (Chapter 4)
- Contracts of employment with their therapists or other service providers (Chapter 9)
- Contracts for the provision of adoption support services to their client groups, e.g. local authorities, adoption agencies, adoptive families, etc. (Chapter 4)
- Enforcement of contracts through legal claims (Chapter 10)

9.6.1 The multi-way contract: agency/local authority/parents/child

The agency or an individual therapist may be commissioned by a local authority to assist an adoptive family. The commissioning contract may therefore involve the local authority, the adoptive parents and the adopted child (for capacity to consent, see below and also Chapter 8).

A therapist employed by an adoption agency, or commissioned by the agency to provide services for a child may, for example, enter into a therapeutic contract with their agency, the child's parents /or the adoptive family and the child, i.e. a multi-way therapeutic contract.

In multi-way contracts, it is important to address any necessary boundaries in sharing information and any other issues that might impact on one of the parties to the contract. Therapists should give consideration of the ability of the child to enter into a therapeutic contract. The age and maturity of the child is relevant, and it may be necessary to identify those who have parental responsibility for the child.

Children aged 16–18

Under s. 8(1) of the Family Law Reform Act 1969, art. 4 of the Age of Majority Act (Northern Ireland) 1969 and s. 1 of the Age of Legal Capacity (Scotland) Act 1991, a child of age 16 or over may make his or her own medical decisions (with some limitations where life-saving treatment is refused, see below) and therefore they may also make therapeutic contracts.

Children under 16

Children who are under the age of 16 may be competent to make certain decisions (and therefore to enter into a therapeutic contract). This principle of law was settled by the House of Lords in the leading case of *Gillick v West Norfolk and Wisbech Area Health Authority and Another* [1986] 1 AC 1212; [1985] 3 All ER 402 (HL) [1986] 1 FLR 224. See also s. 2 (1) and (4) of the Age of Legal Capacity (Scotland) Act 1991. For discussion of the rationale of the *Gillick* case and a child's ability to make an informed decision, see Chapter 8 at 8.2. Consent for a therapeutic contract may be given for a young child under the age of 16 who is not 'Gillick competent' by a person with parental responsibility for the child or an order of the High Court or Court of Session.

Please see Chapter 8 for consideration of situations where therapeutic treatment is considered necessary but the child or those with parental responsibility refuse. If there is any issue about the competence of a child to make an informed decision, the matter can, if necessary, be referred to those with parental responsibility for the child and/or for expert opinion and/or to the High Court. The High Court has the power to make an order in the best interests of the child under s. 8 of the Children Act 1989; in Northern Ireland, under art. 8 of the Children (Northern Ireland) Order 1995; and in Scotland, under s. 11(2)(e) of the Children (Scotland) Act 1995. For further discussion of competence, also see Bond and Mitchels 2008: Chapter 11.

9.7 Practice issues

We are greatly indebted to Joanna North, who runs a registered adoption support agency in Devon, for her comments on some of the issues that she has encountered in practice, and we have addressed some of these issues here.

9.7.1 Assessment of the family situation and needs

Allow time for thorough assessment of both child and adoptive parents, in order to understand their real needs. The needs of the adoptive family may not be fully explored or addressed before the court order is made for adoption. An incompatibility might arise after adoption between the needs of the adopted child and their adoptive family, i.e. the family may need stability and a peaceful environment in which to function, whilst the child needs space and opportunity to test acceptance, and to explore and perhaps to challenge boundaries.

9.7.2 Training and information for adoptive families

New adoptive parents are not necessarily psychologically minded or experienced with children and they may need to be taught how to become aware so that they can recognise when children need help. They may, for example, react to the child's boundary challenges by strict discipline, but not understanding that this may be an expression of feelings of insecurity or a need for attention or affection.

9.7.3 Understanding and accepting the child's history

Children bring to their new parents a great deal of history that has to be accepted. Their child's past is part of their lives. Adoptive parents may be shocked to learn about their child's history and they may have to cope with having their idealism about childhood shattered.

Historical issues for the child that may not be recognised by the adoptive parents may impact on the child's new relationship with adoptive parents. For example, a child who has experienced long-term emotional, sexual or physical abuse may have learned patterns of response to domestic situations which are substantially different from those of a child of the adoptive family who has not experienced abuse. In addition to this, issues may arise throughout the life of the child and could surface years after adoption. The adoptive family may not make links with the past in new (perhaps unexpected) behaviours arising from or triggered by past memories that are surfacing. New parents are adapting to parenting as well as the baggage that the new adoptive child brings with them. A therapist working with an adoptive family has to think of both ends of the spectrum.

9.7.4 Supporting adoptive families

Adoptive parents who do not understand the child's distress may end up becoming part of the problem for the child, instead of being part of the solution. The role of the therapist is often educative and supportive of both child and family and facilitating mutual understanding and adjustment. Where an adopted child presents difficult behaviours, adoptive parents may feel resentful, and feel that they are carrying a burden that has been dumped on them by the local authority. This is exacerbated if there is a lack of information about the child's past leading to unexpected behaviours triggered by shadows of the past, or in cases where there is a lack of funding support for resources for the adoptive family. The therapist may have to liaise with the local authority or adoption agency in order to improve mutual understanding and effective communication.

9.8 Interface and managing movement between adoption support services and other contexts

9.8.1 Liaison with the local authority

In adoption support work, liaison between the agency and the social services department of the local authority is likely to be frequent. The adoption support agency will almost certainly find itself invited to provide feedback on work done, and reporting on work is necessary and required more frequently than in some other types of therapeutic work. Therapists may be invited to attend six-month statutory reviews for new adoptions. Not only is there a need for good reports, but the necessary consents for disclosures and the limits of confidentiality must be negotiated and agreed before commencing therapeutic work.

Getting a good history from social services in relation to the child is sometimes difficult, perhaps because the necessary consents for disclosure may not be forthcoming. As a result, the therapist (and indeed, the adoptive family) may never know the child's full history or experiences, or the information provided may not always be accurate.

9.8.2 Managing differences in attitude and perceptions

The adoptive family may think about their situation in a different way from the perspective of the courts or social services. For example, social services may be driven by perceived pressures and budget constraints to finalise adoption placements quickly, and sometimes when adoption placements suffer difficulties, adoptive parents may express the feeling that they were pushed too quickly into adoption when what they needed was sufficient time for adaptation. Some adopters have felt unable to say to social services or adoption agencies that they were not quite ready yet to make the necessary commitment to permanence, for fear of criticism or even fear of losing the potential adoptive placement. From the therapy point of view, the process of establishing the child's security within their new family requires time, patience, commitment and support.

Social services may work in a practical, systematic, 'tick box' frame of mind whereas an adoption is an emotional experience for the adoptive parents. This can cause resentment for adoptive parents who don't feel understood, and the role of the therapist in adoption support may include that of 'translator' between the adoptive family and social services to help mutual understanding.

9.8.3 Contact issues and managing contact

An Adoption Order may contain provisions for direct or indirect contact between the adopted child and their birth parents several times a year. This may be stressful to negotiate both for the adoptive parents and the child concerned. If it proves to be unduly stressful, it may threaten to cause disruption to the adoptive placement. Therapists providing adoption support need to understand the basic provisions of the legal framework within which they work. They may be able to help the birth parents, adoptive parents and child manage contact in the best way possible for the welfare of the child.

9.8.4 Funding

Getting payment for adoption support services is not always easy. Local authority social care departments have a statutory duty under the Adoption and Children Act 2002 for local authorities to provide a range of post-adoption support services, including financial support. The general duty of local authorities to provide assistance to children in need under s. 17 and Sch. 2 of the Children Act 1989 or art. 8 and Sch. 2 of the Children (Northern Ireland) Order 1995 also allows for financial assistance, but most authorities are unlikely to provide financial assistance for post-adoption support under this section unless other avenues are unproductive. Where funding is sought from the local authority, the therapist may need to conduct an initial assessment and reporting with an estimate of costs in order to obtain the necessary funding.

For further information about adoption support agencies and contacts please see Useful Resources.

10 Forensic Work

Forensic is derived from the Latin term *forensis*, meaning 'of or before the forum'. In the times of the Roman Empire, the forum was the place where criminal cases were usually tried in a public hearing. By the term 'forensic work' in this book, we include all the work of therapists which is directly related to the courts and the judicial system, for example assessments requested by the court, court reports, evidence of fact and evidence given as an expert witness, etc.

In the UK as yet there seems to be no defined clinical role of forensic counselling or forensic psychotherapy, but there is a clear professional role of forensic psychology, for which courses are available at various academic levels. Forensic psychology is the interface between psychology and the legal process of the civil and criminal courts and the prison system, and it therefore may include psychological work in the context of prisons, probation services and other institutions. For forensic psychology in the NHS, see www.nhscareers.nhs.uk. See also www.bps.org.uk for a description of the different types of psychologist, and the Division of Forensic Psychology.

10.1 What is an expert witness?

Some therapists are invited or ordered to come to court to give evidence as an 'expert witness'. The court alone has the right to decide who is regarded as an expert witness or not.

There are different categories of witness:

- A witness of material fact (e.g. someone who saw a traffic accident and tells the court what he personally saw/experienced/did)
- A professional witness of material fact (e.g. a therapist who has treated a client and is now called by that client to give evidence concerning their treatment)
- An expert witness (e.g. a person with some experience in a particular field who is asked to provide evidence of fact and also to give their expert opinion on a matter which is before the court).

In relation to civil cases, s. 3 of the Civil Evidence Act 1972 explains the situation very clearly in England:

3. – (1) Subject to any rules of court … where a person is called as a witness in any civil proceedings, his opinion on any relevant matter on which he is qualified to give expert evidence shall be admissible in evidence.

(2) It is hereby declared that where a person is called as a witness in any civil proceedings, a statement of opinion by him on any relevant matter on which he is not qualified to give expert evidence, if made as a way of conveying relevant facts personally perceived by him, is admissible as evidence of what he perceived.

(3) In this section 'relevant matter' includes an issue in the proceedings in question.

In Scotland, the position is the same. Witnesses give evidence of either fact or opinion. Only experts suitably qualified to do so may provide opinion evidence. Other witnesses must confine themselves solely to matters of fact.

10.2 Why are some therapists treated as experts and others not?

The court has to decide whether a witness may be treated as an expert. A number of criteria may be considered by the court. The first is whether, in relation to the matter before the court, the therapist was acting in a professional capacity, e.g. conducting an assessment requested by the court, or working with a client in a professional capacity. If the witness was not acting in their professional role at the time and was merely a bystander (e.g. they saw a traffic accident on their way to work) then, as a bystander, the therapist would only be regarded as a witness who can give material facts such as the time and place of the accident and what they observed and experienced. But note that acting in a professional capacity does not, in itself, automatically make a therapist an expert.

Therapists acting in their professional capacity may (or may not) be regarded as experts by the court. This will depend on whether the court thinks that they are sufficiently qualified and experienced in a particular modality, area of professional practice, or in their work with a particular person or group of people, to provide the court with their professional opinion on a matter, in addition to simply providing the material facts. For example, we have seen a court regard as expert witnesses not only a highly experienced and famous psychiatrist, but also a newly qualified nursery nurse with little post-graduate experience but who had worked intensively with a young child and therefore she knew that child very well. Usually the court will require the witness to provide a brief outline of their relevant qualifications and experience, which will assist in assessing the status of their evidence. It is usual practice for professional witnesses to attach a brief CV or such an outline to their statement or report to the court.

To avoid embarrassment or worse, it is wise not to ask for inclusion in an expert witness register or promote your services to lawyers or the courts as an expert witness unless you have appropriate experience in the relevant field of practice. It helps to have gained some experience in court.

There always has to be a first time giving evidence, but it helps to watch a few criminal court cases from the public gallery beforehand so that the court layout and procedure is familiar. For first-timers in private hearings in the family court, go and ask the consent of the court and parties to sit in and watch a case or two beforehand, to become familiar with the family court process, and go through the evidence with the lawyer who has given instructions. They can be helpful in pointing out the possible lines of questioning to expect. See 10.7 below for brief notes on courtroom etiquette.

If a court has adjudged that you are an expert, then your evidence must be succinct, strictly accurate and impartial. The GMC has held disciplinary proceedings against medical doctors acting as expert medical witnesses who exceeded their remit, gave inaccurate evidence, or have overstepped their professional expertise – see *Meadow v General Medical Council* [2006] EWHC 146 (Admin)[2006] 1 WLR 1452. See also Bond and Sandhu (2005) and Mitchels and James (2009: 217–25) for details of evidence and report writing.

10.3 Legal features of forensic work

It is difficult to set out all the law which might be relevant to the cases in which forensic work takes place, since evidence is needed in such a wide variety of contexts, each of which has its own evidential rules.

For example, forensic evidence may be required in:

- public law relevant to child protection
- private family law (e.g. contact disputes, parental responsibility and consent issues, divorce, separation, etc)
- education
- residential care
- adoption cases
- criminal cases
- employment
- health and safety
- disability, equality and anti-discrimination cases.

However, certain elements are common to forensic work in many contexts. Other areas of forensic work, e.g. family cases, have their own specific statutory guidance for expert witnesses. We advise that therapists who are called to provide forensic work in any type of court case that is unfamiliar to them, or in which they are uncertain of the evidential rules or form of report which applies to their work, should ask the solicitor instructing them to clarify the parameters of their role, and to provide them with details of any current written or statutory guidance available.

There is no shame in asking for guidance, and it is always helpful to ask colleagues who are familiar with that area of work to share their experience and to point out the possible pitfalls. Professional organisations may have internal specialist groups. BACP has a number of special interest groups which have helped us with information for this book, and are willing to be contacted for information and support; see Useful Resources and the BACP website www.bacp.co.uk. We have also included in Useful Resources a number of forensic science and expert witness societies and organisations which may be approached for assistance or membership.

Some organisations maintain registers of expert witnesses, e.g. the Expert Witness Online Directory at www.expertwitness.co.uk; the Law Society of Scotland Directory of Expert Witnesses 2010, available at www.expertwitnessscotland.info; and the UK Register of Expert Witnesses at www.jspubs.com. The list of expert witness in Northern Ireland can be established by contacting the Law Society of Northern Ireland at www.lawsci-ni.org. There are websites including www.expertsearch.co.uk and www.thelegalhub.co.uk, which have lists and information on getting started as an expert witness.

There are a number of helpful books for witnesses. In *Forensic Science in Court: The Role of the Expert Witnesses* (Wall 2009), the author, who is a well known and highly respected judge, provides a general guide intended for forensic scientists, but which may also be useful for therapists. He explains the different types of court, arbitration, courts martial and the Coroner's court, and then explains the evidential rules and ethics relevant to each of these. In *Therapists in Court* (2005) Bond and Sandhu give detailed guidance specifically written for therapists on report writing, court procedure and giving evidence in court. The law is always moving on and since that book was written, new guidance has been produced for the use of expert witnesses in the family courts, see 10.3.1.below.

10.3.1 Experts in Family Proceedings Relating to Children

The Practice Direction *Experts in Family Proceedings Relating to Children* [2008] 1 WLR 1027 (EFPRC 2008) was made by the President of the Family Division under the powers delegated to him under Schedule 2, Part 1, paragraph 2(2) of the Constitutional Reform Act 2005, and is approved by the Lord Chancellor.

This Practice Direction aims to assist the court with the appropriate use of expert evidence and the instruction of experts in family proceedings relating to children, and came into force on 1 April 2008, superseding all earlier guidance. It applies to public and private law cases involving the welfare of children, including placement and adoption proceedings. The instruction of an expert and provision of documents to the expert requires the permission of the court, and guidance is given on applying for the permission, the duties of the expert, the content of the expert's report, preparation for hearings, response to enquiries, and how the expert's evidence should be provided.

The guidance also includes questions that may be included in letters of instruction to adult psychiatrists and applied psychologists in Children Act 1989 proceedings. The full text can be found at www.justice.gov.uk, and watch that website for updates to the guidance.

10.3.2 'McKenzie Friend'

Therapists may also in some circumstances be asked to accompany a client to court as a 'McKenzie Friend' (MF) (see Box 10.1). A litigant who has no legal representation has the right to be accompanied by a lay person (i.e. not a lawyer), even where the proceedings relate to a child and are in private. Details of applications, rights of audience, the role and duties of a McKenzie Friend can be found at www.hmcourts-service.gov.uk. It is also possible to have someone fulfil the role of McKenzie Friend in the Scottish courts.

Box 10.1 Role of a McKenzie Friend

What a McKenzie Friend may do:

- Provide moral support for the litigant
- Take notes
- Help with case papers
- Quietly give advice on:
  - points of law or procedure;
  - issues that the litigant may wish to raise in court;
  - questions the litigant may wish to ask witnesses

What a McKenzie Friend may not do:

- A MF has no right to act on behalf of a litigant in person. It is the right of the litigant who wishes to do so, to have the assistance of a MF.
- A MF is not entitled to address the court, nor examine any witnesses. A MF who does so becomes an advocate and would need the grant of a right of audience.
- A MF may not act as the agent of the litigant in relation to the proceedings nor manage the litigant's case outside court, for example, by signing court documents.

Advice and support for unrepresented clients is also available from the local Personal Support Units and Citizens' Advice Bureaux. The PSU at the Royal Courts of Justice in London can be contacted on 020 7947 7701, by email at cbps@bello.co.uk or at the enquiry desk. There is also a CAB at the Royal Courts of Justice in London, which can be contacted at the enquiry desk.

10.3.3 Case law on forensic evidence

Re A (Children) (Contact: Expert evidence) [2001] Times Law Reports 27 February was a leading case in which the well-known judge H.H. Mr Justice Wall sought to exercise judicial control over expert evidence, and this was one of the cases that led to the changes in procedure in the Practice Direction discussed earlier in 10.3.1.

The case of *Re B (Minors) (Sexual Abuse: Standard of Proof)* [2008] UKHL 35; [2008] WLR (D) 186, is a leading case in which the House of Lords examined the standard of proof in children cases. Baroness Hale (with all the other Law Lords concurring) delivered a judgment in which she supported the proposition that the burden of proof in civil children cases is the balance of probabilities, i.e. that it is 'more likely than not' than an event did, or did not, occur. She re-iterated the duty of the court not to punish or deter, but to protect children from harm. The implication here for experts is that their duty lies to the court but they must comply with section 1(3) of the Children Act 1989 and consider the welfare of the child as of paramount importance, over and above all other interests. In the Civil Procedure Rules 1998, part 35, the primary duty of an expert is stated to be to the court. The Practice Direction *Experts in Family Proceedings Relating to Children* 13 February, 2008 1 WLR 1027 (EFPRC 2008) para. 3.1 very clearly re-iterates that duty in family cases. In criminal cases, the expert's primary duty to the court and the need for impartiality to any party to the case has also been emphatically stated, e.g. in the *Cannings* case in 10.4. below.

Experts should never go beyond the remit of their instructions or their expertise. There have been cases in which, regrettably, this has happened, to the detriment of a party, the child, justice, or possibly all three. The Court of Appeal gave helpful guidance for experts and lawyers in *R v Cannings* [2004] EWCA Crim 1 [2004] 1 WLR 2607.

The courts also try to protect expert witnesses from exploitation. In one case, an unwilling expert was released because a litigant instructed her as an expert witness but subsequently said that he could not pay her fee. The court held that, save in exceptional circumstances, where a litigant instructed an expert witness but subsequently said that he could not pay her fee, the court would not issue a witness summons to demand that the expert give evidence. See the decision of Mr Justice Neuberger in his judgment on 13 October 2000 in *Brown and Another v. Bennett and Others* [2 November 2000], 1 Times Law Reports, Chancery Division.

The court accepted the proposition in *Phipson on Evidence* (15th edition, 2000: paras 37–49) that: 'an unwilling expert witness will, save in an exceptional case, be released from the operation of a subpoena'. His Lordship said that he was not persuaded that the instant case was 'exceptional' and accordingly he would set aside the witness summons. Please note that this proposition was intended to apply only to experts, and not to witnesses of material fact.

Professional guidance is provided by the government and courts, some of which may be enforceable by the courts, e.g. the Practice Direction *Experts in Family Proceedings Relating to Children* [2008] 1 WLR 1027 (EFPRC 2008), discussed earlier, which was made under Schedule 2, Part 1, paragraph 2(2) of the Constitutional Reform Act 2005. Another form of guidance for a therapist witness is the policy and accepted standards of practice in the therapy profession, e.g. the *Ethical Framework* (BACP 2010a). In cases of alleged breach of duty of care or negligence by an expert witness, accepted professional standards along with guidance for expert witnesses may be taken into account by the courts as a measure of the therapist's competence.

10.4 Contractual issues in forensic work

10.4.1 Contracting for forensic work/services of expert witness

Therapists who are asked to provide forensic work will enter into a contract for their services, whether it is an assessment, the provision of therapy, or another forensic service. That contract may take a variety of forms – perhaps a standard form of contract with a local authority or agency, or a specific contract with a client for provision of services in a private law case, or a contract with a solicitor for services in a criminal, civil or family case on behalf of their client.

10.4.2 Publicly funded work

Experts frequently contract with a solicitor to undertake forensic work that is funded by the Legal Services Commission (LSC), e.g. for an assessment and the subsequent provision of a report and attendance at court to give evidence, or to prepare a report for court on work previously undertaken with a client. The present government is actively planning changes to the system of public funding, so watch out for changes during 2011.Ask the instructing solicitor for details of the current rules regarding public funding that may apply to your work.

The witness's estimate of costs in publicly funded cases for the forensic work should be agreed by the court. If the court has given prior approval for the expenditure, it is less likely to later be reduced on taxation by the court or refused by the Legal Services Commission. In many cases where the case is publicly funded, the court may reserve the power to review the costs of the case, including the expert witness's bills on taxation at the end of the case (taxation of costs is a legal term meaning a review by a District Judge of the bill from the lawyers and others involved in the case, to make sure that the amounts charged are reasonable, before the bill goes to the Legal Services Commission for payment) and the judge may revise and reduce fees if they are considered too high for the work done. Solicitors will advise on taxation procedure in civil and criminal cases. The Practice Direction *Experts in Family Proceedings Relating to Children* [2008] sets out these provisions in detail for family court cases.

The Legal Services Commission may refuse to pay for work they have not first approved, or which was not specifically ordered by the court. We recommend that experts always ask the instructing solicitor to get a court order directing the expert witness's attendance, and supply the court at the same time with an estimate of the costs and time frame of the work, which can then be considered when the court makes the order.

10.4.3 General contract issues for experts

In each case it is advisable to ask about the terms of the contract and consider them carefully, before accepting a forensic role. Ask who is responsible for payment of the fees. Always agree the extent of the work to be done: the planned work and time frame, including deadlines and the fee payable. Agree, too, that revisions in the fee may be made if further work is required. Request a written contract with the person/organisation who will be responsible for making payment, before starting the work. If the task needs, for example, an assessment, followed by a treatment plan, with possible further work later, then make each stage of this absolutely clear, and give the cost of the assessment, and then an estimate for the time frame and cost of the treatment plan, and provide the invoices in stages. Further work should be estimated and agreed before it is carried out.

Always ask for a court order directing and authorising the expert evidence you have been asked to provide, and ask the court for all necessary legal consents. Expert witnesses may not see a child in a family court case without the consent of the court, and evidence gathered without appropriate consent may be disallowed.

10.4.4 Private clients

Where the client is to pay privately, it is wise to be protected from non-payment by a disgruntled (or deliriously happy and forgetful) client after a case has ended and they have then disappeared. It is good practice, therefore, to agree a fee in advance, and to ask the instructing solicitor to obtain payment from the client in advance to hold on account, or to agree with the instructing solicitor that the bill will be paid within 30 days of submission.

10.4.5 Unrepresented clients

A client who is not legally represented may be asked for payment for expert witness and other witness fees in advance, or to agree with the instructing solicitor that the bill will be paid within 30 days of submission.

10.4.6 Court control of evidence

The court controls expert evidence in family matters, and the court would need to give consent for disclosure of relevant papers in the case to the expert witness. Consent of the court would also be required for an expert to see a child, and judicial directions are given covering assessments, possibly including the venue, who is to be present, the timing, dates for filing reports, and disclosure of the results. Instructions for an expert witness should always be agreed by the court and set out in writing.

10.4.7 Obtaining clear instructions

Insist on written instructions, with a clear time frame and objectives, and a list of all the documents supplied (then when something later appears not to have been provided, this can be clearly evidenced). Ask for an undertaking from the instructing solicitor to keep you up to date with developments in events in the case and changes in the parties circumstances, which may affect your work in the case. See practice issues at 10.5 for further discussion.

10.4.8 What if the solicitors haven't paid me?

It is always best to have business contracts in writing for clarity and enforceability.

In publicly funded cases, some solicitors are very slow at getting their bills taxed and may need reminders to get interim payments on account for witnesses. The LSC also has a backlog of work and so payment in publicly funded cases can take time after taxation. Getting prior authorisation and then an interim payment is always best. If you find that the solicitor has actually been paid by the LSC (and therefore has your fees in hand) but is being slow in paying your invoice, the only recourse is repeated reminders and a request for interest on the debt. The Solicitors Regulation Authority governs the standards of solicitors' practice, and may offer advice if necessary. It is the body to which complaints about solicitors may be made. All solicitors in England and Wales must provide on their website and correspondence their firm's SRA number and contact details for the SRA, see www.sra.org.uk. In Scotland complaints should be made to the Law Society of Scotland, see www.lawscot.org.uk. In Northern Ireland, complaints should be made to the Law Society of Northern Ireland www.lawsoc-ni.org. In privately funded cases, there should be a written contract with clear terms (see above), and the invoice to the solicitor can state that payment within 30 days is required, and that interest will be charged for each day after that under the Late Payment of Commercial Debts (Interest) Act 1998. This useful Act, as amended by subsequent legislation, allows interest to be charged for the late payment of contracts for goods or services where both parties are acting in the course of a business. Therapy is a business. Interest (currently at the time of writing set by the rules at the generous rate of 8% over the base rate) is payable from either an agreed date in the contract or within 30 days after delivery or invoice, whichever is the later.

10.5 Practice issues

10.5.1 Planning and timing evidence in the case

Liaise with the lawyers in the case to plan the timing of evidence. With careful planning, the wear and tear on expert witnesses can be saved considerably. Joint expert consultations and jointly compiled experts' lists of agreed and disputed issues are becoming much more commonly used in court cases, saving both time and costs. Arrangement of evidence by the lawyers to fit the needs of witnesses (doctors and therapists have busy lives) and the run of evidence in a logical sequence in the case is vital. Written evidence can be admitted by agreement, and expert witnesses' time saved by reduction of their evidence in chief and more time in cross examination.

If you are acting as an expert witness in a case in Scotland it is likely that you will prepare a written report which the solicitor instructing you will lodge as a production with the court. The joint instruction of experts by both parties in a case is not common in Scottish litigation. In addition to this, you will be required to attend at court to speak to the terms of the report which you have prepared and provide additional information where required. Once you have been examined in chief by those instructing you, it is likely that those instructed for the other party to the case will wish to cross-examine you.

10.5.2 Confidentiality and information sharing

Be aware that there are potentially many parties to a contract for forensic work. The work is directed by the court, commissioned by a client or their solicitor, and may also involve reporting therapeutic outcomes or assessment issues to others. It is vital to be clear about the limits of confidentiality with the client, especially when working with or for children in care, making it clear to them that information will be shared.

A similar situation regarding information sharing will exist when working with clients in the context of an involvement with education/youth offending/probation/social services and police.

10.5.3 Evidence on oath or affirmation

Evidence is given on oath or affirmation. The usher will first discreetly ask if the witness is willing to take the oath or prefers to affirm. The oath is usually taken on the New Testament, but by request for other religions, this may be replaced by the Old Testament, the Koran, the Gita, or the Adi Granth. The court usher will show the witness to the stand, then ask them to take the New Testament, or other holy book, in their hand and to read from a card or repeat after the usher the words 'I swear by Almighty God that the evidence which I shall give, shall be the truth, the whole truth and nothing but the truth' (or alternative wording for other faiths). In Scotland the oath or affirmation is given with an uplifted right hand.

If a therapist is not willing to take the oath for religious or other reasons, they can affirm, with the words 'I do solemnly, sincerely and truly declare and affirm that the evidence which I shall give, shall be the truth, the whole truth and nothing but the truth'.

10.5.4 Authority and reliability of evidence (professional confidence compared with unprofessional arrogance!)

Reports must be thorough because they will be subjected to the close scrutiny of the court, the parties and the lawyers. An appropriate degree of professional confidence in one's own expertise and experience (not the same as unjustified arrogance) is necessary when giving evidence and standing up to cross-examination. Cross-examination in criminal cases can be very challenging (less so in family matters, which should be not so adversarial) and if the witness feels tired or vulnerable, strong cross-examination may be felt as undermining or aggressive. Evidence should be given in a calm, assertive, authoritative manner.

Clarity and absolute integrity is essential in forensic work. It is not a sin to admit that we do not know something, nor to admit that we may have been mistaken about something, if this is the truth. It is also totally acceptable to politely decline to answer a question posed by an advocate, if the answer would take us beyond the limits of our work or our expertise, e.g. if a counsellor is asked for a clinical diagnosis that they are not qualified to give, or for an opinion based on an assessment that has not been carried out. But don't just simply refuse to answer – that would seem discourteous, so briefly explain to the court why the question cannot be answered. Refusal to answer the questions of a court without a good reason may be treated as a contempt of court.

Expert witnesses should be objective in their assessments, and not partisan in any way, however much empathy there may be for a client. It is unethical and not professionally acceptable to try to fudge issues, tell half-truths, or otherwise in any way mendaciously evade difficult issues or questions. Telling the court a direct lie when under oath (or having affirmed) to tell the truth is perjury – a criminal offence.

The court is in charge of the evidence. If necessary, legal issues or other concerns about giving evidence may be discussed in advance, in confidence, with the instructing solicitor. Concerns about evidence may also arise during a case. In these circumstances, tell the instructing solicitor or barrister to speak with the clerk of the court. The judge and the lawyers may, where necessary, discuss any legal issues about the evidence in the absence of the parties and the public.

10.5.5 Keep fully informed and be aware of changes

In forensic assessments, it is vital to have all the information that is available. If vital or relevant information is not provided by solicitors, social workers or others, the assessment and report may be flawed. Experts also need to keep updated on legal and factual developments as the case progresses over time. In the context of forensic work, be prepared to attend regular reviews, which can be time consuming.

We may not know what we are getting into when asked to undertake forensic work, so insist on having copies of all psychological/psychiatric/police reports before starting work, and insist on clarification of the objectives that are expected. Do not take on anything beyond your individual capability or expertise ... and don't attempt the impossible, like promising an assessment and report in a very short time if it is not really feasible, even if someone begs you to!

10.5.6 Client compliance versus openness in the therapeutic relationship

Remember that forensic work with offenders or alleged offenders may not be easy. They may be required as part of a court order to comply with assessment or to work with the therapist, and so they may be outwardly compliant, but inwardly reluctant to engage with therapy or assessment. Clients may be seductive, evasive or downright untruthful about events in an attempt to persuade the therapist that significant change has occurred or to support a particular outcome in court. It is a fine line between being compassionate and being a push over. It helps to constantly re-evaluate the quality of the therapeutic relationship – ask yourself, am I being seduced/manipulated/framed? Here good self-knowledge and reflective awareness supported by effective supervision is essential.

Ensure that the therapeutic or assessment work keeps alive to the goals that are set by the courts, probation services, or Youth Offending Team. Constantly revisit the goals and aims of the work so the client is aware of what is expected of them. One forensic practitioner recommends that we should read the novel *Lying on the Couch* (Yalom 1996). She says that it is a great way to learn about making mistakes!

Therapists working with offenders may be faced with ethical dilemmas, e.g. they may be told about breaches of bail conditions, breach of the terms of their probation, or about new offences for which the client has not been caught, but the therapist may be asked not to mention this in their report because it will cause punishment for re-offending etc. This work therefore needs clear boundaries agreed in advance with the client and good supervision to support the therapist. Contracts with clients may need to be regularly re-negotiated to adjust to changing circumstances.

10.5.7 Risk assessment

Risk assessment for forensic work is absolutely necessary; this is true for all therapy, but particularly so for those working with offenders and clients with severe mental dysfunction. Consider whether any element of risk exists to you or to others, especially to any children in the environment. For risk assessment, see Tasker (2010) (BACP Information Sheet P.13).

> **Checklist: Issues to consider for risk assesment in forensic work**
>
> - Might the client become aggressive?
> - Can aggression be handled safely?
> - What general protections or safeguarding procedures may be appropriate?
> - If the therapist works in premises with children or vulnerable adults present, are they safe from this client?
> - Ensure safe practice by never being in the building on your own.
> - Keep phone numbers private etc.
> - Ensure good security, with alarms if necessary.
> - If necessary, have a third party in the room. This can be negotiated with the client, and can be helpful for the client to feel re-assured.
> - It is useful to have a pre-arranged contact with a colleague who will raise the alarm if not contacted at an agreed time.

10.6 Interface and managing movement between forensic practice and other contexts

Earlier in the chapter we touched on the necessity of information sharing in the context of forensic work. Inevitably, there is sharing of information with the court, and in most cases, even though the court controls dissemination of the evidence, all or part of assessments and reports are likely to be shared with other parties in the case.

Those working with children in hospitals, residential care or secure accommodation may need to liaise with education, social services, or health care personnel. Some children and young people may need the assistance of specialist help for trauma treatment, substance abuse, self-harm, eating disorders, etc.

Therapists working with adult offenders in prison, or young people in young offender institutions, etc. may need to liaise with a range of people including probation services, youth offending teams, police, social services, education, health care personnel and possibly specialist units or organisations (e.g. treatment for trauma, substance abuse, sex addiction, eating disorders etc.). Some of these specialist areas of therapeutic work are addressed in this book.

10.6.1 Managing communication and information sharing between professionals

Witnesses involved in forensic work may get unexpected phone calls from social care workers, other experts, police or lawyers asking for a 'quick off the record chat …'. Take care. In court work, there is no such animal as 'an off the record chat'. All conversations and meetings should be noted or recorded in some way as evidence of what was discussed and opinions given. Many an 'off the record' conversation has later become the subject of question by an enthusiastic advocate to a forensic witness in court, and if anything that was said was unclear, unfair, hasty or inappropriate, then the witness has only themselves to blame for any subsequent embarrassment.

Information relevant to court cases should be shared with other professionals and parties on the basis of a court order with specific directions, or on a genuine 'need to know' basis, which is then carefully noted.

Government and public authority records are regulated by the Freedom of Information Act 2000 and the Data Protection Act 1998, which require that the client should have access to information held about them, with safeguards. Clients should be made aware of the nature and extent of the sharing of information about them and they should have given express consent for this disclosure. See Bond and Sandhu (2005) and Bond and Mitchels (2008), pp. 55–71 for duties with regard to notes and records; pp. 92–102 for sharing information between professionals; and pp. 116–25 for consent and capacity issues in relation to decisions by and for adults, children and young people.

Therapists may find that the 'Caldicott Principles' are helpful in making decisions about when to share information. In 1997, the Caldicott Committee delivered the

Report on the Review of Patient-Identifiable Information (available from the Department of Health website www.dh.gov.uk). That report included recommendations on information sharing within the NHS and between the NHS and non-NHS organisations, embodied in six principles (the 'Caldicott Principles') which are set out in Chapter 1 at 1.4.3 above. The Department of Health produces the *Caldicott Guardian Manual* (DH 2010b), which can be obtained through the DH website. The government's intention to regularly review and update the *Manual* is an example of the present intention to encourage and monitor openness in practice. In pursuance of the Caldicott Report, the Department of Health set up the National Confidentiality and Security Advisory Body in the year 2000 and began to develop protocols for information sharing between agencies and organisations, for example in child abuse investigations (see Chapter 8. The Disclosure Checklist in Chapter 1 at 1.4.1 may also prove helpful).

Most communication between professionals in court cases is by the sharing of reports or by arranged experts meetings. The lawyers will usually arrange these meetings and notes will be taken. If any additional information is required from an expert in a case (for example, a progress report on an assessment and estimate of time when it will be completed), it is good legal practice for the other parties to ask the solicitor instructing the expert to elicit the information from the witness.

10.7 Courtroom etiquette

People entering a court building are likely to be security screened. At court, criminal cases will be listed in a notice in the public area, indicating the number of the court in which they will be heard. Criminal and private family law cases are listed by name. Confidential adoption and child protection cases are listed by the name of the local authority and/or a reference number. The court ushers, known as macers in Scotland (usually in black gowns), are a reliable source of information, and will ask for the names of the advocates and witnesses in each case as they arrive. The ushers will need to know where to find you when required to give evidence, so always let them know where you are, particularly if you are going out of the building or off to the canteen, etc. Be prepared for long waiting times. Be aware of the feelings of others who are waiting, and also the need to maintain confidentiality at court, so avoid getting drawn into inappropriate social conversation, or talking about the case in public places outside court.

Ordinary witnesses of fact have to wait outside the courtroom to prevent them being influenced by hearing what others say. In family cases, expert witnesses may be invited to sit in and hear all the evidence to help them to formulate an opinion on the basis of all available information. Sit near the instructing advocate if possible – they may need your help as the case progresses. In Scotland, expert witnesses may be allowed to sit in to hear the evidence of other experts, or of factual matters, but this is strictly by permission from the bench only. The Advocate representing the party who has instructed you may wish to seek permission for you to sit in during other evidence from the judge.

Switch off pagers and mobiles before entering the courtroom. In the courtroom, find somewhere to put down any coats, bags and other unnecessary items before going into the witness box. Being calm and uncluttered as you walk there helps confidence.

Silence is observed in the court while in session – audible asides or critical comment of other witnesses is highly unprofessional. If you need to communicate urgently with the advocate, you can pass a note or whisper if the comment is short. If a longer consultation is necessary, the advocate may seek a short adjournment.

In the witness box, after taking the oath or affirmation, it is courteous to remain standing until invited to sit. Behave with dignity, and no matter how irritating or irrelevant the questions seem to be, remain calm and courteous. Do not venture opinions on topics unless they can be justified.

Expert witnesses may have to tolerate anger, sarcasm, and sometimes even obtuseness from advocates, but resist the urge to crumble, or to respond with defensiveness or a show of skill. Remember that you are the expert in your field of work, and that the court is genuinely interested in hearing what you have to say. If you can justify your actions professionally as a therapist, then there is nothing to fear in court.

Sometimes advocates may try to interrupt a witness who is mid-way through making a point (perhaps to prevent the witness saying something), but it is difficult for an advocate to interrupt a witness who is speaking directly to the judge. Make a habit of listening to the advocate's question, and then turning round to face the magistrates or judge and direct the answers to them, and not to the advocate who asked the question. It would then be discourteous for an advocate to try to interrupt you whilst you are speaking to the court.

If you are interrupted before saying all you wanted, say so and return to the unfinished point before answering the next question.

Speak clearly and slowly enough for the judge and others to take notes of the points they need to record. Do not rush evidence; take time to think before answering questions. Be prepared to refer to notes or records before answering. Be accurate and concise. If the answer is not known or unclear, do not be afraid to say so. Cross examination provides an opportunity to reconsider, correct or modify previous evidence. Be ready to concede points made by counsel if they are a reasonable interpretation of the facts. Remember that in criminal cases the jury may have to rely on what they hear in court.

Make sure that all notes and records are kept in a folder or easily accessible, and that you know where to find everything, so that you don't have to scrabble around in a file looking for something, or worse, drop all the papers in a heap on the floor! Advocates and others may ask to see your case notes and records. Disclosure of these is a matter for the court to decide. If reluctant to disclose notes, or in doubt, seek directions from the judge or magistrate.

Computer records may be printed and produced, provided they are properly verified. Research findings, references, etc., may be used in court, but be prepared for cross-examination by an advocate who may well question the methodology, research sampling methods, hypotheses, aims, and evaluations, so ensure that any work cited and relied upon is well understood. Bring extra copies to court for the judge and the advocates.

Experts may wish to confer with each other, and it is therefore courteous to do so in the presence of their respective instructing advocates, or at least with their knowledge. Experts should demonstrate their independence by non-partisan behaviour. It is wise to consult the instructing lawyer first about any request to confer with another party or witness. During an adjournment – for example, for lunch – the court does not permit discussion by anyone with a witness when they are still in the process of giving evidence.

Witnesses should not leave the court building until the court has given consent for release. Make a habit of asking for the court's consent to be released at the end of giving your evidence, then if the court might need you to come back again, you will either be asked to stay (in this case you should expect to be paid for your extra time) or the court will make arrangements to contact you if necessary. Try to make a calm, unhurried exit, picking up notes efficiently, and leaving with dignity. Bring a diary; if the case is adjourned it is helpful to know dates available for future hearings.

11 Counselling in Police and Home Office Settings

Work in the context of the police and Home Office includes both care of the professionals involved, and of those who are living in the custodial system. These settings are all potentially intrinsically stressful and traumatic for police officers and staff. Equally, in the Home Office context, perhaps the majority of employees are Prison Officers and staff, who also have stressful jobs, where emotions have to be managed in a highly contained environment.

Both police and prison officers have to work within a highly regulated system, strictly bound by rules and law, with the added stress of the 'goldfish bowl' environment where, for most, their actions are visible to (and may impact on) many others. Their emotional reaction to events or people, therefore, must be managed in accordance with their environment.

Those who are on remand in prison awaiting trial or serving custodial sentences for criminal offences also may receive professional counselling or psychotherapy, which again, is provided in the context of a highly regulated environment in which both therapist and client are bound by rules, regulations and procedures. This has an inevitable impact on the work carried out. We live in times where, in the UK, many young people are locked up and the challenges to those working with young people in custody include not only those inherent in the job, but of public protection, and how to work in close cooperation with other agencies.

The key rehabilitation and other programmes within the prison system and those operated by the Probation Service in the community tend to employ a mainly cognitive behavioural (CBT) approach, but may be integrative. The CBT approach is used in relation to a range of offences, e.g. sexual abuse, domestic and other forms of violence, anger management, etc and for the development of self-awareness and of thinking skills. Longer term specialist therapeutic programmes are available in some prisons. With regard to other forms of therapeutic intervention within the prison system, e.g. one-to-one counselling, provision has been made, in some instances, under mental health care, the NHS being one such body that has provided this service. However, this may be dependent on resources, budgetary considerations and who is responsible for providing and funding the service, and, perhaps, more importantly, being specific as to why this particular therapy may be beneficial. A quantitative measure showing that therapy can produce specific results and change is more likely to be the guiding principle for determining whether a counsellor or therapist is employed in the criminal justice system. This same principle is also evident with regard to the provision of accredited Sex Offender Treatment Programmes, which have been subject to research evaluation. The principle of 'what works best' would guide best practice and achieving the outcome of risk reduction. For useful research reports, see the publications list at www.justice.gov.uk

There is another context, too, that of the staff who work with asylum seekers and refugees who are residing in accommodation awaiting Home Office decisions about their future. Many of the stressors for staff may be similar to those of prison officers, but the stressors for residents in the units are often related to their earlier life experiences, and some may suffer from anxiety, depression and post-traumatic stress.

This chapter explores these specific contexts for therapeutic work, looking at the law and process issues which apply over and above the generic issues applicable to counselling and psychotherapy. Websites for reference include www.hmprison-service.gov.uk which lists several agencies and organisations. Information relating to the prison service in Scotland can be found at www.sps.gov.uk. See also the Counselling in Prison Network at www.pn.counselling.co.uk. Its annual conference in 2010 was hosted by York St John University, and the report on the academic site, www.w3.yorksj.ac.uk, has useful material and connections – see 11.2.6 below. The Lucy Faithfull Foundation, www.lucyfaithfull.org, is a child protection charity committed to reducing the risk of children being sexually abused. Part of its work is to treat known offenders and their families.

BACP has a new Criminal Justice Forum (see www.cjf.bacp.co.uk) which has a list of members, information and resources, useful for therapists with clients involved with the criminal justice system. Other organisations that may be of assistance are listed in Useful Resources at the end of this book.

11.1 Legal features of the context

11.1.1 Support for police officers, prison officers and staff

Many police forces and prison services now use external Employee Assistance Programmes (EAPs) to provide counselling and psychotherapy for their staff. Therapists working for these EAPs will find that their contract is usually carefully drafted to cover issues such as venue for the therapy, payments, record keeping and confidentiality. Staff working for the police, Crown Prosecution Service (CPS) and Home Office may be governed by the official secrets legislation as well as general law and government guidance applicable to the running of the Home Office and the criminal justice system. Therapists working with police and Home Office staff may have constraints relating to the client material disclosed in therapy. This may leave little room for therapists to negotiate the terms of their contracts with EAP providers, and so therapists working for EAPs may have to choose simply whether (or not) to accept the terms of the contract proposed.

Some EAPs now keep record systems that are created and stored electronically, with records sent to the EAP online. We would expect these online systems to lie within the definitions for registration set out in the Data Protection Act, and therapists using them should therefore check whether they are liable to register with the Information Commissioner's Office. Guidance as to the scope of the data protection legislation is available on the Internet at www.dataprotection.gov.uk, and see also Bond and Mitchels (2008: 58–66).

11.1.2 Support for adults resident in a custodial setting

When counselling and psychotherapy are provided for those resident in a custodial setting, there are limits on the work that can be carried out, which are imposed by working within a strict prison system, for example the venue, timing, privacy, record keeping etc.

With regard to Sex Offender Treatment Programmes (SOTP) offering group therapy, this would not be available for prisoners on remand awaiting trial. This only becomes operative once the offender is sentenced, followed by an assessment for suitability by the psychology department. Eligibility is dependent on the offender's motivation to address his offending behaviour, his acknowledgement of culpability or accepting some responsibility for his wrong doing. There are alternative programmes for men with learning difficulties known as SOTP Adapted Programmes. The offender is not under an obligation to attend a prison-based programme but would be aware that his acceptance and acknowledgement of culpability and willingness to address his offending behaviour through an accredited programme would be a major factor in determining his eligibility for parole.

A difficulty that we have seen in our work is that therapists are likely to have little leeway in negotiating the parameters of their work with prisoners. If the prison staff respect and value the provision of therapy, they can make the therapists' work easier by facilitating use of rooms, materials, time, etc.

There is some risk that other prisoners who stigmatise those receiving therapy may openly oppose or try to disrupt therapy. However, this is unlikely in those prisons that provide an exclusive regime solely for sex offenders and programmes of therapeutic work to address the sexual offending. Prisoners who find themselves in these types of institutions are likely to have elected or agreed to be sent there. Practitioners have told us that because of the segregation of sex offenders to these establishments and their motivation to work on their offending behaviour, there is less likelihood of disruption and opposition in these particular institutions.

Support following release

Post-release Sex Offender Programmes available in the community are obligatory and either take the form of a requirement within a Community Order or as a condition of the prison licence following release.

After-care is important. On release, there may be many hardships and temptations for a released prisoner, which can cause reversion to offending behaviour or old habits. Support on 'the outside' is therefore important, and therapists can liaise (with client consent) with support systems in so far as they are available, to organise help before release.

The after-care provision provided by the Probation Service is built into the statutory supervision on prison licence. The purpose of the prison licence is, primarily, to ensure that conditions are adhered to in order to prevent or reduce the risk of further offending. Help and support are provided, in this context, with regard to accommodation and employment. Statutory supervision on release is not applicable to those prisoners who have served all of their sentence in prison, i.e. been released on their Sentence Expiry Date (SED), which means, in effect, that no statutory support from the Probation Service after the SED has passed will be provided. So far as we are aware, there is no voluntary after-care provision once the statutory obligations have passed.

Probation Hostels are known as Probation and Bail Hostels or Approved Hostels. Depending on need or the offence, prisoners may be assessed for hostel accommodation on release.

The Useful Resources section has a list of foundations which may be able to help those who have left prison.

11.1.3 Support for young people in youth custody

In England, Wales and Northern Ireland the age of criminal responsibility is 10 years; in Scotland, the Criminal Justice and Licensing (Scotland) Act 2010 raised the Scottish limit from 8 to 12 years and in Eire it is 12 years. The UN Committee on the Rights of the Child has stated that an age of criminal responsibility below 12 is 'not acceptable'; see Jacobsen and Talbot 2009. These limits are lower than most other countries in Europe and are the cause of some international criticism. In autumn 2010, after a trial of two 11-year-old boys at the Old Bailey on an indictment for rape, there began a political move to raise this age. The youth justice system is different in England, Northern Ireland and Wales. The Youth Justice Agency was established in Northern Ireland in 2003, with restorative justice through 'Youth Conferences' as a strong feature. The courts may refer young people to the youth conferences, with certain restrictions. In Wales, local government structures are devolved and so function differently from England, but the principles on which the Youth Justice Board (YJB) currently operates in the UK are the same. However, the YJB is likely to be abolished and replaced by a new youth justice structure that is yet to be finalised. The www.yjb.gov.uk website is now supported by a much bigger website – www.justice.gov.uk. Information aimed for the general public will go to www. directgov.uk.

The new justice.gov.uk website will encompass content from the Ministry of Justice, Her Majesty's Courts Service, the Prison Service, the Legal Services Commission and many other justice agencies whose websites are also closing. The content of this new justice site will cover the administration, regulation and scrutiny of justice.

Each local authority in England and Wales has a youth offending team, made up of representatives from the police, Probation Service, social services, health, education, drugs and alcohol misuse and housing officers. Each YOT is managed by a YOT manager who is responsible for coordinating the work of the youth justice services.

The YOT will organise pre-trial assessments for the young person. The factors considered in the assessment process are set out in the website, and will include: criminal history (if they have already offended), education, health (including mental health), family, environment and attitudes. The YOT will then:

- make a recommendation to the court on a suitable sentence
- identify the activities that the young person will be required to complete as part of their sentence
- identify whether work needs to be done with their parents/carers
- identify how to protect the public.

If a custodial sentence is made, then the YOT will consider the best secure environment for the young person. For details of the assessment process and criteria used, see *The Common Assessment Framework, Asset and Onset: Guidance for Youth Justice Practitioners* (B295), and see also for guidance *YOT Substance Misuse Worker* (B271), both of which should be available from 31 March 2011 either at www.justice.gov.uk or at www.directgov.uk.

11.1.4 Support for asylum seekers, refugees and the staff caring for them

The UK Border Agency, run by the Home Office, is responsible for securing the UK border and for controlling migration into the UK. It also considers applications for citizenship and asylum. For definitions of its role, see www.ukba.homeoffice.gov.uk.

The website also provides details of refugee, asylum, asylum seeker, the relevant guidance, immigration rules and immigration law. Refugees and asylum seekers may have experienced trauma in their lives – often this will be the reason for their flight to safety. They may suffer from physical illness or mental distress, e.g. anxiety, depression or post-traumatic stress (see 11.1.5). Therapists who work with these experiences may suffer stress, potentially leading to compassion fatigue and burnout, with symptoms including emotional exhaustion, general fatigue, lack of confidence, a sense of helplessness, and perhaps disturbances in appetite or sleep, etc. (Arcel et al. 1998; Franciskovic et al. 1998; Urlic 1999).

Regular reflection on practice, self-awareness and supervision can help to spot the onset of burn out, and to address it.

The Refugee Council offices in London help asylum seekers and refugees in the Greater London Area, see www.refugeecouncil.org.uk. Their specialist team operates an assessment, referral and casework service to help meet the health and mental health needs of vulnerable refugees and asylum seekers. They use the 'Therapeutic Casework Model' which combines advocacy for refugees' practical needs with counselling skills and therapeutic care. There are many other agencies that assist refugees, some linked with specific areas, populations or cultures. Embassies and local authorities may help with contact details.

There are a number of immigration removal centres around the UK, some managed by non-government agencies, where adults, children and families may be held securely while their case is investigated. Following government concerns about the conditions for children and families, a review is currently being held in relation to detention of children for immigration purposes.

Therapists working with asylum seekers and refugees cannot ignore the cultural differences in recognising and addressing aspects of mental health, e.g. the difference between Western and non-Western cultural perceptions and ways of dealing with anxiety, depression and post-traumatic stress (Bracken 1993, 2002; Burchell 2005; Marsella et al. 1996).

11.2 Practice issues

11.2.1 Confidentiality in the context of police and CPS work

Those working for the police and Home Office are subject to the Official Secrets legislation as well as government guidance for the running of the criminal justice system. Section 5 of the Official Secrets Act 1989 (OSA) provides that:

> 5. – (1) Subsection (2) below applies where –
>
> (a) any information, document or other article protected against disclosure by the foregoing provisions of this Act has come into a person's possession as a result of having been –
>
> (i) disclosed (whether to him or another) by a Crown servant or government contractor without lawful authority; or
>
> (ii) entrusted to him by a Crown servant or government contractor on terms requiring it to be held in confidence or in circumstances in which the Crown servant or government contractor could reasonably expect that it would be so held; or
>
> (iii) disclosed (whether to him or another) without lawful authority by a person to whom it was entrusted as mentioned in sub-paragraph (ii) above; and
>
> (b) the disclosure without lawful authority of the information, document or article by the person into whose possession it has come is not an offence under any of those provisions.

(2) Subject to subsections (3) and (4) below, the person into whose possession the information, document or article has come is guilty of an offence if he discloses it without lawful authority knowing, or having reasonable cause to believe, that it is protected against disclosure by the foregoing provisions of this Act and that it has come into his possession as mentioned in subsection (1) above.

From this it seems that, if in the course of personal counselling for staff, therapists come into possession of information that has been disclosed to them in contravention of Section 1 of the OSA, they may also be bound to secrecy by section 5 and subject to criminal penalty for unauthorised disclosure.

Therapists working for staff support services should expect that the provision of therapy will be made subject to the same conditions of confidentiality as those that operate for staff, and look for clauses in their contracts with EAP providers, or with the employing organisation. Therapists and staff are also both bound in civil law by their contracts of service or for services, see Chapter 1 at 1.2 and Mitchels and Bond (2010: Chapter 4).

Therapists who work with police or CPS staff privately (i.e. outside the staff support service of the organisation), should discuss confidentiality issues with their clients, and negotiate their therapeutic contract accordingly. They should be aware that material facts disclosed by clients in therapy which are relevant to any criminal investigations with which their client is (or has been) involved, may be subject to a request for disclosure in the public interest, or conversely, to a requirement under the OSA not to do so. Note that the principle of lawful disclosure in the public interest does not afford a defence in cases involving unlawful disclosure of official secrets, see the House of Lords decision in *R v Shayler* [2002] HL The Times Law Reports 22 March 2002. For general discussion of confidentiality and disclosure, see Bond and Mitchels (2008), Bond and Sandhu (2005) and Bond et al. (2010).

Checklist: Practical approaches to OSA issues

- Check (in general terms, not related to a specific client) with the employer if OSA applies to the work situation and how it affects the work of the clients.
- If the OSA applies, discuss with each client before starting work with them, whether the material they want to bring to therapy might be OSA-sensitive.
- Where it is known that material may be OSA-sensitive, client and therapist should discuss the issue of confidentiality at the outset of their work and to agree a practical way forward. Often, for example, clients can work effectively in therapy by focusing on their internal psychological processes but sometimes it is hard to do this without also revealing external factors that raise issues of security. Therapy for post-traumatic stress, if caused by a work-related incident, might be very difficult to manage without drifting into OSA-sensitive areas.
- With the client's consent, see if there is a possibility of agreement with the employer that the client may work with OSA-sensitive material and the therapist also agrees to be subject to a duty of confidentiality under the OSA.

- If a client discloses OSA-sensitive material unlawfully in therapy (i.e. without appropriate clearance), then it is our view that the therapist will be under an obligation to maintain secrecy under s. 5 OSA. An issue then arises as to how the therapist deals with any OSA-sensitive information in the context of their own therapeutic supervision. If any therapist or supervisor is concerned about their legal position in such a situation, take legal advice on the specific circumstances of your case. Professional insurers will often provide or fund legal advice, as part of their cover.

11.2.2 Confidentiality in the context of work in the prison system

Those working in the prison system may be subject to the official secrets legislation as well as to government guidance. See the discussion of Section 5 of the Official Secrets Act 1989 in 11.2.1 above.

There may be additional internal rules for the running of the prison. Therapists working for staff support services should expect that the provision of therapy for staff will be made subject to those conditions, and look for clauses in any contracts of employment or for services. Therapists and staff are bound by their contracts – see Chapter 1 at 1.2 and Mitchels and Bond (2010: Chapter 4). There are criminal sanctions for non-compliance with the official secrets legislation.

Maintaining confidentiality of client identity, information, case notes and other information from therapy is vital in a custodial setting. Officers and staff will not wish those in custody to be aware that they receive counselling, and off-site provision of services is important.

Those in custody may be stigmatised, either by receiving therapy, or by the nature of their offence or lifestyle, once it becomes known, and this may be exacerbated by provision of specialist therapy, e.g. if paedophiles or addicts receive group therapy in a certain place, on specific days, etc.

Records of therapy may be targeted for all sorts of purposes and should be strictly safeguarded. Any sexually explicit material of any sort (i.e. from publications, court papers or notes from therapy) can acquire a 'sale-value' as masturbatory material and therapists working in this context should be aware that attempts may be made to copy or steal such material.

11.2.3 Fitness to work: Advice, feedback and management issues

Much of police and Home Office work is, in itself, stressful. Where therapists employed in this context are returning to work following illness or stress, they should balance any desire to return to work as quickly as possible against the legal expectation that they should be fit to practise on their return.

Employees who are clients may also feel a pressure to return to work as soon as possible, particularly in times of staff shortage or where they have expertise in short supply. When referrals for therapy are made by occupational health departments, they may expect feedback about the client's progress in therapy. Some therapists may be under a contractual duty from their EAP or the workplace to report back to occupational health, personnel or human resources departments about the client's progress. This feedback should be provided only with the knowledge and consent of the client. The therapist should also be aware of the terms of their work with the organisation and agree these terms with the client before starting therapy. Staff will usually have a clause in their contract of employment allowing such feedback to be given, where necessary. If a client does not wish feedback about their progress to be given (but the therapist is obliged contractually to provide it), then this issue should be clarified as part of the therapeutic contract at the outset, before therapy begins.

11.2.4 Substance misuse in the prison system

The misuse of drugs and alcohol continues, even in the closed context of the prison system, despite any routine safeguards that are put in place. Remedial therapeutic work may be necessary for addicts to prevent substance misuse in prison and prepare clients for continuing abstinence on leaving custody.

The Rehabilitation for Addicted Prisoners Trust (RAPt) runs 12 Steps programmes in prisons, requiring total abstinence, see www.rapt.org.uk. It earned Home Office accreditation in 2000. One of us has experience as a group supervisor for the counsellors providing a RAPt prison programme, and in that time, learned much about the prison system, the nature of addiction, and the difficulties facing the therapists in the project!

The standardised RAPt programme is a three-stage intervention: assessment, primary treatment and after-care. The first assessment stage gives basic information about drugs and their effects. It also motivates participants to start examining the effect of their using on their lives, and introduces them to the 12 Steps concepts. The 12-week primary treatment phase is mainly based around group work, employing a range of cognitive behavioural treatment processes, and focusing on creating awareness of the issues around drug use and its impact, effects of past behaviour on others, positive goal-setting, relapse prevention strategies and personal responsibility. The steps take clients through breaking down denial, encouraging motivation to build a new life, looking at obstacles, strengths, challenges, etc. and to make plans for change. The programme includes therapy groups, lectures meditation and, where available, complementary therapies and sports activities. There may be specific pieces of work to complete where necessary, e.g. anger or grief assignments. On completion of the primary programme, clients are invited to have an ending ceremony where they invite the counselling team, family members, their prison officer and their peers to give their honest feedback on their progress.

The Aftercare programme focuses on a package of compulsory workshops covering a number of elements, including specific elements of relapse prevention and skills training. These are delivered from within the primary treatment teams at each location and no prisoner can be said to have formally graduated from RAPt until he or she has completed these workshops.

Following completion of the three-stage programme, graduates are expected to move on to other wings and to help to create an anti-drug culture, looking for work in the prison workshops or participating in other structured or therapeutic activities. Some may help other prisoners through the programme and act as peer role models. After release, they should be linked into proper support services in the community, and have a stable address in which to live.

11.2.5 Violence, harassment and abuse in custodial contexts

The potential causes of violence in a custodial setting are many and varied. They may include: the stress of being deprived of liberty, sexual frustration, the impact of stressors, post-traumatic stress from earlier experiences triggered by current events, and also the dynamics of shame.

Some people in custody (and some of their custodians) will have suffered from abuse and violence in their childhood and/or adult lives. Some will be serving sentences for violence to others. Research suggests that there may be links between the symptoms of post-traumatic stress – see the *Diagnostic and Statistical Manual of Psychiatric Disorders* (APA 2000: 463–468) – and subsequent violence. The 'avoidance of stimuli', an emotional numbing restricting the range of feelings and emotions, may lead to a lack of empathy with others (seeing their point of view) and a failure to notice or interpret the signals of others accurately. The 'hypersensitivity' of post-traumatic stress may lead to volatility, which if coupled with certain personality traits or emotional lability in a person who is sensitive to perceived threats, might, if uncontrolled, lead to outbursts of violence. Therapists will be aware of clients (some of whom may be survivors of prolonged or repeated violence or abuse) who say they have 'a short fuse' and when aroused by a perceived threat or insult can, instead of seeking discussion or apology, become angry and react quickly, with little consideration of the circumstances or impact of their behaviour on others (Mitchels 2006: 102–4; 108–10).

The UK National Advisory Group on Sexual Violence and Trauma was founded to research and to develop best practice in the engagement, management and treatment of female and male offenders who are resident in the custodial setting. Currently Chaired by Peter Jones FBACP, the organisation includes specialism in the treatment of those who have suffered sexual abuse or violence, and the website has useful research information for practitioners.

Jonathan Asser founded the Shame/Violence Intervention project (SVI), which won the 2008 BACP Innovation Award. SVI is a programme that works with violently enacting prisoners in a new way, inhabiting the dynamics of violent gang culture in the heat of the escalating moment to achieve de-escalation, alongside the capacity to nurture and repair social bonds. See BACP's Criminal Justice Forum website for more details.

People in custody, especially for long periods, may experience sexual frustration and seek outlets for this, and this, with power struggles, may be reasons for the development of various forms of violence within prisons. Harassment and bullying may take sexual forms. A response to this by staff may be segregation of the perpetrator(s) or, more usually, isolation of the victim, for their own protection. Such treatment may in itself feel punitive, and it is possible that if segregation is perceived to be unfair or deleterious to the client's mental health, it may perhaps be challenged under the prison rules by the client with the support of their therapist.

11.2.6 Equality issues and the balance of power

In a custodial setting, the custodians hold considerable power. They may exercise this power over those in custody or over other staff or therapists working in custodial settings. We would expect that the abuse of power will be prohibited in the prison rules, but it may be difficult to see and take action against it. Victims may be reluctant to report it for fear of reprisals or staff may feel ashamed that they cannot prevent it occurring and feel at risk of being told that they are not good enough at their job. We have been told by practitioners of instances of the abuse of power by prison officers and by prisoners, at many levels. Aggressive acts range from pushing and shoving, to threats or direct violence.

Aggressive acts by staff or other prisoners are not always overt. They may also be subtle, and therefore difficult to prove. They may be motivated by punitive intent or disapproval of the offender or of the therapy, e.g. keeping back someone on a treatment programme until they are late for groups; withholding materials intended for writing, drawing, or creative expression; by making people wait in cold or uncomfortable places for long periods of time, perhaps without access to toilet facilities; or, in one instance, walking past a hospital wing where mentally ill patients were deprived of smoking materials and blowing cigarette smoke in through open windows. Such subtle acts of aggression are difficult to prove, and so complaints about those situations are much more difficult to make. The impact of such acts on their victims, however, can be immense, particularly when the incidents are cumulative or prolonged.

List of Cases, Practice Directions, Government and Professional Guidance, Statutes, Statutory Instruments and EEC Directives

Cases

A v B plc and C ('Flitcroft') [2002] EWCA Civ 337; 3 WLR 542, reversing [2001] 1WLR 2341

Associated Provincial Picture Houses Ltd v Wednesbury Corpn [1948] 1 KB 223

Boehringer Ingelheim Ltd and Others v. Vetplus Ltd [2007] Times Law Reports 27 June

Brown and Another v. Bennett and Others [2 November 2000] 1 Times Law Reports, Chancery Division

Council for the Regulation of Healthcare Professionals v *General Medical Council and Southall* [2005] EWHC 579 (Admin)

Dunlop v Selfridge [1915] AC 847 at 855

Gillick v West Norfolk and Wisbech Area Health Authority and Another [1986]1 AC 1212; [1985] 3 All ER 402 (HL) [1986] 1 FLR 224

Hatton v Sutherland; Barber v Somerset County Council; Jones v Sandwell Metropolitan Council; Bishop v Baker Refractories Ltd. [12 February 2002] CA, Times Law Reports, the Court of Appeal (CA)

Hippolyte v Bexley L.B.C. [1995] PIQR (309) CA

Kelly v DPP [2002] EWHC Admin 1428 166 JP 621

Lampleigh v Braithwait [1615] Hob 105

London Borough of Lewisham v Malcolm [2008] UKHL 43

Majrowski v Guy's and St Thomas's NHS Trust [2006] UKHL 34

Meadow v General Medical Council [2006] EWHC 146 (Admin)[2006] 1 WLR 1452

Melhuish v Redbridge Citizens Advice Bureau [2005] IRLR 419, EAT

Nally v Grace Community Church of the Valley (1980) No NCC 15668-B, L.A. County Super. Ct, Cal. filed March 31, 1980; 157 Cal. App. 3d 912, 204 Cal. Rptr. 303 (1984)

Portsmouth Hospitals NHS Trust v. Wyatt and another [2005] EWCA Civ 1181, [2005] 1 WLR 3995

Pratt v DPP [2001] EWHC 483

R v Cannings [2004] EWCA Crim 1 [2004] 1 WLR 2607

R v Clark [2003] EWCA Crim 1020, CA

R v Ealing District Health Authority, ex parte Fox [1993] 3 All ER 170

R v East Sussex County Council ex parte Tandy [1998] 2 All ER 769; *Re T (A Minor)* [1998] 1 CCLR 352.

R v Gloucestershire County Council ex parte Barry [1997] 1 CCLR 40; [1997] 2 WLR 459 HL

R v Islington LBC ex parte Rixon (Jonathan) [1998] 1 CCLR 119, (1996) The Times 17 April

R v Manchester CC ex parte Stennett and two other actions [2002] 2CCLR 500; [2002] UKHL 34

R v Shayler [2002] HL The Times Law Reports 22 March 2002.

Re A (Children) (Contact: Expert evidence) [2001] Times Law Reports 27 February

Re B (Minors) (Sexual Abuse: Standard of Proof) [2008] UKHL 35; [2008] WLR (D) 186

Re C (a Minor) (Medical Treatment: Court's jurisdiction), 21 March 1997 The Times Law Reports

Re K (Secure Accommodation Order: Right to Liberty) [2001] 1 FLR 526

Re L (Medical Treatment: Gillick Competency, [1998] 2 FLR 810, [1998] Fam Law 591

Re O (a Minor) (Care Order: Education Procedure) [1992] 2 FLR 7

Re O (a Minor) (Medical Treatment), 19 March 1993 The Times Law Reports

Re W (A Minor) (Medical Treatment: Court's Jurisdiction) [1992] 3 WLR 758

S v DPP [2008] EWHC (Admin) 438

W v Edgell and others [1990] 1 All ER 835; Ch 359 (CA) affirming [1989] 1 All ER 801

X v Y [1988] 2 All ER 648

Williams v Eady (1893) 10 TLR

X (Minors) v Bedfordshire County Council ELR WLR [1995] 2 AC 633; [1995] 3 WLR 152; [1995] 3 All ER 353, HL(E)

YL (by her litigation friend, the Official Solicitor) v Birmingham City Council [2007] 1MHLR 85

Practice Directions

Practice Direction: Experts in Family Proceedings Relating to Children [2008] 1 WLR 1027 (EFPRC 2008)

Government and Professional Publications and Guidance

General Government publications and news

For England and Wales see www.official-documents.gov.uk, www.direct. gov.uk, www.hmso.gov.uk, www.publications.parliament.uk, www.legislation.gov.uk and www.wales.gov.uk/

National Assembly for Wales Information on guidance in Wales: www.wales.gov. uk/

For Northern Ireland see www.northernireland.gov.uk

For Scotland see www.scotland.gov.uk/Publications and www.scottish parliament.uk.

UK Government changes to websites: the government is making major changes to their websites in an effort to reduce the complexity of numbers and gather information together in one place. Watch for updates in response to fresh government website changes. We hope that there will also be redirections in place from the obsolete sites to make searches easier.

For all Department of Health (DH) and Department for Education (DfE) (prior to May 2010, the Department for Children, Schools and Families [DCSF], and prior to June 2007, the Department for Education and Skills, [DfES]) publications, including those listed below, see websites www.dh.gov.uk and www.education. gov.uk for pdfs

From 31 March 2011, much of the Youth Justice Board website entries at www.yjb. gov.uk will move to www.justice.gov.uk and to www.directgov.uk.

The new justice.gov.uk website will encompass content from the Ministry of Justice, Her Majesty's Courts Service, the Prison Service, the Legal Services Commission and many other justice agencies whose websites are also closing. The content of this new justice site will cover the administration, regulation and scrutiny of justice. The website www.directgov.uk will contain material aimed for the general public.

Assessing Children in Need and Their Families – Practice Guidance (DH 2000) (companion volume to the *Framework*).

Building Bridges – A Guide to Arrangements for Inter-agency Working for the Care and Protection of Severely Mentally Ill People (DH 1995).

Care Management and Assessment: Practitioner's Guide (Department of Health and Social Services Inspectorate, 1991).

The Child's World: Assessing Children in Need, Training and Development Pack (DH 2000).

Community Care Assessment Directions 2004 (DH 2004) available as pdf at www.dh.gov.uk; *Confidentiality: NHS Code of Practice* (DH 2003); see also *The NHS Confidentiality Code of Practice: Supplementary Guidance: Public Interest Disclosures* (DH 2010).

Co-operating to Safeguard Children (DHSSPS 2003) available as a pdf at www.dhssp-sni.gov.uk.

Fair Access to Care Services – Guidance on Eligibility Criteria for Adult Social Care (DH 2002).

Framework for Assessment of Children in Need and Their Families (DH 2000).

The Gender Agenda – Research and Evidence (DCSF 2008) for this and reflections in the Gender Agenda Conference 2010, see websites www.education.gov.uk, and www.teachernet.gov.uk.

Information Sharing: Guidance for Practitioners and Managers (DCSF 2008).

Modern Standards and Service Models – Older People – National Service Framework for Older People (DH 2001).

Modernising Adult Social Care – What's Working (DH 2007).

Needs, Wishes and Feelings Pack, and the *Domestic Violence Tool Kit*. These are among the 'tools' produced by the Children and Family Court Advisory Service (CAF-CASS) for working with both children and adults.

People First: Care Management Guidance on Assessment and the Provision of Community Care (DH 1993).

Prioritising Need in the Context of Putting People First: a whole system approach to eligibility for social care – guidance on eligibility criteria for adult social care, England (DH 2010).

Protecting all God's Children: The Policy for Safeguarding Children in the Church of England (4th Edition 2010) see www.churchofengland.org/media/37378/protectingallgodschildren.pdf

Provision of Therapy for Child Witnesses Prior to a Criminal Trial: Practice Guidance and *Provision of Therapy for Vulnerable or Intimidated Adult Witnesses Prior to a Criminal Trial: Practice Guidance*, both available as pdfs at www.cps.gov.uk.

Safeguarding Children: Working Together under the Children Act 2004 (National Assembly for Wales 2007).

Special Report NHS Funding for Long Term Care – Investigation into complaints Nos E208/99-00 (DH 1995).

What to Do If You're Worried a Child Is Being Abused (DfES 2006).

Working Together to Safeguard Children: A Guide to Inter-Agency Working to Safeguard and Promote the Welfare of Children (DCSF 2010).

Disability Rights Commission

Making Access to Goods and Services Easier for the Disabled: a Practical Guide for Small Business and Other Small Service Providers (DRC, n.d.), available as a pdf at www.direct.gov.uk.

Equality and Human Rights Commission

Code of Practice on Equal Pay (Equal Opportunities Commission 2003), available as a pdf at www.equalityhumanrights.com.

Northern Ireland Office

Achieving Best Evidence in Criminal Proceedings (Northern Ireland): Guidance for Vulnerable Witnesses, including Children, available as a pdf at www.nio.gov.uk.

Scottish Government

Scottish Government publications are available as pdfs at www.scotland.gov.uk.

Code of Practice to Facilitate the Provision of Therapeutic Support to Child Witnesses in Court Proceedings (Scottish Executive 2006)

Interviewing Child Witnesses in Scotland – Supporting Child Witnesses Guidance Pack (Scottish Executive 2003)

Protecting Children – A Shared Responsibility: Guidance on Inter-Agency Co-operation (The Scottish Office 1998)

National Assembly for Wales

Information on guidance in Wales: www.wales.gov.uk/

Youth Justice

For young people in the secure estate monthly figures, see the Youth Justice Board monthly report at www.yjb.gov.uk, but note that from 31 March 2011, much of the Youth Justice Board website entries for England and Wales at www.yjb.gov.uk will move to www.justice.gov.uk and to www.directgov.uk

Information on Youth Justice in Northern Ireland: www.youthjusticeagencyni.gov.uk.

Information on Youth Justice in Scotland, see www.scotland.gov.uk, www.cjscotland.org.uk, and www.restorativejusticescotland.org.uk.

Professional Guidance

For Professional Guidance, see Useful Resources below.

Statutes and Statutory Instruments

Please note that these statutes and statutory instruments, with any updates to them, can be found by searching the title and date on www.legislation.gov.uk.

Statutes

Academies Act 2010

Adoption and Children Act 2002

Adoption and Children (Scotland) Act 2007

Adoption (Northern Ireland) Order 1987

Adults with Incapacity (Scotland) Act 2000

Age of Legal Capacity (Scotland) Act 1991

Age of Majority Act (Northern Ireland) 1969

Care Standards Act 2000

Children Act 1989

Children Act 2002

Children Act 2004

Children (Scotland) Act 1995

Children and Adoption Act 2006

Children and Young People (Northern Ireland) Order 2003

Children (Northern Ireland) Order 1995

Children (Leaving Care) Act (Northern Ireland) 2002

Children's Commissioner for Wales Act 2001

Civil Evidence Act 1972

Civil Partnership Act 2004

Commissioner for Children and Young People (Northern Ireland) Order 2003

Community Care (Delayed Discharges etc.) Act 2003

Community Care and Health (Scotland) Act 2002

Constitutional Reform Act 2005

Contracts of Employment and Redundancy Payments Act (Northern Ireland) 1965

Data Protection Act 1998

Data Protection (Processing of Sensitive Personal Data) Order 2000

Data Protection (Subjects Access Modification) (Education) Order 2000

Data Protection (Subjects Access Modification) (Health) Order 2000

Data Protection (Subjects Access Modification) (Social Work) Order 2000

Disabled Persons (Northern Ireland) Act 1989

Disabled Persons (Services Consultations and Representations) Act 1986

Disability Discrimination Act 1995

Disability Discrimination Act 2005

Discrimination Act 1995

Discrimination Act 2005

Domestic Violence, Crime and Victims Act 2004

Education Act 1944

Education Act 1972

Education Act 1981

Education (Scotland) Act 1980

Education (Northern Ireland) Order 2006

Education (Support for Learning) (Scotland) Act 2004

Electronic Communications Act 2000

Employment Act 2002

Employment Act 2008

Employment Act (Northern Ireland) 2010

Employment (Northern Ireland) Order 2003

Employment Relations Act 1999

Employment Relations (Northern Ireland) Order 1989

Employment Rights (Northern Ireland) Order 1996

Employment Tribunals Act 1996

Employers' Liability (Compulsory Insurance) Act 1969

Employers' Liability (Defective Equipment and Compulsory Insurance) (Northern Ireland) Order 1972

Equal Pay Act 1970

Equal Pay Act (Northern Ireland) 1970

Fair Employment and Treatment (Northern Ireland) Order 1998

Family Law Act (Northern Ireland) 2001 (FLA(NI) 2001)

Family Law (Scotland) Act 2006 (FL(S)A 2006)

Family Law Reform Act 1969

Freedom of Information Act 2000

Health Act 1999

Health and Personal Social Services Act (Northern Ireland) 2001

Health and Personal Social Services (Northern Ireland) Order 1977

Health and Personal Social Services (Quality Improvement and Regulation) (Northern Ireland) Order 2003

Health and Safety at Work Act 1974

Health and Safety at Work (Northern Ireland) Order 1978

Health Services (Northern Ireland) Order 1972

Health and Social Care Act 2008

Health and Social Care (Northern Ireland) Act 2009

Health and Social Care (Community Health and Standards) Act 2003

Human Rights Act 1998

Human Fertilisation and Embryology Act 1990 (HFEA 1990)

Human Tissue Act 2004

Human Tissue (Scotland) Act 2006

Industrial Tribunals (Northern Ireland) Order 1996

Interpretation Act 1978

Late Payment of Commercial Debts (Interest) Act 1998

Law of Property Act 1925

Limitation Act 1980

Limitation (Northern Ireland) Order 1989

Local Authority Social Services Act 1970

Mental Capacity Act 2005

Mental Health Act 1983

Mental Health Act 2007

Mental Health (Care and Treatment) (Scotland) Act 2003

Mental Health (Northern Ireland) Order 1986

Minors' Contracts Act 1987

Minors' Contracts (Northern Ireland) Order 1988

Misrepresentation Act 1967

Misrepresentation Act (Northern Ireland) 1967

National Assistance Act 1948

National Health Service and Community Care Act 1990

Occupiers' Liability Act 1957

Occupiers' Liability Act 1984

Occupiers' Liability (Northern Ireland) Act 1957

Occupiers' Liability (Scotland) Act 1960

Occupiers' Liability (Northern Ireland) Order 1987

Official Secrets Act 1989

Part-time Workers (Prevention of Less Favourable Treatment) Regulations 2000

Part-Time Workers (Prevention of Less Favourable Treatment) Regulations (Northern Ireland) 2000

Prescription and Limitation (Scotland) Act 1973

Protection from Harassment Act 1997

Protection from Harassment (Northern Ireland) Order 1997

Protection of Children and Vulnerable Adults (Northern Ireland) Order 2003

Protection of Vulnerable Groups (Scotland) Act 2007

Race Relations Act 1976

Race Relations (Northern Ireland) Order 1997

Redundancy Payments Act 1965

Regulatory Reform (Fire Safety) Order 2005

Rehabilitation of Offenders Act 1974

Rehabilitation of Offenders (Northern Ireland) Order 1978

Requirements of Writing (Scotland) Act 1995

Safeguarding Vulnerable Groups Act 2006

Safeguarding Vulnerable Groups Act 2006 (Commencement No 1) Order 2007

Safeguarding Vulnerable Groups (Northern Ireland) Order 2007

Sale of Goods Act 1979

Serious Organised Crime and Police Act 2005

Sex Discrimination Act 1975

Sex Discrimination (Northern Ireland) Order 1976

Sex Offenders Act 1997

Sexual Offences Act 2003

Sexual Offences (Northern Ireland) Order 2008

Social Services Act 1970

Statute of Frauds (Ireland) Act 1695

Safeguarding Vulnerable Groups (Northern Ireland) Order 2007

Sex Discrimination Act 1975

Sex Discrimination (Northern Ireland) Order 1976

Terrorism Act 2000

Trade Descriptions Act 1968

Unfair Contract Terms Act 1977

Statutory Instruments

Adoption Agencies Regulations 2005

Adoption Agencies (Northern Ireland) Regulations 1989

Adoption Agencies (Miscellaneous Amendments) Regulations 2005

Adoption Support Agencies (England), Adoption Agencies (Miscellaneous Amendments) Regulations 2005

Adoption Support Agencies (England) (Amendment) Regulations 2010

Adoption Support Services Regulations 2005

Business Protection from Misleading Marketing Regulations 2008

Care Quality Commission (Registration) Regulations 2009

Care Standards Act 2000 (Establishments and Agencies) (Miscellaneous Amendments) Regulations 2002

Children (Leaving Care) (England) Regulations 2001

Children (Secure Accommodation) Regulations 1991

Children (Secure Accommodation) Regulations (Northern Ireland) 1996

Children (Secure Accommodation) (No 2) Regulations 1991

Community Care Assessment Directions 2004

Consumer Protection from Unfair Trading Regulations 2008

Control of Asbestos Regulations 2006

Control of Asbestos Regulations (Northern Ireland) 2007

Control of Misleading Advertisements (Amendment) Regulations 1998

Control of Misleading Advertisements (Amendment) Regulations 2000

Electronic Commerce (EC Directive) Regulations 2002

Electronic Signatures Regulations 2002

Employers' Liability (Compulsory Insurance) Regulations 1998

Employment Act 2002 (Dispute Resolution) Regulations 2004

Employment (Northern Ireland) 2003 (Dispute Resolution) Regulations 2004

Employment Equality (Age) Regulations 2006

Employment Equality (Age) Regulations (Northern Ireland) 2006

Employment Equality (Religion or Belief) Regulations 2003

Employment Equality (Sex Discrimination) Regulations 2005

Employment Equality (Sexual Orientation) Regulations 2003

Employment Equality (Sexual Orientation) Regulations 2003 (Amendment) Regulations 2004

Employment Equality (Sexual Orientation) Regulations 2003 (Amendment)

Employment Equality (Sexual Orientation) Regulations (Northern Ireland) 2003

Fair Employment Treatment Order Regulations (Northern Ireland) 2003

Fair Employment Treatment Order (Amendment) Regulations 2003

Health and Social Care Act 2008 (Regulated Activities) Regulations 2010

Her Majesty's Chief Inspector of Education, Children's Services and Skills (Fees and Frequency of Inspections) (Children's Homes etc.) Regulations 2007

Ireland, Employment Equality (Sexual Orientation) Regulations (Northern Ireland) 2003

Maternity and Parental Leave, etc. Regulations 1999

Maternity and Parental Leave etc. Regulations (Northern Ireland) 1999

Maternity and Unfair Terms in Consumer Contract Regulations 1999

Mental Capacity Act 2005 (Appropriate Body) (England) Regulations 2006

Misleading Marketing Regulations 2008

National Care Standards Commission (Registration) Regulations 2001

NHS Trusts and Primary Care Trusts (Sexually Transmitted Diseases) Directions 2000

Part-time Workers (Prevention of Less Favourable Treatment) Regulations 2000

Part-time Workers (Prevention of Less Favourable Treatment) Regulations (Northern Ireland) 2000

Paternity and Adoption Leave Regulations 2002

Paternity and Adoption Leave Regulations (Northern Ireland) 2002

Safeguarding Vulnerable Groups Act 2006 (Commencement No 1) Order 2007 Sex Discrimination Order 1976 (Amendment) Regulations (Northern Ireland) 2004

Social Care Act 2008 (Regulated Activities) Regulations 2010

Unfair Trading Regulations 2008

Voluntary Adoption Agencies Regulations (Northern Ireland) 2010

Working Time Regulations 1998

Working Time (Amendment) Regulations 2001

Working Time Regulations (Northern Ireland) 1998

Working Time (Amendment) Regulations (Northern Ireland) 2002

EEC Directives

Equal Opportunities Directive (2006/54/EC)

Equal Treatment Directive (76/207/EEC)

Useful Resources

Postal addresses and contact numbers inevitably change over time. We have included here websites for offices in England, but many organisations have separate offices in Wales, Scotland and Northern Ireland. We cannot include them all here, but for additional offices and also for address and contact numbers, please see the relevant websites.

To find list of charities in the UK

Charities Portal www.charityportal.org.uk
Charity Commission www.charity-commission.gov.uk

Organisations listed under their areas of work

Abuse – helping victims and survivors of abuse

Child abuse victims
Bernados www.barnardos.org.uk
Childline www.childline.org.uk
NSPCC www.nspcc.org.uk

Elder abuse victims
Age UK www.ageuk.org.uk
Action on Elder Abuse in England and Wales www.elderabuse.org.uk
The Commissioner for Older People in Wales www.olderpeoplewales.com
Scottish Independent Advocacy Alliance www.siaa.org.uk produces the Guide to Independent Advocacy for Older People and Elderly Abuse Advocacy Guidelines

General help for victims of abuse
Respond www.respond.org.uk – supports people with learning difficulties, their carers, and professionals affected by trauma and abuse
Victim Support www.victimsupport.org

Adoption

Information and help for adopting and adopted parents and children, and the birth families of adopted children
Adoption UK www.adoptionuk.org

British Association for Adoption and Fostering (BAAF) – Email: mail@baaf.org.uk; www.baaf.org.uk/

Adopt or foster a child www.bemyparent.org.uk (a service from BAAF)

Tracing adopted children and family

For help for adopters and prospective adopters in Scotland, www.adoptionuk.org

To trace family in Scotland: General Register Office www.gro-scotland.gov.uk and National Archives Scotland www.nas.gov.uk

Birthlink – Scottish Adoption Services www.birthlink.org.uk

To trace family in England and Wales: Adoption Contact Register www.ukbirth-adoptionregister.com

Elderly – helping the aged and their carers maintain quality of life

Age UK www.ageuk.org.uk (amalgamates Age Concern and Help the Aged)

Alzheimer's Society www.alzheimers.org.uk

Alert – defending vulnerable people's right to live www.alertuk.org

Care Quality Commission www.cqc.org.uk

Carers UK www.carersonline.org.uk

Commission for Social Care Inspection (CSCI) www.csci.org.uk/

Contact the Elderly www.contact-the-elderly.org

Court of Protection *see* Office of the Public Guardian Office, below

The Clinic for Boundaries Studies (formerly POPAN and WITNESS) helps those who are abused by people in a position of trust, including those abused by health or care workers www.professionalboundaries.org.uk and www.popan.org.uk

Dementia Care Trust www.dct.org.uk

Dignity in Dying (formerly the Voluntary Euthanasia Society) www.dignityindying.org.uk/

Exit (formerly Voluntary Euthanasia Society of Scotland) www.euthanasia.cc/vess.html

Counselling, psychotherapy and psychologogical help and information for professionals and the public

British Association for Counselling and Psychotherapy (BACP) www.bacp.co.uk

BABCP – British Association for Behavioural and Cognitive Psychotherapies www.babcp.org.uk

British Psychological Society (BPS) www.bps.org.uk

Childline www.childline.org.uk

CPC – Counsellors and Psychotherapists in Primary Care www.cpc-online.co.uk

COSCA – Confederation of Scottish Counselling Agencies www.cosca.org.uk

College of Psychoanalysts (CPUK) www.psychoanalysts.org.uk

CRUSE – Cruse Bereavement Care www.crusebereavementcare.org.uk

Counselling Society www.counsellingsociety.com

General Hypnotherapy Register www.general-hypnotherapy-register.com

Hypnotherapy Association www.thehypnotherapyassociation.co.uk

Hypnotherapy Society www.hypnotherapysociety.com

Irish Association for Counselling and Psychotherapy (IACP) www.irish-counselling.ie

Irish Association of Humanistic and Integrative Psychotherapy www.iahip.com
IPN – Independent Practitioners Network www.i-p-n.org
Institute of Transactional Analysis www.ita.org.uk
United Kingdom Council for Psychotherapy (UKCP) www.psychotherapy.org.uk
Samaritans (for those contemplating suicide) www.samaritans.org

For a comprehensive list of counselling organisations in the UK see www.counselling.ltd.
    uk/organisations/

Medical – help and information for professionals and the public

British Medical Association (BMA) www.bma.org.uk
General Medical Council www.gmc-uk.org

Children and young people

Barnados www.barnardos.org.uk
Childline www.childline.org.uk
Childrens' Trust www.thechildrenstrust.org.uk/
NSPCC www.nspcc.org.uk
Connexions www.connexions-direct.com

Crime

Crown Prosecution Service (CPS) (England and Wales) www.cps.gov.uk – has headquarters
    in London and York, and operates under a structure of 42 areas
Scotland: (Crown Office and Procurator Fiscal) www.crownoffice.gov.uk
Northern Ireland: (Public Prosecutions) www.ppsni.gov.uk

Help for those leaving prison

Housing in Northern Ireland www.housingadviceni.org
Help for those leaving prison in Ireland www.citizensinformation.ie
Mentoring Scheme www.princestrust.org.uk
Release dates, discharge grants, getting work, etc. www.adviceguide.org.uk
Resettlement – HM Prison Service www.hmprisonservice.gov.uk
A–Z list of support groups see www.hmprisonservice.gov.uk

Help for people with mental illness, learning difficulties, or with physical or mental disability

British Deaf Association www.bda.org.uk
British Medical Association (BMA) www.bma.org.uk
Deafblind Scotland www.deafblindscotland.org.uk
Down's Syndrome Association www.downs-syndrome.org.uk (for those with Down's
    Syndrome and their carers in England and Northern Ireland. In Scotland, see also Downs
    Syndrome Scotland www.dsscotland.org.uk)
Equality and Human Rights Comission www.equalityhumanrights.com

Foundation for People with Learning Disabilities www.learningdisabilities.org.uk

General Medical Council www.gmc-uk.org

Headway (Brain Injury Association) www.headway.org.uk, and for Northern Ireland, see www.headwayni.org

Help the Hospices www.helpthehospices.org.uk

Independent Safeguarding Authority (ISA) www.isa-gov.org.uk

In Scotland, for implementation of the Protection of Vulnerable Groups Scheme, see www.scotland.gov.uk and www.disclosurescotland.co.uk

Learning and Skills Council www.lsc.gov.uk

MDF The Bipolar Organisation www.mdf.org.uk

MedicAlert Foundation www.medicalert.org.uk

MENCAP www.mencap.org.uk – helping those with mental disability

Mind (National Association for Mental Health) www.mind.org.uk. For Scotland see Mind Scotland – www.supportinmindscotland.org.uk

Motor Neurone Disease Association www.mndassociation.org.uk

National Autistic Society www.nas.org.uk

Office of the Public Guardian (OPG) www.publicguardian.gov.uk

Official Solicitor www.officialsolicitor.gov.uk/ and for

Northern Ireland www.courtsni.gov.uk and for Scotland www.scotland.gov.uk

Respond www.respond.org.uk – supports people with learning difficulties, their carers, and professionals affected by trauma and abuse

Rethink (the National Schizophrenia Fellowship) UK www.rethink.org

Royal National Institute for the Deaf www.rnid.org.uk

Royal National Institute for the Blind www.rnib.org.uk (includes RNIB Scotland)

SANE www.sane.org.uk – provides practical help to improve quality of life for those with mental illness

Scope www.scope.org.uk – major UK disability charity for children and adults with cerebral palsy

Speakability www.speakability.org.uk – helps aphasic people rebuild communication through training, groups, treatment, and information

Stroke Association www.stroke.org.uk

Voice UK www.voiceuk.org.uk – supports people with learning disabilities

Patients Association www.patients-association.com

Patient Concern www.patientconcern.org.uk

Patient Information Advisory Group (PIAG) www.dh.gov.uk/piag – provides the minutes of PIAG meetings and guidance on the use of powers provided under section 60 of the Health & Social Care Act 2001 which allow confidentiality requirements to be set aside in limited circumstances for purposes such as research and public health work. PIAG also provides guidance on issues of major significance that are brought to its attention

Law and legislation

Bar Council www.barcouncil.org.uk

Law Society (England and Wales) www.lawsociety.org.uk

Northern Ireland www.lawsoc-ni.org

Law Society (Scotland) www.lawscot.org.uk;

Legislation.gov.uk www.legislation.gov.uk – brings together the legislative content formerly held on the OPSI website and revised legislation from the Statute Law Database to provide a single legislation service

Judicial Studies Board www.judiciary.gov.uk; www.judicialstudies-scotland.org.uk; www.jsbni.com

Solicitors Regulation Authority www.sra.org.uk

Statutes, statutory instruments and other law

England and Wales www legislation.gov.uk

Scotland www.scotland.gov.uk, www legislation.gov.uk and www.scottishlaw.org.uk

Northern Ireland www.legislation.gov.uk/nisr

Expert witness lists, organisations and assistance

Expert Witness Directory (Sweet and Maxwell) www.legalhub.co.uk

ExpertSearch.co.uk www.expertsearch.co.uk (online register of expert witnesses)

Expert Witness www.expertwitness.co.uk (website with witness lists)

The Law Society of Scotland Directory of Expert Witnesses www.expertwitness scotland.info

UK Register of Expert Witnesses www.jspubs.com

Glossary

Acquired Immune Deficiency Syndrome (AIDS) is a term that is used to describe the latter stages of HIV infection, when the immune system has been seriously weakened and the person develops an AIDS defining illness, such as pneumonia (infection of the lungs).

Burden of proof To secure a conviction in a criminal prosecution, the case for the prosecution has to be proved 'beyond reasonable doubt'. The burden of proof in civil cases is on the balance of probabilities, i.e. 'that it is more likely than not' that the events occurred.

Contract Legally enforceable agreement, usually regulating the sale, lease or transfer of land, or the provision of goods, advice or services for an agreed price. In legal terms, the 'promisor' (or 'offeror') promises or offers to do something, in return for which the 'promisee' (or 'offeree') agrees to do (or forbear from doing), or provide something in return (the 'consideration'). For example, a therapist may offer to provide therapy in return for which the client agrees to provide payment, or a shop may provide goods in exchange for the release of a debt.

CRB and the CRBS (The Criminal Records Bureau and Central Registered Body in Scotland) Executive agency of the Home Office which maintains criminal records. Further information, including details of how to apply for disclosures, is available at www.crb.gov.uk. In Scotland, the Central Registered Body in Scotland (CRBS) provides enhanced disclosures in the voluntary sector for those working with children, young people and adults at risk – see www.crbs.org.uk. Disclosure Scotland provides criminal records disclosures upon request and payment of a fee, see www.disclosure-scotland.co.uk/apply/. In Northern Ireland, a similar service is provided by Access Northern Ireland, see www.accessni.gov.uk/.

Crown Prosecution Service (CPS) A government department that advises the police on evidence and law, and prepares cases for prosecution. The CPS provides its own staff or agents to act as advocates in some cases, and instructs barristers (counsel for the prosecution) to represent the Crown in others. The Director of Public Prosecutions (DPP) heads up the prosecution service. In Scotland, the head of the criminal prosecution system is the Lord Advocate, supported by the Solicitor General and Crown Counsel. The Procurator Fiscal's Service processes criminal prosecutions in Scotland and investigates a range of other matters including fatal accidents and sudden or suspicious deaths.

Disability/Disabled   Disability is defined in Section 1(1) of the Disability Discrimination Act (DDA) 1995, subject to the provisions of Schedule 1, as 'a person who has a physical or mental impairment that has a substantial and long term adverse effect on his ability to carry out normal day-to-day activities'. The effect of an impairment is long term if it has lasted at least 12 months, or if it is likely to last at least that long, or for the rest of the person's life, or if it is likely to recur if in remission, DDA 1995 Sch 1 paras 2(1) & (2). For further discussion of the Disability Discrimination Acts 1995 and 2005, with resources for information and help, see website www.direct.gov.uk. In the context of employment, see the *Disability Discrimination Act 1995 Code of Practice: Employment and Occupation* (the Code), issued on 1 October 2004, setting out the rights of disabled workers and duties of their employers.

Employee Assistance Programme (EAP)   EAPs help to make the workplace more efficient and improve the work experience for both the workforce and management by assisting individuals and organisations to fulfil many functions, including: addressing workplace problems, improving performance, productivity, motivation and morale, reducing conflict in the workplace and providing therapy for staff. For a detailed consideration of EAP roles, see the Employee Assistance Professional Association website: www.eapa.org.uk. See Chapter 2.

Exposure-prone procedures   Invasive procedures where there is a risk that injury to the health care worker may result in the exposure of the patient's open tissue to the blood of the worker. They include procedures where the worker's gloved hand may be in contact with sharp instruments, needle tips or sharp tissue (e.g. spicules of bone or teeth) inside a patient's open body cavity, wound or confined anatomical space, where the hands or fingertips may not be completely visible at all times.

Financial Year/Fiscal Year   The name for the accounting year chosen by a business for tax purposes. This may not be a calendar year, and it may run from the business starting up date, or be chosen to coincide with other convenient dates, e.g. the government fiscal year which runs from 1 April to 30 March, or a school or university year.

Forensic   Describes things that are directly related to the courts and the judicial system, for example assessments, court reports, witness evidence of fact and evidence given as an expert witness, etc. Forensic is derived from the Latin *forensis*, meaning of or before the forum, the place where criminal cases were tried in a public hearing. See Chapter 11.

'Gillick competence'   The colloquial expression for a principle of law settled by the House of Lords in the leading case of *Gillick v West Norfolk and Wisbech Area Health Authority and Another* in 1986. Under this law, children under the age of 16 may be legally competent to make certain decisions. See Box 8.1 in Chapter 8 for a detailed discussion of the principle. In Scotland, the principle in the *Gillick* case, and in particular the judgment and explanation of the principle by Lord Fraser, was embodied in statute in sections 2(1) and (4) of the Age of Legal Capacity (Scotland) Act 1991.

Government   In England, Scotland and Wales, in practice, although the Queen is the Head of State, the supreme authority of the Crown is carried by the government of the day. The government comprises the Prime Minister (appointed by the Queen), the Ministers with departmental responsibilities, and those Ministers of State who form the Cabinet by the invitation of the Prime Minister. The legislature comprises the two Houses of Parliament – the House of Lords and the House of Commons, see Chapter 1. For details of the government in Northern Ireland by the Assembly and the Executive Committee, devolved on 8 May 2007, see www. northernireland.gov.uk. For the Northern Ireland Office, which represents Northern Ireland interests at UK level, see www.nio.gov.uk. For government services see www.nidirect.gov.uk. For details of the devolved government to Welsh National Assembly see www.direct.gov.uk

Judicial precedent   In case law in England and Wales, there is a hierarchy in judicial precedent, in which the decisions of the House of Lords bind every court below it (including the Court of Appeal) and the decisions of the Court of Appeal bind all lower courts. There are also constitutional conventions which have binding force but do not have statutory authority, see Chapter 1. For Scotland, see www.scotcourts.gov.uk/ and for Northern Ireland see www.northernireland. gov.uk.

Judiciary   The collective name for all judges, at all levels. The judiciary should be independent of government, and of politics, and are appointed from among experienced lawyers. Most of the present senior judges were formerly QCs, but the judiciary makes appointments from both branches of the profession. For further information see the Bar Council, Law Society and Judicial Studies Board websites (for web addresses, see Useful Resources).

Lawyer   The term 'lawyer' has a very wide meaning, and includes Judges, Queens Counsel (known as QCs – 'senior' barristers), barristers ('junior' members of the Bar), solicitors (solicitors of the Supreme Court), each Notary Public, and legal executives (legal personnel qualified in law who assist solicitors and the courts). In Scotland, the term lawyer includes attorney, solicitor and Sheriff. See Useful Resources for a list of websites for further information on the law and lawyers.

McKenzie Friend   If a litigant has no legal representation they have the right to be accompanied by a lay person (i.e. not a lawyer), even where the proceedings relate to a child and are in private. Details of applications, rights of audience, the role and duties of a McKenzie Friend can be found at: www.hmcourts-service.gov. uk. It is also possible to have someone fulfil the role of McKenzie Friend in the Scottish courts. See Chapter 10 at 10.3.2.

Negligence The legal concept of negligence in the context of therapy is based on the failure to reach appropriate professional standards and/or breach of a professional duty of care, causing quantifiable damage. In order to establish a case against a therapist, the plaintiff would have to prove:

- That a duty of care exists
- Breach of that duty of care (conduct falling below the standards that the law demands)
- In the case of advice, that the defendant could have foreseen that any advice given would be relied upon (foreseeability)
- That, as a result of the action/omission complained of, the plaintiff suffered damage
- That the actions/omissions complained of were the cause of the damage.

Self-employed The distinction between self-employment and employment is not always easy to make, see the HMRC booklet *Employed or Self-employed?* IR56. For help, ask local taxation offices, or ask for leaflets ES/FS1 and HMRC CIS349. There is useful government advice on how to make the decision at www.hmrc. gov.uk.

Sex Offenders Register Notification under Part 2 of the Sexual Offences Act 2003 (known as the Sex Offenders Register) is an automatic requirement on offenders who receive a conviction or caution for certain sexual offences. The notification requirements are intended to ensure that the police are informed of the whereabouts of offenders in the community. Current legislation requires that any sex offender sentenced to a prison term of at least 30 months is placed on the register for life and has a duty to keep the police informed of any change of address or travel abroad. Up to April 2009, there were more than 44,700 people on the sex offenders register for England and Wales. All offenders must reconfirm their details at least once every 12 months, and notify the police seven days in advance of any travel overseas for a period of three days or more. Failure to comply with these requirements is a criminal offence, with a maximum penalty of 5 years' imprisonment.

Soft law Soft law includes the codes of practice issued by government departments; recommendations from official reports; and protocols adopted by statutory services. This type of law has no legal status in the courts in the sense that courts are not obliged to follow it until such time as Parliament gives it full legal status.

Starting up date Term used for the legal date from which a business first starts its existence and trading.

Tipping off Section 39 of the Terrorism Act 2000 creates an offence colloquially known as 'tipping off' which, in relation to the investigation of terrorist activities, means disclosure of anything likely to prejudice the investigation, or interference with material which is likely to prejudice the investigation. The courts take this seriously, and the current maximum penalty for tipping off is 5 years' imprisonment, a fine or both (see Chapter 5).

Tort   The law of tort in England and Wales is the general law of civil liability (in Scotland, it is called 'delict'). The word 'tort' (colloquially meaning 'wrong') was probably imported into our law from old French, having evolved from the Medieval Latin *tortum* derived from *torquēre* (to twist) and *tortus* (meaning twisted, crooked, dubious) – see Mitchels and Bond 2010: Chapter 2.

Vetting and Barring Scheme (VBS) and the Independent Safeguarding Authority (ISA)   The Safeguarding Vulnerable Groups Act 2006 (SVGA) set up the Vetting and Barring Scheme, which was gradually being brought into force in England, Scotland, Wales and Northern Ireland. From 12 October 2009, the Independent Safeguarding Authority (ISA) has maintained 'Child First', a list of individuals barred from working in regulated activity with children, and 'Adult First', a list of those barred from working in regulated activity with vulnerable adults. The ISA makes decisions about inclusion on the lists. Inclusion may happen automatically on caution or conviction for certain offences, or for meeting other specified criteria set out in Sch. 3 of SVGA. The legislation can be found at www.legislation.gov.uk. However, following a change of government in May 2010, the implementation of the legislation was suspended and changes are to be made. Watch www.isa-gov.org.uk for developments.

Whistle-blowing   Colloquial term for giving information about bad practice by colleagues. Several professional organisations have published guidance on 'whistle-blowing' procedures, for example the General Medical Council (GMC 2006: 43–5), and the British Psychological Society's Division of Psychology's *Professional Practices Guidelines* (BPS 2005).

References and Further Reading

Allen (2007) *Making Sense of the New Adoption Law: A Guide for Social and Welfare Services*. Lyme Regis, Russell House Publishing.

Alleyne, A. (2009) G.10: *Working with Clients who are Experiencing Harassment in the Workplace*. Lutterworth, British Association for Counselling and Psychotherapy.

American Psychiatric Association (2000) *Diagnostic and Statistical Manual of Psychiatric Disorders*, 4th edition, Text Revision (DSM-IV-TR). Washington, DC, APA.

Anthony, K. (2007) P.6: *Introduction to Online Counselling and Psychotherapy*. Lutterworth, British Association for Counselling and Psychotherapy.

APSCC (Association for Pastoral & Spiritual Care & Counselling) (2002) *Guidelines for the Pastoral Care of Lesbian, Gay and Bisexual People in Faith Communities*. Lutterworth, BACP/APSCC.

Arcel, L.T., Folnegović-Šmalc, V. Tocilj-Šimonković, G., Kozarić-Kovačić, D. and Ljubotina, D. (1998) 'Ethnic cleansing and post-traumatic coping. War violence, PTSD, depression, anxiety and coping in Bosnian and Croatian refugees: A transactional approach.' In L.T. Arcel and G. Simunkovic (eds), *War, Violence and the Coping Process*. Zagreb, International Rehabilitation Council for Torture Victims (IRCT) 45–78.

Aston, M. (2009) G.9: *Recognising Asperger's Syndrome: Its Implications for Therapy*. Lutterworth, British Association for Counselling and Psychotherapy.

BACP (2004) *Ethical Guidelines for Researching Counselling and Psychotherapy*. Rugby, British Association for Counselling and Psychotherapy.

BACP (2009) C.1: *What Is Counselling?* Lutterworth, British Association for Counselling and Psychotherapy.

BACP (2010a) *Ethical Framework for Good Practice in Counselling and Psychotherapy*. Lutterworth, British Association for Counselling and Psychotherapy.

BACP (2010b) A.1: *Guidelines for Writing Information Sheets*. Lutterworth, British Association for Counselling and Psychotherapy.

BACP (2010c) A.2: *Guidelines for Writing Client Information Sheets*. Lutterworth, British Association for Counselling and Psychotherapy.

Bamber, L. (ed.) (2008) *The Health and Safety at Work Handbook*. London, Lexis Nexis.

Bond. T. (2010) *Standards and Ethics for Counselling in Action*. London, Sage

Bond, T. and Jenkins, P. (2009) G.1: *Access to Records of Counselling and Psychotherapy*. Lutterworth, British Association for Counselling and Psychotherapy.

Bond, T. and Mitchels, B. (2008) *Confidentiality and Record Keeping in Counselling and Psychotherapy*. London, Sage and BACP.

Bond, T., Brewer, W. and Mitchels, B. (2010) G.2: *Breaches in Confidentiality*. Lutterworth, British Association for Counselling and Psychotherapy.

Bond, T. and Sandhu, A. (2005) *Therapists in Court: Providing Evidence and Supporting Witnesses*. London, Sage.

Bower, P. (2010) R.2: *Evidence Based Practice in Counselling and Psychotherapy*. Lutterworth, British Association for Counselling and Psychotherapy.

Bower, P. (2010) R.11: *Undertaking Systematic Reviews in Counselling and Psychotherapy*. Lutterworth, British Association for Counselling and Psychotherapy.

Bracken, P. (1993) 'Post empiricism and psychiatry: meaning and methodology in cross-cultural research' *Social Science and Medicine* 36: 265.

Bracken, P. (2002) *Trauma, Culture Meaning and Philosophy*. London, Whurr.

Brettle, A. (2009) R.1: *How to Do a Literature Search*. Lutterworth, British Association for Counselling and Psychotherapy.

British Psychological Society (2005) *Professional Practice Guidelines for Counselling Psychologists* (BPS INF75/01/05) at www.bps.org.uk

Buckroyd, J. and Rother, S. (2009) R.10: *How to Write a Research Paper and Get It Published*. Lutterworth, British Association for Counselling and Psychotherapy.

Burchell, S. (2005) *Counselling Asylum Seekers and Refugees*. Lutterworth, British Association for Counselling and Psychotherapy.

Burchell, S. (2009) G.8: *Counselling Asylum Seekers and Refugees*. Lutterworth, British Association for Counselling and Psychotherapy.

Butler, J. (2008) *Community Care Law and Local Authority Handbook*. Bristol, Jordans Publishing.

Cahill, J. (2009) R.8: *Counselling in Higher and Further Education*. Lutterworth, British Association for Counselling and Psychotherapy.

Cardew, P. (2005) DG.10: *The Ethical Framework for Good Practice in Counselling and Psychotherapy in the NHS*. Lutterworth, British Association for Counselling and Psychotherapy.

Carter, M. (2003) DG.9: *Clinical Governance in Counselling and Psychotherapy in the NHS*. Lutterworth, British Association for Counselling and Psychotherapy.

Church of England (2003) *Guidelines for the Professional Conduct of the Clergy*. London, Church House Publishing. Available as a pdf at www.churchofengland.org

Clafferty, A. (2009) V.1: *Managing Volunteers – a Guide for Those Managing Volunteer Counsellors in Voluntary Organisations*. Lutterworth, British Association for Counselling and Psychotherapy.

Clark, J. (2002) *Freelance Counselling and Psychotherapy: Competition and Collaboration*. London, Routledge.

Coate, M. A. (2009) T.3: *Guidance for Trainee Placements*. Lutterworth, British Association for Counselling and Psychotherapy.

Coleridge, L. and ISEB (2009) P.11: *Making Notes of Counselling and Psychotherapy Sessions*. Lutterworth, British Association for Counselling and Psychotherapy.

CPS (Crown Prosecution Service) (2005a) *Provision of Therapy for Child Witnesses Prior to a Criminal Trial: Practice Guidance*. Available at www.cps.gov.uk/publications; accessed 11 February 2011.

CPS (Crown Prosecution Service) (2005b) *Provision of Therapy for Vulnerable or Intimidated Adult Witnesses Prior to a Criminal Trial: Practice Guidance*. Available at www.cps.gov.uk/publications; accessed 11 February 2011.

CQC (Care Quality Commission) (2010) *Position Statement and Action Plan for Mental Health 2010-2015*. London, Care Quality Commission. Available as a pdf at www.cqc.org.uk/_db/_documents/20100315_Mental_health_5_year_action_plan_final.pdf

Dale, H. (2009a) P.2: *Charging for Therapy in Private Practice – Pitfalls and Ethical Issues*. Lutterworth, British Association for Counselling and Psychotherapy.

Dale, H. (2009b) P.9: *Am I Fit to Practise as a Counsellor?* Lutterworth, British Association for Counselling and Psychotherapy.

Dale, H. (2009c) P.11: *Making the Contract for Counselling and Psychotherapy*. Lutterworth, British Association for Counselling and Psychotherapy.

Daniels, D. and Jenkins, P. (2000) *Therapy with Children*. London, Sage.

DCSF (Department for Children, Schools and Families) (2007) *The Children's Plan: Building Brighter Futures*. London, The Stationery Office. Available at www.dfes.gov.uk/publications/childrensplan

DCSF (Department for Children, Schools and Families) (2008a) *Information Sharing: Guidance for Practitioners and Managers*. Nottingham, DCSF Publications. Available as a pdf at www.education.gov.uk

DCSF (Department for Children, Schools and Families) (2008b) *The Gender Agenda – Research and Evidence*. Nottingham, DCSF Publications.

DCSF (Department for Children, Schools and Families) (2010) *Working Together to Safeguard Children: A Guide to Inter-Agency Working to Safeguard and Promote the Welfare of Children*. Nottingham, DCSF Publications. Available as a pdf at www.education.gov.uk

Despenser, S. (2009) P.15: *Guidance on How to Bring Professional Obligations to a Close*. Lutterworth, British Association for Counselling and Psychotherapy.

DfES (Department for Education and Skills) (2004) *Every Child Matters: Change for Children Programme*. London, DfES.

DfES (Department for Education and Skills) (2006) *What to Do If You're Worried a Child Is Being Abused*. Nottingham, DfES Publications. Available as a pdf at www.education.gov.uk

DH (Department of Health) (1995) *Building Bridges – A Guide to Arrangements for Inter-agency Working for the Care and Protection of Severely Mentally Ill People*. London, Department of Health.

DH (2000a) *Assessing Children in Need and Their Families – Practice Guidance*. London, Department of Health.

DH (2000b) *Framework for the Assessment of Children in Need and their Families*. London, Department of Health.

DH (Department of Health) (2001) *Modern Standards and Service Models – Older People – National Service Framework for Older People*. London, Department of Health. Available as a pdf at www.dh.gov.uk

DH (Department of Health) (2002a) *Fair Access to Care Services – Guidance on Eligibility Criteria for Adult Social Care*. London, Department of Health. Available as a pdf at www.dh.gov.uk

DH (Department of Health) (2002b) *Health Clearance for Serious Communicable Diseases: Report from the Ad Hoc Risk Assessment Expert Group*. Department of Health. London, Department of Health. Available at www.dh.gov.uk

DH (Department of Health) (2003) *Confidentiality: NHS Code of Practice*. London, Department of Health. Available as a pdf at www.dh.gov.uk

DH (Department of Health) (2007) *Modernising Adult Social Care – What's Working*. London, Department of Health. Available as a pdf at www.dh.gov.uk

DH (Department of Health) (2008) *Refocusing the Care Programme Approach: Policy and Positive Practice*. London, Department of Health. Available as a pdf from www.dh.gov.uk

DH (2009a) *Improving Health, Supporting Justice: The National Delivery Plan of the Health and Criminal Justice Programme Board*. London, Department of Health. Available as a pdf at www.dh.gov.uk

DH (Department of Health) (2009b) *Living Well with Dementia: A National Dementia Strategy*. London, Department of Health. Available as a pdf at www.dh.gov.uk

DH (Department of Health) (2009c) *New Horizons: A Shared Vision for Mental Health*. London, Mental Health Division, Department of Health. Available as a pdf at www.dh.gov.uk

DH (Department of Health) (2010a) *Confidentiality: NHS Code of Practice. Supplementary Guidance: Public Interest Disclosures*. London, Department of Health. Available as a pdf at www.dh.gov.uk

DH (Department of Health) (2010b) *The Caldicott Guardian Manual 2010*. London, Department of Health for the UK Council of Caldicott Guardians.

DH (Department of Health) and Social Services Inspectorate (1991) *Care Management and Assessment: Practitioner's Guide*. London, Department of Health. Available as a pdf at www.dh.gov.uk

DHSSPS (Department of Health, Social Services and Public Safety) (2003) *Co-operating to Safeguard Children*. Belfast, DHSSPS Publications. Available at www.dhsspsni.gov.uk

Frankiscovic, T., Pernar, M., Moro, L. and Ronceric-Grezeta, I. (1998) 'Aggravating and mitigating factors in the "burn out" syndrome'. In L.T. Arcel, *War, Violence, Trauma and the Coping Process*. Zagreb, International Rehabilitation Council for Torture Victims (IRCT).

Freeth, R. (2007) *Humanising Psychiatry and Mental Health Care: The Challenge of the Person Centred Approach*. Oxford, Radcliffe Publishing.

Freeth, R. (2009) P.8: *Psychopharmacology and Counselling and Psychotherapy*. Lutterworth, British Association for Counselling and Psychotherapy.

Gabriel, L. (2009) P.5: *The Challenge of Working in a Multi-tasked Job*. Lutterworth, British Association for Counselling and Psychotherapy.

Gabriel, L. and Casemore, R. (2009a) E.1: *Practical Aspects of Setting Up a Counselling Service*. Lutterworth, British Association for Counselling and Psychotherapy.

Gabriel, L. and Casemore, R. (2009b) P.4: *Guidance for Ethical Decision Making: A Suggested Model for Practitioners*. Lutterworth, British Association for Counselling and Psychotherapy.

GMC (2004) *Confidentiality: Protecting and Providing Information*. London, General Medical Council. Also available at www.gmc-uk.org

GMC (2006) *Good Medical Practice*. London, General Medical Council. Also available at www.gmc-uk.org

GMC (2009) *Confidentiality: Supplementary Guidance*. London, General Medical Council. Also available at www.gmc-uk.org

Goss, S. and Rose, S. (2004) R.2: *Evidence Based Practice*. Lutterworth, BACP.

Harborne, L. (2009) G.13: *Working with Issues of Spirituality, Faith or Religion*. Lutterworth, British Association for Counselling and Psychotherapy.

Hershman, D. and McFarlane, A. (2010) *Hershman and McFarlane: Children Law and Practice*. Bristol, Family Law.

Hill, A. (2009) R.3: *Counselling Older People: Information for Practitioners and Policy Makers*. Lutterworth, British Association for Counselling and Psychotherapy.

HM Prison Service (2009a) *Enhanced Thinking Skills Programme: Outcomes and Implementation of a Randomised Controlled Trial* www.justice.gov.uk/publications/research.htm

HM Prison Service (2009b) *Evidence-based Practice? The National Probation Service's Work with Alcohol Misusing Offenders*. www.justice.gov.uk/publications/research.htm

HM Prison Service (2010a) *Impact Evaluation in the Enhanced Thinking Skills Programme*. www.justice.gov.uk/publications/research.htm

HM Prison Service (2010b) *Sexual Offenders Risk Assessment Tool Pilot*. www.justice.gov.uk/publications/research.htm

Inspectorate of Prisons, Chitsabesan et al. (2006) 'Mental health needs of young offenders in custody and in the community', *British Journal of Psychiatry*, 188, 534–540.

ISEB (2009a) S.2: *What is Supervision?* Lutterworth, British Association for Counselling and Psychotherapy.

ISEB (2009b) T.1: *Training and Careers in Counselling and Psychotherapy*. Lutterworth, British Association for Counselling and Psychotherapy.

Jackson, H. and Chaytor, D. (2009) G.5: *Personal Safety for Practitioners Working in High-risk Environments and with High-risk Clients*. Lutterworth, British Association for Counselling and Psychotherapy.

Jacobs, M. (2010) G.3: *Dual Roles – Blurring the Boundaries in Professional Relationships*. Lutterworth, British Association for Counselling and Psychotherapy.

Jacobson, J. with Talbot, J. (2009) *Vulnerable Defendants in the Criminal Courts: A Review of Provision for Adults and Children*. London, Prison Reform Trust.

Jacobson J. Bhardwa, B., Gyateng, T., Hunter, G. and Hough, M. (2010) *Punishing Disadvantage: a Profile of Children in Custody*. London: Prison Reform.

Jenkins, P. and Bond, T. (2009) E.6: *Confidentiality Guidelines on Reporting Child Abuse for College Counsellors and Psychotherapists in Further Education and Sixth Form Colleges.* Lutterworth, British Association for Counselling and Psychotherapy.

Joseph, S., Dyer, C. and Coolican, H. (2009) *R.13: Statistics in Counselling and Psychotherapy.* Lutterworth, British Association for Counselling and Psychotherapy.

Lane, M. (2006) *Adoption Law for Adopters.* London, British Association for Adoption and Fostering.

Lawton, B., Bradley, A-M., Collins, J., Holt, C. and Kelly, F. (2010) *AUCC Guidelines for University and College Counselling Services*, 2nd edn. Lutterworth, BACP.

Lendrum, S. (2009) *P.10: Satisfactory Endings.* Lutterworth, British Association for Counselling and Psychotherapy.

Litchfield, K. (2006) *Tend My Flock: Sustaining Good Practice in Pastoral Care.* Norwich, Canterbury Press.

Marsella, A.J. (1982) 'Culture and mental health: an overview'. In A.J. Marsella and G.M. White, *Cultural Conceptions of Mental Health and Therapy.* Dordrecht, Reidal Publishing Company.

Marsella, A. J., Friedman, M. J., Gerrity, E. T. and Scurfield, R. M. (1996) *Ethnocultural Aspects of Post Traumatic Stress Disorder: Issues, Research and Clinical Applications.* Washington D.C., American Psychological Association.

McGuiness, J. (2009) *P.16: Setting Up a Therapy Room.* Lutterworth, British Association for Counselling and Psychotherapy.

McLeod, J. (2009) *R.7: Writing a Practice Based Study for Publication.* Lutterworth, British Association for Counselling and Psychotherapy.

Mearns, D. (2009) *S.1: How Much Supervision Should You Have?* Lutterworth, British Association for Counselling and Psychotherapy.

Mearns, D. and Syme, G. (2008) *G.4: Counselling and Psychotherapy Workloads.* Lutterworth, British Association for Counselling and Psychotherapy.

Mitchels, B. (2006) *Love in Danger: Trauma,Therapy and Conflict.* Oxford, Jon Carpenter.

Mitchels, B. and Bond, T. (2010) *Essential Law for Counsellors and Psychotherapists.* London, Sage and BACP.

Mitchels, B. and James, H. (2009) *Child Care and Protection: Law and Practice.* London, Wildy, Simmonds and Hill.

Moore, S. (2009) *P.1: Professional Aspects of Setting up a Counselling and Psychotherapy Service.* BACP Information Sheets. ISEB. Lutterworth, British Association for Counselling and Psychotherapy.

New Oxford Dictionary of English (2001) Oxford, Oxford University Press.

Ofsted (2011) *Introduction to Adoption Support Agencies: A Children's Social Care Guide to Registration.* Available at www.ofsted.gov.uk

OFT (Office of Fair Trading) (2006) 'Press Release: Misleading magnetic therapy claims stopped', 28 April. www.oft.gov.uk/news-and-updates/press/2006/82-06; accessed 11 February 2011.

Palmer, I. and Mander, G. (2009) *P.3: Time Limited to Open Ended Counselling – How to Handle the Transition.* BACP Information Sheets. ISEB. Lutterworth, British Association for Counselling and Psychotherapy.

Pattenden, R. (2003) *The Law of Professional-client Confidentiality: Regulating the Disclosure of Confidential Personal Information.* Oxford, Oxford University Press.

Pattison, S. and Harris, B. (2009) *R.5: Research on Counselling Children and Younger People.* BACP Information Sheets. ISEB. Lutterworth, British Association for Counselling and Psychotherapy.

Perren, S. (2009) *R.9: How to Write a Research Proposal.* BACP Information Sheets. ISEB. Lutterworth, British Association for Counselling and Psychotherapy.

Phipson, S.L. and Howard, M. (2000) *Phipson on Evidence*, 15th edn. London, Sweet & Maxwell.

Prison Reform Trust (2010) *Report December 2010.*

Raffles, K. (2009) P.14: *The Impact of Personal Crisis on Independent Therapists' Practice – What is your Contingency Plan or Plan B?* BACP Information Sheets. ISEB. Lutterworth, British Association for Counselling and Psychotherapy.

Redstone, J. (2009) G.15: *Working with Clients with Addictive Behaviours.* BACP Information Sheets. ISEB. Lutterworth, British Association for Counselling and Psychotherapy.

Reeves, A. and Seber, P. (2009) P.7: *Working with the Suicidal Client.* BACP Information Sheets. ISEB. Lutterworth, British Association for Counselling and Psychotherapy.

Richards, K. (2009) R.12: *Finding Research Funding.* BACP Information Sheets. ISEB. Lutterworth, British Association for Counselling and Psychotherapy.

Roth, T. (2009) R.4: *Using Measures, and Thinking about Outcomes.* BACP Information Sheets. ISEB. Lutterworth, British Association for Counselling and Psychotherapy.

Rowland, N. (2004) E.7: *Clinical Guidelines for Treatment Choice Decisions in Psychological Therapies and Counselling.* BACP Information Sheets. ISEB. Lutterworth, British Association for Counselling and Psychotherapy.

Roxborough, T. (2010) C.1: *How to Get the Best out of Your Therapist.* BACP Information Sheets. ISEB. Lutterworth, British Association for Counselling and Psychotherapy.

Rusello, A. (2009) G.7: *Recognising Mental Health and Mental Health Problems.* BACP Information Sheets. ISEB. Lutterworth, British Association for Counselling and Psychotherapy.

Sharman, K. (2003) DG.11: *Guidance on Good Practice for the Management of Post Graduate Counsellor Trainee Placements in Healthcare Settings.* BACP Information Sheets. ISEB. Lutterworth, British Association for Counselling and Psychotherapy.

Sharman, K. (2004) DG.3: *Guidance on Good Practice for the Management of Counselling Placements in Healthcare Settings.* BACP Information Sheets. ISEB. Lutterworth, British Association for Counselling and Psychotherapy.

Slade, E. (2008) *Tolley's Employment Handbook.* London, Lexis Nexis.

Tasker, B. (2010) P.13: *Assessment in Counselling and Psychotherapy.* BACP Information Sheets. ISEB. Lutterworth, British Association for Counselling and Psychotherapy.

Triskel, N., Jade, R., Weston, H., Patterson, W. and Atkins, S. (2009) *G.11: Making Therapy Accessible to Disabled People.* BACP Information Sheets. ISEB. Lutterworth, British Association for Counselling and Psychotherapy.

Trivasse, M. (2009) G.6: *An Interpreter in the Therapy Room.* BACP Information Sheets. ISEB. Lutterworth, British Association for Counselling and Psychotherapy.

UKCP (2009) *UKCP Ethical Principles and Code of Professional Conduct.* Available at www.psychotherapy.org.uk

Urlic, L. (1999) 'Aftermath of war experience: Impact of anxiety and aggressive feelings of the group and the therapist' *Croatian Medical Journal*, 40(4): 486–92.

Wall, W. (2009) *Forensic Science in Court: The Role of the Expert Witnesses.* Chichester, Wiley–Blackwell.

Walley, S. (2009) P.17: *Making Referrals.* BACP Information Sheets. ISEB. Lutterworth, British Association for Counselling and Psychotherapy.

West, W. (2004) *Spiritual Issues in Therapy.* Basingstoke: Palgrave Macmillan.

Yalom, I.D. (1996) *Lying on the Couch.* London, Harper Perennial.

Youth Justice Board (2008) *Accommodation Needs and Experiences, 2007*, as cited in *Legal Action*, February 2008.

Youth Justice Board (2009) *Children and Young People in Custody 2008-2009: An Analysis of the Experiences of 15–18 year olds in Prison*, see www.justice.gov.uk

Youth Justice Board (2010) *Children and Young People in Custody 2009-1010: An Analysis of the Experiences of 15–18 year olds in Prison*, see www.justice.gov.uk

Youth Justice Board (2011) *Review of the Complaints System in the Secure Estate for Children and Young People.* Youth Justice Board for England and Wales, see www.justice.gov.uk

Ward, S. and Eden, C. (2009) *Key Issues in Education Policy.* London, Sage.

Index

A v. B plc and C ('Flitcroft')
   [2002], 108
accounts, 4
Adams, John Bodkin, 102
Adamson, Kirstie, 88
adoption, 143–54
   adoptive family
      accepting child's history, 152–3
      and contact with birth parents,
         154
      readiness, 153–4
      situation and needs, 152
      supporting, 153
      training and information, 152
   parental responsibility, 128–9
   step-parents, 129
   support services, 144, 146–54
      agencies: definition, 146
      contracts, 150–2
      documents required for
         registration as agency
         (Box 9.2), 148–9
      exceptions to requirements for
         registration, 147
      funding, 154
      inspections, 149
      legislation (Box 9.1), 145
      and local authorities, 153
      multi-way contracts, 151
      registration, 148–9
      self-employed therapists, 147
      standards enforcement, 149–50
Adoption and Children Act 2002,
   143, 144, 145, 146
*Adoption guidance: Provision of
   Adoption Support Services*, 145
*Adoption Support Agencies: National
   Minimum Standards*, 146, 149
'Adult First' list, 85, 134
advertising, 5–7
   definition of, 6
   and misleading information, 5–6
Advisory, Conciliation and
   Arbitration Service (ACAS), 50
age discrimination, 10, 103

Allen, 143
Allitt, Beverley, 102
Anglican Association of Advisors
   in Pastoral Care and
   Counselling (AAAPCC), 117
Anthony, K., 5
appointments
   cancelled, 29–30
   missed, 29
Arcel and Tocilj-Simunkovic, 175
Asser, Jonathan, 180
assertive outreach teams, 97
*Assessing Children in Need and Their
   Families* (DH), 74
*Associated Provincial Picture Houses
   Ltd v. Wednesbury Corpn*
   [1948], 61
Association for Pastoral and
   Spiritual Care and Counselling
   (APSCC), 117
asylum seekers, 172, 175–6
Audit Commission, 73

BACP
   advertising, 5
   'Being trustworthy', 7
   contracts, 22, 27
   counselling in schools, 86
   Criminal Justice Forum, 172
   discrimination, 10, 11
   dual roles, 118
   fees, 28
   general standards, 41
   harassment, 11
   insurance, 14
   keeping records, 19
   record keeping, 142
   refusal of disclosure, 130
   starting-up, 5
   supervision of practitioners, 54
   working with children, 124
Bamber et al.: *Health and Safety at
   Work Handbook*, 13
Bamford Committee, 59
Barber v. Somerset County Council, 35

Bichard Inquiry, 134
Bishop v. Baker Refractories Ltd, 35
*Boehringer Ingelheim Ltd and Others
   v. Vetplus Ltd* [2007], 6
Bond, T., 54
Bond, T., Brewer, W. et al., 20, 67
Bond, T. et al., 122
Bond, T. and Jenkins, P., 5, 20,
   67, 122
Bond, T. and Mitchels, B.
   children and consent, 152
   confidentiality, 22, 66, 67
   consent, 34, 90
   data protection, 20, 42
   disclosure, 31, 45, 47, 88, 122, 167
   disclosure and children, 130, 136
   ethics in contracts, 27
   inter-agency co-operation, 32
   parental responsibility, 127
   record keeping, 21, 173
   written contracts, 27
Bond, T., Mitchels, B. et al., 5
Bond, T. and Sandhu, A., 114, 130,
   136, 157, 158, 167
Bracken, P., 176
Bracken, P. et al., 176
British Association for Adoption
   and Fostering (BAAF), 145
*Brown and Another v. Bennett and
   Others* [2000], 160
Browne-Wilkinson, Lord, 61–2
Building Bridges (DH), 59
Burchell, S., 176
burden of proof, 199
Butler, J, 59

Caldicott Guardian Manual (DH),
   100, 168
Caldicott Principles, 31, 33, 100, 167
*Care Management and Assessment:
   Practitioner's Guide*, 62
care orders, 135–6
*Care Planning, Placement and Case
   Review Regulations* 2010, 76
care proceedings, 136

Care Programmes, 59, 60
Care Quality Commission (CQC),
    57–8, 146
    five-year plan, 94–7
    statistics, 96
Care Standards Act 2000, 56,
    144, 149
child and adolescent mental health
    service (CAMHS), 97
Child Exploitation and Online
    Protection (CEOP), 133
'Child First' list, 85, 134
children
    adoption *see* adoption
    assessment framework, 75–6
    capacity to enter contracts, 124–5
    in care, 135–7
        care orders, 135–6
        care proceedings, 136
        residential mental health care,
            136–7
        voluntary care, 136
    care plans, 76–7
    'child', 'adult': definitions,
        79, 123–4
    children as witnesses, 79
    consent, 122, 125–6, 129–31, 141
    CRB checks, 84–6
    in criminal proceedings, 140
    criminal responsibility, 140, 174
    Family Assessment Pack of
        Questionnaires and
        Scales, 75
    in family proceedings, 140–1
    in hospital, 141–2
    information sharing, 33–4
    inter-agency roles, 78
    local authority referral
        procedures, 77
    mental capacity (Box 8.1), 125–6
    parental responsibility, 79–80,
        126–9, 135–6
    protection, 83–6, 121–2
        conference procedure, 78
        guidance, 131–2
        from harm, 132, 133
        legislation, 131, 132–3
        from sexual abuse, 132–3
        vetting and safeguarding
            procedures, 134–5
    referrals, 83–4
    refusal of disclosure, 130–1
    refusal of therapy by guardians,
        131
    refusal of therapy/medical
        treatment, 130–1, 141
    in secure accommodation, 137–9
    serious situations, 82

children *cont.*
    services, 74–6
    supervision orders, 139–40
    teachers and child welfare, 71–3
    see also adoption; education
        system
Children Act 1989, 34
    adoption, 144, 154
    capacity to consent, 80–1
    care plans, 76
    child protection, 121
    'children': definition, 124
    children in need, 74, 75, 144
    disability, 61
    duty of care of teachers, 71
    emergency care, 82
    family proceedings, 158
    forensic evidence, 160
    parental responsibility,
        80, 126, 127
    recovery orders, 107
    refusal of therapy, 152
    secure accommodation, 138
Children Act 2002, 121
Children Act 2004, 70, 121, 132
Children and Adoption Act 2006,
    143
Children and Family Court
    Advisory Service (CAFCASS),
    75, 145
Children and Young Persons Act
    1969, 139
Children's Commissioners, 132
Children's Plan (DCSF), 70
Church of England, 114, 116–17
    *Guidelines for the Professional
        Conduct of the Clergy*, 114
Churches Agency for Safeguarding
    (CAS), 121, 122
Churches' Child Protection
    Advisory Service (CCPAS),
    121, 122
Citizens Advice Bureau, 27, 43–4, 50
Civil Evidence Act 1972, 155
civil partnerships
    acquisition of parental
        responsibility, 128–9
    discrimination, 11
Civil Partnership Act 2004, 11
Clark, J., 3
cognitive behavioural therapy
    (CBT)
    with offenders, 171
Cohen, 5
*Commission for Healthcare Audit and
    Inspection* (CHAI), 56
Commission for Social Care Inspection
    (CSCI), 56

*Common Assessment Framework,
    Asset and Onset*, 175
community care, 60
Community Care Assessment
    Directions 2004, 60
community mental health teams, 97
compensation claims, 88–9
computer records, 20
confidentiality
    in child welfare, 80–1
    and contracts, 22–3
    in the education system, 86–8
        in further and higher
            education, 87–8
    and employment assistant
        programmes (EAP), 44, 46
    forensic work, 164, 167–8
    and information about third
        parties, 66–7
    and information sharing, 31
    limits of, 65, 66
    not absolute, 66
    in police and CPS work, 176–8
    in the prison system, 178
    recording breaches, 32
    in spiritual/pastoral setting,
        113–15
        confessions, 114–15
    and tribunals, 45
    and vulnerable adults, 90
    see also disclosure
consent
    and mental capacity, 24–5, 59,
        80–2, 90, 103, 124–6, 141–2
    refusal of treatment, 31, 34, 81,
        87–8, 102
consideration: 'price of a promise',
    23
Constitutional Reform Act
    2005, 160
contracts
    and client's mental capacity, 24–5
    and confidentiality, 22–3
    in conflict with the law, 45–6
    consensus in idem, 21
    defined, 199
    and electronic communications,
        26
    of employment, 27
    and employment assistant
        programmes (EAP), 41–4
    enforceability, 23
    ethical issues, 26–7
    fees, 23–4
    and legal claims, 27, 43–4
    for minors, 25
    in schools, 79
    terms, 21, 22

contracts *cont.*
  therapeutic, 21–4
  therapeutic, counter to terms of
    employment, 93
  verbal or written, 22, 25–6, 52
  for voluntary work, 27, 43, 51, 52
Core Assessment Records, 74
*Council for the Regulation of
  Healthcare Professionals v.
  General Medical Council and
  Southall* [2005], 102
Counselling in Prison Network, 172
'counsellor's will', 30
crimes
  confessed by clients, 107
  reported about a client, 108–9
  reported by clients, 107–9
Criminal Records Bureau (CRB),
  84–6, 199
criminal responsibility, 140
crisis resolution/home treatment
  teams, 97
Crown Prosecution Service (CPS),
  172, 199

Dale, H., 5
data protection, 19–20, 31, 173
  legislation (Box 1.3), 19
Data Protection Act 1998, 19, 20, 31,
  42, 167
death or illness of therapist,
  21, 29–30
Department for Children, Schools
  and Families (DCSF), 70
Department of Education (DfE),
  69, 70
Department for Innovation,
  Universities and Skills
  (DIUS), 70
*Diagnostic and Statistical Manual of
  Psychiatric Disorders* (APA), 180
disability discrimination, 10,
  103, 200
  and premises, 16, 17
Disability Discrimination Act 1995,
  10, 16, 17, 200
Disability Discrimination Act 2005,
  10, 16, 17, 38
Disability Rights Commission, 17
'disabled': definition, 61
disclosure, 46, 47, 87–8, 100
  of abuse, 64–5, 66–7
  for child protection, 122
  clients with communicable
    diseases, 109–11
  in forensic work, 167–8
  and Official Secrets Act 1989,
    176–7

disclosure *cont.*
  refusal by child, 130–1
  of reported crimes, 107–9
  reporting bad practice, 102–3
discrimination, 9–12
  legislation (Box 1.2), 10
  in NHS, 103–4
Domestic Violence, Crime and
  Victims Act 2004, 133
Dratch, Rabbi Mark, 120
Dunlop v. Selfridge [1915], 23
duty of care, 13, 16, 29–30, 115, 202
  employers, 40, 99
  and negligence, 41, 52, 63, 64
  and record keeping, 46, 88
  teachers, 71, 72–3

early intervention services, 97
Education Act 1880, 70
Education Act 1902 ('Balfour'), 70
Education Act 1918 ('Fisher'), 69
Education Act 1944, 70
Education Act 1972, 70
Education Act 1981, 70
Education Act 2002, 83
education supervision orders, 139
education system
  academies, 70–1
  child protection, 83–4
  compulsory education, 69–70
  confidentiality, 86–8
  conflict between institutions and
    therapeutic practice, 91
  counselling
    ethics, 86
    length and frequency, 86
    and parental consent, 81–2
    space for, 86
  CRB checks, 85
  development of, 68–71
  gender differences, 69
  inspectorates and agencies, 73–4
  learning environments, 70–1
  record keeping, 88–9
  state control, 70–1
  teachers *in loco parentis*, 71–3
  therapeutic contracts, 79
  vulnerable adults, 89–90
  see also adoption; children
Electronic Communications Act
  2000, 26
Electronic Signatures Regulations
  2002, 26
Employee Assistance Programmes
  (EAP), 35–47, 200
Employers' Liability (Compulsory
  Insurance) Act 1969, 8,
  15, 39

employment
  contracts, 27
  equal opportunities/
    discrimination, 9–12
  health and safety, 13, 16, 35–6
  insurance, 15
  legislation, 7–8
  part-time, 11
  regulations checklist, 9
  and self-employment, 7–8, 40
  vulnerable groups, 8
  see also employee assistance
    programmes (EAP);
    voluntary work
Employment Act 2002, 8
Employment Act 2008, 8, 38
employment assistant programmes
  (EAP), 35–47
  commissioned by business, 39
  confidentiality, 44
  contracts, 41–4
    for goods and services, 42
    and legal claims, 43–4
    therapeutic with EAP
      clients, 43
    for volunteer workers, 43
  emergence of, 35–7
  employees as providers, 38–9
  forms of, 38
  law and guidance, 40–1
  for police and prison staff,
    172, 173
  and record keeping, 42
  record keeping, 46, 47
  and record keeping, 42
  record keeping, 46, 47
  role of (Box 2.1), 37, 37–8
  and self-employment, 40
  statutes and subsidiary
    legislation (Box 2.3), 38
  and subsequent private
    sessions, 46–7
  therapists as external
    consultants, 39–40
  unfair terms in contracts, 42
  'whistle-blowing', 45
Employment Relations Act 1999, 38
Employment Tribunals Act 1996, 38
equal opportunities, 9–12, 103
Equal Opportunities Commission:
  Code of Practice on Equal Pay, 11
Equal Pay Act 1970, 11, 39
equal pay for women, 11
Equality and Human Rights
  Commission, 17
*Essential Standards of Quality and
  Safety* (CQC), 57
ethics in contracts, 26–7

Every Child Matters (DfES), 70
Experts in Family Proceedings Relating to Children, 158
exposure-prone procedures, 200
external supervision, 54

Factory Act 1833, 69
Fair Access to Care Services (DH), 62
Family Court, 127, 140–1
Family Law Reform Act 1969, 25, 125, 151
family proceedings, 140–1, 158
fees
    assessing and negotiating, 23, 28
    late payment, 24
finance, 12
financial (fiscal) year, 4, 200
first aid training, 13
forensic work
    being informed, 165
    case law, 159–60
    categories of witnesses, 155
    in civil cases, 155–6
    compliance of client, 165–6
    confidentiality, 164
    contracts, 161–3
    control of evidence, 162, 165
    courtroom etiquette, 168–70
    criteria for treatment as 'expert', 156–7
    definition, 200
    information sharing, 167–8
    instructions, 162–3
    'McKenzie Friends' (Box 10.1), 158–9
    oath or affirmation, 164
    objectivity, 165
    payment of fees, 162, 163
    planning evidence, 163–4
    Practice Direction, 158, 160, 161
    publicly funded, 161, 163
    records: availability, 169–70
    refusal to answer questions, 165
    registers of witnesses, 158
    reliability of evidence, 164–5
    risk assessment, 166
    types of, 157
Framework for Assessment of Children in Need and their Families (DH), 34, 74
Franciskovic et al., 175
Freedom of Information Act 2000, 19, 20, 31, 88, 167
Freeth, Rachel, 95

Gabriel, L. and Casemore, R., 5
Gender Agenda – Research and Evidence (DCSF), 69

General Medical Council (GMC), 41, 66, 110, 157
    Confidentiality: Supplementary Guidance, 110
    Good Medical Practice, 110
General Social Care Council, 57
Gillick competence, 200–1
Gillick v. West Norfolk & Wisbech Area Health Authority and Another [1986], 81, 126
GMC guidance, 41
group support for patients, 93
Guidance on Offences Against Children (HO), 133

harassment, 11, 104–6
Harborne, L., 112
Hatton v. Sutherland, 35, 36, 40
Health Act 1999, 13
Health Clearance for Serious Diseases (DH), 110
Health Professions Council, 142
health and safety, 13, 16
Health and Safety at Work Act 1974, 39
Health and Safety at Work Act 1978, 16
health and social care
    elderly, 62–3
    legislation, 56–9
    mental illness, 59–60
    new regulations, 58
    special needs, 60–3
Health and Social Care Act 2001, 56
Health and Social Care Act 2003, 56
Health and Social Care Act 2008, 56, 62, 63, 96, 144
Health and Social Care Trust, 146
Hershman and McFarlane, 124, 135, 143
Hippolyte v. Bexley L.B.C. [1995], 71
Home Office staff, 172
hospitals
    children in, 141–2
    record keeping, 142
Human Rights Act 1998, 9, 10, 31

immigration removal centres, 176
Improving Access to Psychological Therapies (IAPT), 97, 98
Improving Health, Supporting Justice (DH), 98
Independent Mental Health Advocacy, 97
Independent Safeguarding Authority (ISA), 8, 85, 134, 203

information about third parties, 66–7
information in advance of therapy, 22
Information Commissioner, 20
Information Sharing: Guidance for Practitioners and Managers (DCFS), 83
information sharing
    Caldicott Principles, 31, 33
    and child welfare, 33–4
    with consent, 66
    and inter-agency working, 32–3, 66–7
Inspectorate of Prisons, 137
insurance, 14–16
    checklist for cover, 14
    indemnity cover, 15, 64
inter-agency working, 32–3, 66
    Caldicott Principles, 31, 33
interest for late payment of fees, 24
Interpretation Act 1978, 26

Jackson, H., 5
Jacobs, M., 54, 86
Jacobsen, J. and Talbot, 174
Jacobson, J. et al., 137
Joint Strategic Needs Assessments (JSNAs), 95
Jones v. Sandwell Metropolitan Council, 35
Judgement Framework (CQC), 57
judicial precedent, 201
judiciary, 201

Kelly v. DPP, 11
Kelly v. DPP [2002], 11, 104

Lampleigh v. Braithwait, 24
Lane, 143
Late Payment of Commercial Debts Act 1998, 24, 163
Law of Property Act 1925, 25
Lawton et al., 91
legal claims, 27, 43–4
Legal Services Commission (LSC), 161
life event trauma, 93
Limitation Act 1980, 23
Litchfield, K., 114, 118, 122
Living with Dementia (DH), 98
Local Authorities Social Services Act 1970, 34
Local Authority Social Services Act 1970, 34, 76, 83, 133
London Borough of Lewisham v. Malcolm, 10
Lucy Faithfull Foundation, 172

'McKenzie Friends' (Box 10.1), 158–9, 201
Magna Jewellery Ltd., 6
Majrowski v. Guy's and St Thomas's NHS Trust [2006], 11, 12, 105
marital status: discrimination, 11
Marsella, A.J. et al., 176
maternity and paternity leave, 11, 104
Meadow v. General Medical Council [2006], 102, 157
Mearns, D., 5
Melhuish v. Redbridge Citizens Advice Bureau, 49, 51
mental capacity, 24–5, 59, 80–2, 90, 103, 124–6, 141–2
Mental Capacity Act 2005, 24, 25, 59, 97, 125–6
Mental Health Act 1983, 59, 97
Mental Health Act 2007, 24, 125
mental illness, 59–60
Minors' Contracts Act 1987, 25
Misrepresentation Act 1967, 21
missed appointments, 29
Mitchels, B., 77, 124, 131, 135, 141, 180
Mitchels, B. and Bond, T.
  children and contracts, 124
  civil liability insurance, 52, 64
  confidentiality, 65
  contracts, 22, 23, 25, 26, 41, 46, 150
  disclosure, 107
  discrimination, 103
  duty of care, 64, 120, 131
  employment, 9
  legal claims, 44
  mental capacity, 90
  prison staff support, 178
  reporting crimes, 107, 108
  rights of employees, 39, 50
  safety of premises, 17
  self-employment, 40, 50, 99
  starting up business, 5
  volunteer workers, 43, 49
Mitchels, B. et al., 5, 177
Mitchels, B. and James, H., 77
Modern Standards and Service Models (DH), 62
Moore, S., 5
mortgages and working from home, 17

National Assistant Act, 1948
National College for Leadership of Schools and Children Services, 73

National Confidentiality and Security Advisory Body, 168
National Health and Community Care Act 1990, 60
National Health Service (NHS)
  changes in, 93
  counselling careers in, 93, 98–106
  and agency policies, 106
  and clients with communicable diseases, 109–11
  conflict of procedures, 100–1
  counselling for offenders, 171
  discrimination, 103–4
  with GPs, 99, 106
  harassment, 104–6
  in hospitals: record-keeping, 100–1
  'whistle-blowing', 101–2
  law and guidance, 97–8
  mental health services, 97
  statistics on mental health treatment, 96–7
National Institute for Clinical Excellence (NICE), 96, 98
National Insurance, 12
negligence, 41, 52, 63, 64, 202
New Horizons (DH), 94, 95, 97
Northern Ireland
  Access Northern Ireland, 84
  Achieving Best Evidence in Criminal Proceedings, 122
  adoption agency registration, 150
  adoption support services, 146, 150
  Age of Majority Act, 125, 151
  Age of Majority Act 1969, 25
  Audit Office, 73
  care provision for children, 75
  Children Order 1995, 76, 80, 82, 126, 154
  Children Order 2005, 107, 121
  Contracts of Employment and Redundancy Payments Act 1965, 8
  Disabled Persons Act 1989, 61
  Education Order 2006, 83
  Education and Training Inspectorate, 73
  Employer's Liability Order 1972, 8
  Employment Act 2010, 8, 38
  employment legislation, 8
  Employment Order 2003, 8
  Employment Relations Order 1989, 38
  Employment Rights Order 1996, 39
  Equal Pay Act 1970, 8

Northern Ireland *cont.*
  Health and Personal Social Services Order 1977, 61
  Health and Safety at Work Order 1978, 13, 16
  Health Services Order 1972, 59
  health and social care, 57, 58–9
  Health and Social Care Act 2009, 56, 58–9
  Industrial Tribunals Order 1996, 38
  Limitation Order 1989, 23
  mental capacity, 24–5
  Mental Health Order 1986, 59
  Minors' Contracts Order 1988, 25
  Occupiers' Liability Act 1957, 13, 17
  Occupiers' Liability Order 1987, 13, 17
  Our Children and Young People, 70
  Protection from Harassment Order 1997, 11, 104
  Race Relations Order 1997, 10
  Rehabilitation of Offenders Order 1978, 8
  religion and belief, discrimination in, 12
  Safeguarding Vulnerable Groups Order 2003, 8, 85
  Sex Discrimination Order 1976, 10, 11
  Sexual Offences Order 2008, 132
  Statute of Frauds Act 1695, 25–6
  Voluntary Adoption Agency Regulations 2010, 150
  vulnerable witnesses in court, 18
  Youth Justice Agency, 174
note keeping *see* record keeping
NSPCC, 122
  Faith, Religion and Safeguarding, 122
  Home Alone, 133
NSPCC and University of Sheffield, 75

Occupiers' Liability Act 1957, 13, 16, 17
Occupiers' Liability Act 1984, 13, 16, 17
offenders
  confidentiality, 178
  in custody, 173–5, 179–81
  in custody, violence, 180–1
  Sex Offender Treatment Programmes (SOTP), 173
  substance misuse in prison, 179–80
  support after release, 173–4

offenders *cont.*
  therapy services for, 171–2
  in youth custody, 174–5
Office of Fair Trading (OFT), 6
Office of the Qualifications and
    Examinations Regulator
    (Ofqual), 73
Office of Standards in Education
    (Ofsted), 69, 73, 145, 146, 147
  inspections of adoption
    agencies, 149
Official Secrets Act 1989, 176–8
  practical approaches checklist, 17
Optional Protocol of the United
    Nations Convention Against
    Torture (OPCAT), 97

parental responsibility, 79–80, 135–6
  acquisition of, 128–9
  adoption, 128–9
  and child counselling in school,
    81–2
  and confidentiality, 82
  and consent, 80–2
  legislation (Box 8.2), 127
  mothers and fathers, 127–8
  no-one with parental
    responsibility, 129
  unmarried fathers, 128
Parental Responsibly Agreement, 128
part-time employment, 11, 104
police and prison staff
  confidentiality for, 176–8
  illness and fitness for work, 178–9
  support for, 172–3
Poor Law Reform Act 1834, 69
*Portsmouth Hospitals NHS Trust v.
    Wyatt and another [2005]*, 142
Pratt v. DPP, 11
Pratt v. DPP [2001], 11, 104
pregnancy, discrimination on
    grounds of, 11
premises, 16–18
Prevention of Cruelty to and
    Protection of Children Act
    1889, 69
Prison Reform Trust, 137
Probation Hostels, 174
Probation Service, 174
Protection from Harassment Act
    1997, 11, 104
*Provision of Therapy for Child
    Witnesses Prior to Criminal Trial*
    (CPS), 52, 79, 98, 122
*Provision of Therapy for Vulnerable or
    Intimidated Adults Prior to
    Criminal Trial* (CPS), 52, 98, 122
Putting Care into Practice 2011, 76

Qualifications and Curriculum
    Development Agency
    (QCDA), 73
'Quality Protects Programme', 74

R v. Cannings [2004], 160
R v. Clark [2003], 102
*R v. Ealing District Health Authority,
    ex parte Fox* [1993], 60
*R v. East Sussex County Council ex
    parte Tandy* [1998], 61
*R v. Gloucestershire County Council
    ex parte Barry* [1997], 61
*R v. Islington LBC ex parte Rixon
    (Jonathan)* [1998], 62
R v. Shayler [2002], 177
race discrimination, 10, 103
Race Relations Act 1976, 10
*Re A (Children) (Contact: Expert
    evidence)* [2001], 159
*Re B (Minors) (Sexual Abuse:
    Standard of Proof)* [2008],
    159–60
*Re C (a Minor) (Medical Treatment:
    Court's Jurisdiction)*, 141
Re O (a Minor) (Medical Treatment),
    141
*Re W (a Minor) (Medical Treatment:
    Court's Jurisdiction)* [1992], 141
record keeping, 18–21
  of contracts, 22
  and data protection, 19–20
  disclosure, 46, 47, 64–5, 100
  in the education system, 88–9
  and employment assistant
    programmes (EAP),
    42, 46, 47
  in hospitals, 142
  'out-of-hours', 21
  reasons for not keeping, 19
  registration, 20
  storage, 20–1, 46, 173
  by therapists in hospitals,
    100–1
records of referrals, 32
Redundancy Payments Act 1965, 8
referrals, 67
*Refocusing the Care Programme
    Approach* (DH), 97
Refugee Council, 176
refugees, 175–6
Register of Expert Witnesses, 158
registration of personal records, 20
regulations for employment, 9
Rehabilitation for Addicted
    Prisoners Trust (RAPt), 179
Rehabilitation of Offenders Act
    1974, 8

Reinhold, Robert, 120
religion: definition, 113
religious discrimination, 10, 11, 103
reporting bad practice *see*
    'whistle-blowing'
Risk of Sexual Harm Orders, 133
Roman Catholic Church, 114, 115

S v. DPP, 11
Safeguarding Children Boards,
    83, 132
Safeguarding Vulnerable Groups
    Act 2006, 8, 85, 86, 134
Safety at Work Act 1974, 13
school trips, 73
Scotland
  Adoption and Children Act
    2007, 144
  Adults with Incapacity Act 2000,
    24, 126
  Age of Legal Capacity Act 1991, 151
  Care Commission, 58
  child witnesses in court, 18
  Children Act 1995, 80, 126
  children entering contracts, 125
  Community Care and Health Act
    2002, 61
  CRBS, 84, 85
  criminal responsibility, 140
  Directory of Expert
    Witnesses, 158
  Disclosure Scotland, 84, 85
  Education Act, 1980
  Education (Support for Learning)
    Act, 2004
  late payment of fees, 24
  Mental Health Act 2003, 24, 126
  Prescription and Limitation Act
    1973, 23
  prison service, 172
  Protecting Vulnerable Groups
    Act 2007, 8, 19, 85
  Protection of Vulnerable Groups
    Act 2007, 8, 19
  Requirements of Writing Act
    1995, 26
secure accommodation, 137–9
Secure Children's Homes, 137
Secure Training Centres, 137
self-employment, 7–8, 202
  accounts, 12
  and employment assistant
    programmes (EAP), 40
  National Insurance, 12
  premises, 16–18
  self-employed in schools, 89
  tax, 12
  working with GPs, 99

Serious Organised Crime and
    Police Act 2005, 133
Setting the Bar (CQC), 57
sex discrimination, 10
Sex Discrimination Act 1975, 10, 11
Sex Offender Treatment
    Programmes (SOTP), 172, 173
sex offenders, 132–3
Sex Offenders Act 1997, 132
Sex Offenders Register, 132–3, 202
Sexual Offences Act 2003, 132
Shame/Violence Intervention
    project (SVI), 180
Shipman, Harold, 102
Slade, 12, 105
social care
    complaints, 64
    contracts, 64
    disclosures of abuse, 64–5
    elderly, 62–3
    information sharing, 66
    insurance, 64
    legislation, 56–9
    mental illness, 59–60
    new regulations, 58
    reporting bad practice, 65
    special needs, 60–3
Social Services Act 1970, 62
soft law, 202
Solicitors Regulation Authority, 163
special needs, 60–3
    and 'reasonableness', 61
spiritual/pastoral settings
    child protection, 121–2
    confidentiality, 113–15
    dual roles of counsellors,
        117–18, 119
    listening, 116
    misunderstanding of religious
        terms, 120
    needs of clergy, 116–17
    sexual orientation, 117
    team ministry, 119
    use of power, 118–19
starting date, 4, 202

starting up in business, 4–5
    checklist, 30–1
step-parents, 129
storage of records, 20–1
stress at work, 36
supervision orders, 139–40
supervisors, 30

Tasker, 166
tax, 3–4, 12
teachers, 71–3
    duty of care, 71, 72–3
    school trips, 73
    and student teachers, 72
Therapeutic Casework Model, 176
therapeutic contracts, 21–4
therapeutic intervention for
    offenders, 171–2
tipping off, 202
Torbay Council, 72
tort, 203
Trade Descriptions Act 1968, 5
Training and Development Agency
    for Schools (TDA), 73
trustworthiness of therapists, 18

UK Border Agency, 175
UK National Advisory Group
    on Sexual Violence and
    Trauma, 180
UKCP, 41
Urlic, L., 176

VAT, 12
'Vetting and Barring' scheme,
    85, 203
voluntary work, 48–55
    clarity of roles, 53
    and contracts, 27, 43
    contracts, 27, 43, 51, 52
    and contracts, 27, 43
    contracts, 27, 43, 51, 52
    employed/self-employed, 50
    legal definition, 49
    meaning of 'worker', 50

voluntary work *cont.*
    and professional bodies, 51–2
    receiving gifts, 49, 54
    relevant law, 51, 52
    rights in the workplace, 50–1
    supervision, 53–4
    training, 55
vulnerable adults
    CRB checks, 85, 134
    disclosure of abuse, 64–5
    in further education, 89–90

W v. Edgell and others [1990], 66
Wade, Christine, 6
Wall, 158
*What to Do If You're Worried a Child
    Is Being Abused* (DfES), 83
'whistle-blowing', 44–5, 65,
    90, 203
    legal requirements, 65
    by therapists working in health
        care, 101–2
Williams v. Eady (1893), 71
working from home
    premises, 16–18
*Working Together to Safeguard
    Children* (DCSF), 34, 40, 52, 78,
    83, 84, 122, 133, 150

*X (Minors) v. Bedfordshire County
    Council* [1995], 102

Yalom, 166
*YL (by her litigation friend, the
    Official Solicitor) v. Birmingham
    City Council* [2007], 97
YOT Substance Misuse Worker, 175
Young Offender Institutions, 137
Young People's Training Agency
    (YPLA), 74
Youth Court, 124, 140
Youth Justice Board, 137, 174
youth offending teams (YOTs),
    140, 175
youth workers, 124

'This excellent book should do much to offer reassurance and to provide the guidance and information which can bolster therapeutic confidence.'
Brian Thorne, co-founder, The Norwich Centre, Emeritus Professor of Counselling, University of East Anglia

Helping practitioners move between different practice settings, this book explores how the legal framework within which they work varies across contexts. Work settings covered include:

- Private practice
- Commercial organisations – Employee Assistance Programmes
- Voluntary sector
- Government health settings (NHS): primary and secondary
- Private health settings: primary and secondary
- Education – schools/FE/HE
- Social care
- Police and Home Office.

For each setting, the book considers the statutory structure and the impact of the legal framework on the therapist and on the provision of services to clients. It draws on examples from practice to explore systemic issues and the restrictions and empowerment of therapists and clients in different work contexts.

An essential reference for counselling practitioners, including those with portfolio careers, the book provides useful information for counselling, psychotherapy or clinical psychology trainees.

Barbara Mitchels is a Solicitor providing on-line legal advice for therapists at www.therapylaw.co.uk. She is also a psychotherapist and Director of Watershed Counselling Service, Devon. **Tim Bond** is a Professorial Teaching Fellow at the Graduate School of Education, University of Bristol.

Tim and Barbara have both written widely on topics relevant to law, therapy and ethical professional practice.

⑤SAGE www.sagepublications.com
Los Angeles • London • New Delhi • Singapore • Washington DC

bacp
British Association for
Counselling & Psychotherapy

ISBN-13: 978-1-84920-624-2
9 781849 206242

FSC